WAC for the New Millennium

WAC for the New Millennium

Strategies for Continuing
Writing-Across-the-Curriculum Programs

Edited by

SUSAN H. McLEOD
University of California, Santa Barbara

ERIC MIRAGLIA
Washington State University

MARGOT SOVEN
La Salle University

CHRISTOPHER THAISS
George Mason University

National Council of Teachers of English
1111 W. Kenyon Road, Urbana, Illinois 61801-1096

We gratefully acknowledge Luis J. Rodríguez, who generously gave us permission to reproduce his poem "The Calling," © by Luis J. Rodríguez, from *Poems across the Pavement*, published 1989 by Tia Chucha Press, Chicago.

Staff Editor: Bonny Graham
Interior Design: Jenny Jensen Greenleaf
Cover Design: Pat Mayer

NCTE Stock Number: 56487-3050

Library of Congress Cataloging-in-Publication Data

WAC for the new millennium : strategies for continuing writing-across-the-curriculum programs / edited by Susan H. McLeod.
    p. cm
  Includes bibliographical references and index.
  "NCTE stock number: 56487-3050"—T.p. verso.
  ISBN 0-8141-5648-7 (pbk.)
    1. English language—Composition and exercises—Study and teaching. 2. Interdisciplinary approach in education. I. Title: Strategies for continuing writing-across-the-curriculum programs. II. McLeod, Susan H.

LB1576 .W23 2001
808'.042'071—dc21

                                              2001032712

CONTENTS

FOREWORD vii
 Elaine P. Maimon

1 *Writing Across the Curriculum in a Time of Change*
 Susan H. McLeod and Eric Miraglia. 1

2 *Accommodating Complexity: WAC Program
 Evaluation in the Age of Accountability*
 William Condon 28

3 *WAC Wired: Electronic Communication Across
 the Curriculum*
 Donna Reiss and Art Young 52

4 *Writing Across the Curriculum and Service Learning:
 Kairos, Genre, and Collaboration*
 David A. Jolliffe 86

5 *Is It Still WAC? Writing within Interdisciplinary
 Learning Communities*
 Terry Myers Zawacki and Ashley Taliaferro Williams 109

6 *ESL Students and WAC Programs: Varied
 Populations and Diverse Needs*
 Ann M. Johns 141

7 *The Politics of Literacy Across the Curriculum*
 Victor Villanueva 165

8 *Writing Centers and WAC*
 Joan A. Mullin 179

9 *Curriculum-Based Peer Tutors and WAC*
 Margot Soven 200

10 *Writing Intensive Courses and WAC*
 Martha A. Townsend 233

11 *Where Do the Naturalistic Studies of WAC/WID
 Point? A Research Review*
 David R. Russell 259

Contents

12 *Theory in WAC: Where Have We Been,*
Where Are We Going?
Christopher Thaiss 299

INDEX 327
EDITORS 341
CONTRIBUTORS 343

FOREWORD

ELAINE P. MAIMON
Arizona State University West

T he signs are positive that WAC has staying power. *WAC for
the New Millennium* itself testifies that the National Council of Teachers of English believes that writing across the curriculum has a future as well as a past. The first chapter, Susan McLeod
and Eric Miraglia's "Writing Across the Curriculum in a Time of
Change," gets at the heart of the matter. Like every educational
reform movement, WAC has developed within the paradox of
the academy, the simultaneous commitment to conservatism (the
preservation of knowledge) and to radicalism (the generation of
new knowledge). WAC's staying power as an educational reform
movement is based on its resilience in resolving this paradox.

In addition to resolving the paradox inherent in the mission
of higher education, leaders of the WAC movement have also
navigated well through a key administrative paradox, or Lesson
Six, to paraphrase Michael Fullan and Matt Miles's "Eight Basic
Lessons for the New Paradigm of Change": Neither Centralization nor Decentralization Works Alone (both top-down and bottom-up strategies are necessary) (see Chapter 1 of this volume).
My own academic career allows me to reflect on WAC from the
bottom up and from the top down. As Joni Mitchell might say,
I've looked at WAC from both sides now.

I can date my own work in writing across the curriculum to
1974, when as a very junior faculty member at Beaver College (I
was on part-time appointment) I was made director of first-year
composition and simultaneously the flash point for faculty complaints about student writing. To my innocent and much younger
eyes, it seemed neither sensible nor fair to hold only one department—English—responsible for students' progress in something

so complex and various as writing. If it took a village to educate a child, it certainly took a university to educate a writer.

In those early days, I was frequently astonished by allegations that the idea of university-wide responsibility for writing was nothing more than a fad. How could something fundamental be called a fad? As I reflect on those early days from my current vantage point of campus leadership at Arizona State University West, I see that writing across the curriculum has deep roots in long-standing principles of the academy; yet the act of reminding people of those roots necessitates strategies for change. The early leaders of writing across the curriculum—Harriet Sheridan, Toby Fulwiler, Art Young, Barbara Walvoord, Christopher Thaiss, Charles Moran, Anne Herrington, Susan McLeod, Margot Soven—understood that fulfilling the promise of the academy's traditions requires strategies for renewal and change. Moreover, the early leaders exercised a student-centered pragmatism, reflecting the virtues of common sense.

It simply made sense, for example, to develop faculty writing workshops. Yet creating this special nonhierarchical space within the university for exchanging ideas about everything from educational values to writing style proved to be revolutionary. Who would have thought? As Michael Fullan, who is cited in McLeod and Miraglia's essay, pointed out two decades later, effective change depends on work done at the local level—with individual teachers on their pedagogic practice, in collaborative workshop settings.

It also made sense to emphasize connections. E. M. Forster's guiding principle, "Only connect," was a motto of the early WAC movement. Connections across disciplines, among faculty members, and among students were fundamental to learning. Even etymologically a university expressed wholeness, unity among fragments. We saw ourselves as bridge builders, and as such we discovered numerous chasms—between disciplines, between colleagues, between students and professors, between the academy and the community.

The paradox of tradition and change became a special puzzle to me in 1976, when I discovered the disconnects within accepted public definitions of writing. I was developing a major grant proposal for submission to the National Endowment for the Humanities (NEH) to fund faculty writing workshops at Beaver College. NEH program officers told me that reviewers might not understand that college writing was related to rhetoric—one of the most ancient and fundamental of the humanities. Writing instead was thought to be a "skill" and therefore not under the mandate of NEH. Here was another chasm, this one between writing as a technology (like typing?) and writing as an essential component of discovering and generating ideas. It was a great day for bridge building when, in 1977, NEH funded not only the Beaver College program but also the National Writing Project, which has done so much to bring writing across the curriculum to K–12 institutions.

The very fact that writing across the curriculum resolves paradoxes of tradition and change has led to misinterpretation and false dichotomies. Those of us who were early leaders of writing across the curriculum, in our reading of James Britton, James Kinneavy, Edward P. J. Corbett, and Mina Shaughnessy, did not see an opposition between expressivism and social construction. Expressivism—writing to learn—was integrally related to learning to write. Yet, as writing across the curriculum moved from practice to theory, some theorizers in the 1980s and 1990s focused on only half the paradox, emphasizing the traditional, socially constructed features of the movement. Now, in this new century and new millennium, we are clearing the air and reasserting the interconnections between expressivism and social construction, tradition and change. This volume is a landmark step in that direction.

WAC for the New Millennium also reminds us that the educational reform movements most frequently discussed as the twenty-first century begins have their roots in writing across the curriculum. WAC programs moved the sage from the stage by advising instructors to guide from the side. "Course clusters," as we called them at Beaver College in 1977, established linkages among courses—e.g., Nineteenth-Century British Literature; Nineteenth-Century British History; Evolution—through reading and writing assignments, in this case on Charles Darwin. Faculty members and students formed *ur*-learning communities. Collaborative learning and peer tutoring were essential to establishing the student-to-student connections necessary to writing across the curriculum. Writing as problem solving; writing as critical thinking; writing within pragmatic contexts rather than in five-paragraph themes; writing as a way to individualize instruction for a multicultural and multilingual student body—all of these ideas were part of the earliest writing-across-the curriculum programs.

In 1991, when I read David R. Russell's *Writing in the Academic Disciplines, 1870–1990: A Curricular History*, I was both discouraged and encouraged—discouraged because so many educational reform movements had passed from the scene and encouraged because it was clear that writing across the curriculum had emerged from a fascinating history of precursors and that it demonstrated evidence of resilience. I feel even more encouraged today. Russell's historical perspective has a certain linearity, and we may, as the first essay in this volume points out, require a paradigm of change modeled on chaos theory. (I have become a stronger adherent of chaos theory since becoming a campus provost.) McLeod and Miraglia paraphrase James Gleick to explain that "chaos in a scientific sense is not disorder, but a process by which complexities interact and coalesce into periodic patterns which are unknowable in advance." This postmodern paradigm of change encompasses paradox. Writing across the curriculum is a complex set of ideas that have stimulated change at the local, classroom level, from grade school through grad school. As the new century moves along, we might even say that writing across the curriculum occurs at the point where chaos meets common sense.

ACKNOWLEDGMENTS

We would like to thank all the contributors to this volume, the anonymous reviewers of the manuscript, and the editors at NCTE, in particular senior editor Zarina Hock, who guided us through the process of publication with unfailing helpfulness. We would also like to thank all those who come to the WAC Special Interest Group sessions at conventions of the Conference on College Composition and Communication. As a result of their questions and concerns, they inspired us to keep abreast of new developments in WAC in order to meet the needs of emerging and developing WAC programs, and showed us what needed to be included in a book like this.

CHAPTER ONE

Writing Across the Curriculum in a Time of Change

Susan H. McLeod

University of California, Santa Barbara

Eric Miraglia

Washington State University

Change is mandatory, growth is optional.
Michael Fullan, *Change Forces*

Not long ago, writing across the curriculum (WAC) passed its silver anniversary.[1] As an educational reform movement, it has had remarkable staying power, outlasting other institutional initiatives in higher education and enduring beyond the life expectancy that might have been predicted given the fate of similar movements in the past. Although David Russell in his history of writing in the disciplines has pointed to some of the parallels between now-defunct movements such as Deweyan progressive education, the social efficacy movement, or the cooperation movement, he and others (Thaiss; McLeod "Writing"; Walvoord; Herrington and Moran) have noted positive signs for its future prospects: its institutionalization in many universities, its capacity to link up with and inform other initiatives in higher education, and the positive effect teachers say it has on their pedagogy.

Yet if the prognosticators are correct, higher education is facing massive change in the next few decades, which could spell trouble for WAC programs. Change is already evident. State funding priorities are shifting from higher education to Medicaid, prisons, and K–12 schooling (Gold and Ritchie). Legislators and boards of trustees are admonishing universities to emulate corporate models and do more with less—increase enrollments, cut faculty lines, and increase teaching loads; the use of cheaper adjunct faculty to fill vacant faculty lines, already a common feature of many institutions, is increasing (see Faigley; Leatherman). Tenure, which most academics see as essential to academic freedom, is under attack; the president of the National Association of State Universities and Land-Grant Colleges argued in an opinion piece for the *Chronicle of Higher Education* that "tenure, as it currently operates, has become more of a problem than a help to our endeavors" (Magrath), and a keynote speaker at the 1997 National WAC Conference predicted that tenure would simply disappear in the near future (Sturnick). Public opinion, always mixed with regard to higher education, now seems more negative than positive; two essays in the *Wilson Quarterly* under the heading "What's Wrong with the American University?" succinctly summarize the litany of complaints against higher education: the escalation of tuition costs, the emphasis on research at the expense of teaching, the feudal culture of the professorate (Finn and Manno; Wolfe). Peter Drucker, the management guru who predicted the effect of the GI Bill on U.S. higher education, is the gloomiest prognosticator with regard to the fate of higher education. In a 1997 interview, he stated flatly: "Thirty years from now the big university campuses will be relics. Universities won't survive" (Lenzner and Johnson 127).

These developments, along with continuing low salaries and the poor job market for new Ph.D.s in almost all areas, have contributed to sinking morale among faculty. Those involved with WAC are not unaffected by the general atmosphere of gloom. The foreword to a recent WAC book has a fin de siècle tone:

> The waning years of the twentieth century mark higher education's winter of discontent, a bleak time of scarce resources and few bright days. Survival is most on our minds, not doing extras that help our students learn more and better. The quest for students, external funding, and ways to save money saps most of our institutional energy while faculty busily sandbag against rising teaching loads and class sizes. . . . Missing motivation, low morale,

and declining salary dollars engender cynicism about
hood of imminent pedagogical change. (Weimer xviii)

In a time of retrenchment and of competition for scar̶
in higher education, will WAC survive in this new millennium?

We believe it can and will. One of the reasons for its continuing staying power is the fact that WAC, broadly conceived, focuses on writing as an essential component of critical thinking
and problem solving, key elements in a liberal education. If writing is a mode of learning, if it is a way of constructing knowledge, then the integration of writing with learning will continue,
in one way or another, to be seen as a central feature of the learning process. The Boyer Commission Report, one of the latest
policy documents from the Carnegie Foundation for the Advancement of Teaching, recognizes this fact in its recommendations
for a new model of undergraduate education at research universities; one of its recommendations is that such institutions need
to link communication skills with course work (Boyer Commission 24)—a mandate for WAC if there ever was one. Further, as
Russell points out, the WAC movement has been at heart more
of an attempt to reform pedagogy than curriculum.

> In most of its theory and much of its practice, writing to learn
> overshadows learning to write. This is one reason WAC has
> eclipsed all of its predecessors. It asks for a fundamental commit-
> ment to a radically different way of teaching, a way that requires
> personal sacrifices, given the structure of American education,
> and offers personal rather than institutional rewards. . . . A group
> of faculty who are personally committed to WAC can ride out
> any administrative changes (and perhaps increase their numbers),
> for the reforms are personal and not institutional, and their suc-
> cess depends on conversion not curriculum. (295)

What needs to be done, then, for WAC to continue to involve faculty in this sort of pedagogical transformation in the
postmodern, or at least postindustrial, university? Discussing the
future of WAC, Barbara Walvoord states that in an atmosphere
of changing institutional priorities and funding opportunities,
those of us involved in WAC must learn to collaborate with those
involved in new initiatives, to "dive in or die" (70). Using an-

other metaphor, the National Association of State Universities and Land-Grant Colleges recently issued a report that called on public institutions to become architects of the coming change so as not to be its victims (Haworth). In the spirit of becoming architects of change, we find it fruitful to rephrase the question about WAC's future from "Will WAC survive?" to "*How* will WAC survive?" How will it grow and change—what new forms will WAC programs take, and how will they adapt some of the present program elements and structures to the changing scene in higher education? What new WAC theories and research will help lay the groundwork for future WAC programs? The essays in this book, written for all who are interested in what will happen to the WAC movement in this new millennium, attempt to answer these questions.

In this book, we focus on some important recent initiatives or developments in higher education (assessment, technology and teaching, service learning, learning communities, changing student demographics), showing how WAC can be involved with or already has adapted to and informed them; we also focus on some continuing program elements or structures (writing centers, peer tutoring, writing-intensive courses), examining how these have adapted to the changing scene in higher education. Finally, we highlight some of the most recent research and theory about WAC, speculating about the implications of such research and theory. We will say a few words in the following paragraphs about the topics of the essays that make up this collection, and then about the paradigm of change we need to keep in mind as we think about the future of WAC programs. But first, let us define more specifically what we mean by "writing across the curriculum."

What Is WAC?

Like the term "general education," "writing across the curriculum" has come to have a vaguely positive aura, seen as something that is good for students even if faculty and administrators aren't sure what it is, precisely. Like general education programs,

WAC programs are defined in part by their intended outcom. helping students become critical thinkers and problem solvers, as well as developing their communication skills. But unlike general education, WAC is uniquely defined by its pedagogy. Indeed, one might say that WAC, more than any other recent educational reform movement, has aimed at transforming pedagogy at the college level, at moving away from the lecture mode of teaching (the "delivery of information" model) to a model of active student engagement with the material and with the genres of the discipline through writing, not just in English classes but in all classes across the university.

When we speak of WAC, we are talking about two different but complementary pedagogical approaches; we may think of these under the headings of "writing to learn" and "writing to communicate" (see Reiss and Young, Chapter 3, in this volume). The former is most identified with WAC programs. Based on the theories of language and learning articulated by James Britton and by Janet Emig in her article "Writing as a Mode of Learning," this pedagogy encourages teachers to use ungraded writing (writing to the self as audience) in order to have students think on paper, to objectify their knowledge, and therefore to help them discover both what they know and what they need to learn. The latter approach, writing to communicate, is based on theories of the social construction of knowledge, best summarized in Kenneth Bruffee's article "Collaborative Learning and the 'Conversation of Mankind.'" This approach encourages teachers to take into account analysis of disciplinary discourse and of genre theory (see Russell, Chapter 11, in this volume) as they construct and evaluate writing assignments. We cannot emphasize too strongly that it is an error to see writing to learn and writing to communicate as somehow in conflict with each other. Most of us who have been involved in WAC programs from the beginning see "writing to learn" and "writing to communicate" as two complementary, even synergistic, approaches to writing across the curriculum, approaches that can be integrated in individual classrooms as well as in entire programs.

Now let us turn our attention to the new directions WAC is taking, may take, or should take as we face the changes that are inevitable in higher education. Each of the essays in this volume addresses one of the initiatives or forces now affecting writing across the curriculum; of these, none has been so public as assessment.

Assessment

Assessment is not new in U.S. higher education—we have always assessed students in terms of how well they do in our classes, and the accreditation process has ensured periodic review of particular programs and of universities themselves. What *is* new is that assessment has been coupled with accountability in a competition for state and federal resources committed to higher education (see Zook; Lively). Legislators and taxpayers quite rightly want to know, in the face of steeply rising educational costs, that colleges are using public money wisely. The 1990s might be termed "the assessment decade," with various states instituting their own methods for assessing higher education programs and student outcomes, and a call for a national assessment program which would determine whether students gain sufficient skills in their postsecondary education (Blumenstyk and Magner; Jaschik). The American Association for Higher Education now hosts an annual meeting which focuses just on issues of assessment,[2] and it has sponsored a number of useful publications on the topic.

Although there has been some resistance to the assessment movement by those who see it as interference in the educational enterprise, WAC directors have for the most part understood that it is wise not to resist, but instead to jump on the assessment bandwagon and attempt to steer it in the right direction. The danger of all assessment initiatives in education is that they become reductive; legislators and the general public have a good deal of misplaced trust in standardized tests and in the resultant tidy charts, graphs, and percentiles. WAC directors know that student or faculty outcomes in a WAC program cannot be reduced to a number. The challenge for WAC, then, is to develop assessment instruments for both students and programs that satisfy the stakeholders and also avoid positivist measures that do not adequately reflect the complexity of both student learning and the WAC programs which are structured to facilitate that learning. In "Accommodating Complexity: WAC Program Evaluation in the Age of Accountability" (Chapter 2) William Condon discusses how WAC has adapted itself to the assessment movement, arguing that a constructivist paradigm is the most useful for WAC assessment.

Technology and Teaching

The advent of networked computing, more than any other single factor, characterizes the postindustrial university at the dawn of the new millennium. What new technologies bring to pedagogy, and how these technologies might redefine the role of the teacher, have been issues of some speculation (see Young). College writing classrooms, which were among the first to embrace the heady experimentation of word processors twenty years ago, are often at the center of the debate about the worth of technology. Amid the promise of the revolution and democratization of writing in the digital age (Bolter; Landow; Lanham), and amid simultaneous warnings of the demise of serious writing as a central thread in our cultural fabric as a result of the ascendance of new media (Birkerts), the ultimate impact of computer technology on writing and the teaching of writing is still an open question.

Underlying the pedagogical debate are concerns that what digital technology makes possible in the guise of networked communications and transactions is *different* from what it is proposed to replace. Can a chat room on the World Wide Web serve as a functional analog to the verbal exchange of ideas that takes place between students in a classroom? Electronic mailing lists, newsgroups, bulletin boards, and customized virtual classroom spaces elicit similar questions, but in spite of the questioning, the technology juggernaut rolls on. One of the most useful WAC resources is now electronic: the *Academic.Writing* site at http://aw.colostate.edu. Indeed, technology and WAC have become so intertwined that one of the more recent books on WAC, *Electronic Communication Across the Curriculum* (Reiss, Selfe, and Young), doesn't even have the word *writing* in its title; WAC has become ECAC.

There is concern in some quarters that legislators and corporate donors may see technology as a panacea for all they believe is wrong with U.S. higher education. Recently a college president told a group of administrators (which included one of us) that a prominent banker in his state welcomed the advent of computer technology in the university since it would clearly save money. In his own bank, for example, they had replaced tellers with ATM machines, at a considerable savings. The implication was that one could replace expensive (and sometimes troublesome) professors with machines—Freire's banking model of education run amok.

Taking advantage of the technological revolution, the University of Phoenix and the University of Colorado Online have been early out of the gate in delivering online curricula, offering practical alternatives, according to the University of Phoenix's Web-based promotional materials, to "the traffic, confining class schedules, and overall lack of flexibility associated with a traditional educational setting" (*University of Phoenix; University of Colorado Online; Teaching/Learning Model*). How should those of us in traditional educational settings respond to what many college administrators see as a new market force?

In many ways, WAC as a movement is poised as a counterbalance to these online efforts, which work from a model of delivery of information and focus on independent study rather than on the learner as part of a social setting that promotes critical thinking and problem solving. Long an agent for the enrichment of education in traditional venues, WAC's mission must now adapt to meet the challenges associated with this shifting spatial terrain—the challenges associated with maintaining the centrality of cognitively rich activity and writing and learning as a group rather than as a solo activity. In addition to shaping the integration of new learning technologies within the proximal world of the traditional university classroom, the WAC community must now look to apply its profound transformational strategies to new models of student-teacher and student-student interaction. With technology, as with assessment, it is essential for teachers to be involved so that the technology is put to good pedagogical use. In "WAC Wired: Electronic Communication Across the Curriculum" (Chapter 3), Donna Reiss and Art Young provide a short history of ECAC and reflect on its effect on both writing to learn and writing in the disciplines.

Service Learning

Service learning is one of the newest institutional initiatives on the higher education horizon—so new that when a special Modern Language Association session was proposed on the subject in 1995, the panel was rejected on the grounds that none of the members of the evaluating committee had heard of service learning or understood why a session on the topic would be relevant to MLA (Adler-Kassner, Crooks, and Watters 1). The service learning movement is growing, however; a recent volume on service learning published by the American Association for Higher Education (Adler-Kassner, Crooks, and Watters's *Writing in the Community*) has an appendix listing twenty-five program descriptions. There is now a service learning special interest group at the Conference on College Composition and Communication, with (of course!) a listserv devoted to service learning and writing.[3] Community service learning programs are popular with administrators because they involve outreach, mitigating the ivory tower image of the institution.

Service learning programs vary considerably across institutions, but they all have one thing in common: they attempt to connect the classroom to the community in a way that encourages experiential learning on the part of the students. In other words, they attempt to link town and gown in ways that simultaneously help the community and fulfill educational objectives. The goals of such programs are to help students understand the connection of learning to life, to stimulate students' social consciences (Herzberg 58), and to help establish writing as social action—to teach civic discourse (Heilker 72). The service component of courses is not meant in the spirit of noblesse oblige, but in the American spirit of volunteerism and social responsibility. At Washington State University, for example, we linked the research writing class and an introductory environmental science course; students sign up for both classes and conduct research in the writing class about the environmental issues raised in the science class. The service component involves working with a local environmental group on tree planting and environmental cleanup projects.

Not all service learning programs are also WAC programs, but there are some important congruencies that make WAC and service learning natural partners. First, many service learning programs, like WAC programs, have faculty development as a key component; they involve meetings of an interdisciplinary group of faculty who learn from one another or learn together about the project to which they will assign their students. Faculty members are given the opportunity to be learners as well as teachers. Second, both programs provide students with meaningful writing tasks—real projects for real audiences—rather than what James Britton and his colleagues call "dummy runs," or writing to the teacher as examiner (Britton et al.). Both service learning and WAC programs help students function not as students but as writers. Finally, both programs link writing to a particular social context and knowledge base, demonstrating the importance of contextual issues in learning how to write. In "Writing Across the Curriculum and Service Learning: *Kairos*, Genre, and Collaboration" (Chapter 4), David A. Jolliffe discusses further the congruencies of service learning and WAC, suggesting ways in which these programs might work in concert or adapt to one another.

Learning Communities

One of the more sweeping educational reform movements in the past decade was the revival of general education, the third such revival in the twentieth century. Led in part by the Association of American Colleges and Universities and aided by grants from the Lilly Endowment, a number of institutions worked together to develop principles that lead to strong general education programs (Magner). Of interest in this latest general education reform is the fact that the principles developed focused not just on curriculum, but also on pedagogy, advocating a teaching tool already familiar (perhaps in other guises) to writing teachers—learning communities.

These learning communities take many forms (linked courses, first-year seminars, configurations in which students taking the same classes also live together in the same residence hall). Sometimes they unite disparate course offerings into a cluster (Science, Technology, and Human Values, or The American Myth of Success); in other cases, students might be assigned the same book in several different classes and meet periodically to discuss that common text. The main point of creating a community of learners is to help students see the connections among the various general education requirements in the curriculum. But in many cases, the creation of learning communities has the same effect on pedagogy as do WAC approaches: the teacher moves from being the sage on the stage to the guide on the side, as students learn together and from each other. Courses move from being lectures to conversations (see Finkel and Monk).

The state of Washington, under the leadership of the Washington Center for the Improvement of the Quality of Undergraduate Education, has been the leader in this movement (see Graff; Gabelnick et al.), but institutions elsewhere have also developed innovative learning community programs. In "Is It Still WAC? Writing within Interdisciplinary Learning Communities" (Chapter 5), Terry Myers Zawacki and Ashley Taliaferro Williams discuss the learning community movement and its intersections with WAC, and examine two of these programs—the New Century College and the College of Arts and Sciences Linked Courses Program at George Mason University—to show those intersections.

Changing Student Demographics: Non-native Speakers of English

Changing demographics in higher education mean that the "traditional student" (middle class, eighteen to twenty-four years old) will no longer be in the majority in the next century. We are seeing more adult students, and because of recent immigration patterns, we are also seeing large numbers of students whose first or home language is not English.[4] A 1997 *New York Times* article cited statistics showing that between 1984 and 1994, the number of students classified as "minority" or "foreign" rose

27.8 percent (Menad 48). Particular institutions often top those percentages. At the University of California, Irvine, for example, the Office of Analytical Studies data show that the ESL population at the undergraduate level now averages over 60 percent, primarily students of Asian ethnic background. WAC techniques that work well for native speakers do not work at all for ESL learners. Teachers in the disciplines who are told they do not need to know about grammar in order to use writing in their classes feel betrayed when faced with a non-native speaker's grammatical and syntactic tangles in a write-to-learn assignment. Many WAC directors themselves feel at the edge of their competence in dealing with such situations.

Yet little research has been done on ESL and WAC. ESL pedagogy and composition pedagogy are quite different—indeed, sometimes at odds with one another with regard to the focus on detection and correction of error. Tony Silva and his colleagues argue that the composition community has much to learn from the ESL community (Silva, Leki, and Carson). As Ann Raimes points out, the research and pedagogical foci of the ESL community have been roughly parallel to those of the composition community, moving from a focus on the writer during the mid-1970s to mid-1980s, then to a focus on content (often pairing ESL courses with subject matter courses), to a present academic focus on socializing students into the academic discourse community— a focus known as "English for academic purposes."

What should WAC directors do to help teachers in all disciplines work well with ESL students? In "ESL Students and WAC Programs: Varied Populations and Diverse Needs" (Chapter 6), Ann M. Johns examines the issue of ESL and WAC, discussing how WAC programs have adapted and also need to adapt to the needs of ESL learners.

The Voices at the Margins

The Conference on College Composition and Communication published "Students' Right to Their Own Language" in 1974, but the research community in composition studies is still grappling with the implications of this document for issues of race,

class, and ethnicity (see Royster and Williams
recent backlash against affirmative action in
fornia and Washington and the end of open a
York point toward a future in which many u
dents of color who might previously have been
tutions of higher education will now find the~~..... ...~~ ~~.... ....~~
The national trend toward doing away with courses seen as "remedial" by legislators and trustees indicates that students who
are at risk by virtue of speaking and writing something other
than Standard English will not find the curriculum they need to
succeed even if they are admitted. The emphasis on proficiency
testing, in some cases mandated by states for high school graduation or entrance to college, has been blasted as militating against
social justice (Tierney), and standardized tests have come under
increasing criticism for discriminating against students of color
(Haney), but such testing shows no signs of disappearing. What
should WAC directors, administrators, and teachers in the disciplines be doing to address some of these thorny issues? In "The
Politics of Literacy Across the Curriculum" (Chapter 7), Victor
Villanueva examines the political economy of the academy from
a historical perspective. He suggests a "third stage" for WAC,
one in which all of us are more conscious of issues of cultural
identity as those issues intersect with our focus on discourse analysis and the teaching of disciplinary discourse across the curriculum.

Writing Centers

The history of writing centers in U.S. higher education in many
ways parallels the history of WAC programs. As David Russell
points out in his history of writing in the disciplines, the early
1970s were a time when social pressures—in particular, the boom
in higher education and the increased access for students from
diverse backgrounds (many first-generation college students)—
brought about a "writing crisis" in higher education. This perceived crisis was immortalized in a December 9, 1975, "Why
Johnny Can't Write" *Newsweek* cover story on the apparent
decline of writing abilities, shown in the results of the 1974
National Assessment of Education Progress (Russell 274–76).

As a result of the new focus on student writing in the late 1970s and early 1980s, student support services for writing became as necessary to institutions as faculty workshops and the development of curricular elements (such as writing intensive courses). Writing centers as well as WAC programs sprang up at institutions across the country (see Carino; Boquet); sometimes the two appeared together, and sometimes one developed from the other or within the other. Writing centers were not new in the late 1970s and early 1980s, of course—Stephen North tells us they have been around since the 1930s (436). But today's full-service writing center model may be dated in the literature from 1984, when North's "The Idea of a Writing Center," Gary Olson's *Writing Centers: Theory and Administration,* and Bruffee's "Collaborative Learning and 'The Conversation of Mankind'" all appeared. The relationship between WAC and writing centers, as Burkland and Freisinger pointed out in one of the earliest books on WAC, is a synergistic one. Our own institution, Washington State University, provides an example. In the early 1980s, the writing center began as a tutorial center for students enrolled in composition courses. It was headed at first by our harried director of composition and then by a part-time temporary instructor, and was staffed by four undergraduate and six graduate tutors. Its advertised purpose was to help weaker writers. As WSU's WAC program (begun in 1986) has flourished, so has the writing center, which is now advertised as a place for all writers to get feedback on their writing; it serves the entire university, not just the Department of English (in 1991–92 it recorded more than 2,500 tutorial contacts; by 1998–99 it had more than double that number). It is staffed by a permanent full-time director on a twelve-month appointment, an assistant director, a permanent clerical staff person, and a phalanx of tutors from across the university. The writing center director reports to our new director of writing programs and works with the three-quarter-time coordinator of writing assessment and two coordinators of some curricular elements (one-credit tutorial classes) of our WAC program. WAC and the Writing Center at WSU have grown up together and are now firmly bound by administrative and curricular ties.

As university budgets contract and outside funding for WAC programs becomes rare, writing centers and WAC programs at many institutions have formed a natural alliance. In some cases, the writing center is a physical and budgetary entity where the WAC program, an interdisciplinary effort with no departmental home, may be housed and sheltered from budget storms. In some cases, the writing center can provide the springboard for a new WAC effort. In "Writing Centers and WAC," Joan A. Mullin traces the parallels of writing center theory and practice to the WAC movement, discussing how writing centers can support an existing WAC program or provide scaffolding for a developing one.

Peer Tutoring

Programs of peer tutoring, like learning community programs, grow out of the same rather simple conceptual base: students can learn from each other as well as from teachers and books. As Bruffee traces the history of peer tutoring (and its result, collaborative learning), the idea first developed in the 1950s and 1960s in London, in a study of British medical education. Briefly, the study found that when medical students examined a patient together and discussed the case, arriving at a diagnosis by group consensus, that process was more effective in teaching good medical diagnosis than the usual practice of asking each student to diagnose individually (Abercrombie 19). The origin of peer tutoring programs in U.S. colleges is more mundane, however. The 1970s was a decade when underprepared students were entering college in increasing numbers; one symptom of their difficulty adjusting to college life was that they did not seek out help or even refused it when it was offered in tutorial or counseling centers. The solution: offer help in alternative venues—from peers rather than from professionals, who might be seen as extensions of traditional classroom structures (Bruffee 637). Administrators liked peer tutoring programs because they were cost effective as well as learning effective; hence the idea spread rapidly. Although some of these programs are run out of writing centers, some are independent, based in the curriculum.

One of the earliest curriculum-based peer tutoring efforts that can be identified as a WAC program started at Carleton College under the administrative leadership of Harriet Sheridan. In 1974,

n response to a newly established writing proficiency
at the institution—set up a program of undergradu-
rs, called "writing fellows," to work with students
in all disciplines on their writing assignments (Russell 283). When
Sheridan became an administrator at Brown University, she helped
establish a similar program at that institution, a program that
continues to be the model for curriculum-based peer tutoring.

Curriculum-based peer tutoring programs continue to be
popular in institutions for a number of reasons: they are relatively inexpensive to run, they benefit not only those served by
the tutors but also the tutors themselves, they reinforce collaborative composition pedagogy, and they are generally adored by
faculty, who find that such programs aid their teaching. As the
university is pressured to increase class size and teacher workload,
the pressures on peer tutoring programs will also increase. In
"Curriculum-Based Peer Tutors and WAC" (Chapter 9), Margot
Soven examines various models for curriculum-based peer tutoring programs and some of the questions they raise, as well as the
future of such programs.

Writing Intensive (WI) Courses

One of the most interesting curricular developments that have
sprung from the WAC movement is the "writing intensive" course
as a university requirement. The rationale for such courses is usually stated as follows: Students do not learn how to write by
taking just one writing class, but instead need continual practice
with writing in order to improve. A further rationale is sometimes that students learn the general features of academic writing
in a first-year composition course, but then need to learn the
more specific conventions of the discourse communities in their
chosen fields of study—which are known best by faculty in the
disciplines. A third rationale, however, one that is often not stated
in plans approved by faculty senates but that is at the heart of the
WAC movement, is this: writing disrupts the traditional pattern
of classroom instruction, what Freire called the "banking model,"
in which the students are the passive recipients of knowledge
(Farris and Smith 72). Writing intensive courses as defined by

most WAC programs do not simply involve more w
other courses; they are designed to engage students me
in their own learning through writing.

Writing intensive courses can take many forms, but the general guidelines, as summarized by Farris and Smith (73–74), have
some or all of the following elements. First, class size is limited,
or the student-teacher ratio is low, to permit the intensive interaction necessary and make the teacher's workload a reasonable
one. The course is usually taught by faculty rather than teaching
assistants. The guidelines for such courses usually specify the
numbers of papers (or words) and the kinds of papers, as well as
what part revision should play in the process of writing and how
the writing will affect the grade. Sometimes the guidelines suggest or specify particular assignments or approaches to assignments (such as research papers assigned in stages). Finally, these
courses often suggest or require that students and faculty make
use of support services such as writing centers or consultation
with WAC staff. Many institutions, even large research institutions, have been able to implement these courses with remarkable success.

But faculty workload has been an abiding issue with writing
intensive courses. As pressures increase on institutions to increase
class size and teaching loads, what will happen to WI courses? In
"Writing Intensive Courses and WAC" (Chapter 10), Martha A.
Townsend discusses various models for courses in which faculty
in the disciplines use writing, examines the case of one institution where writing intensive courses have successfully become
the centerpiece of the WAC program, and discusses theoretical
and practical considerations for such courses in the future.

Qualitative Studies

A major strength of the WAC movement has been its theory-into-practice approach to encouraging writing in all disciplines.
From the beginning, starting with the work of Britton and his
associates, the movement has been grounded in research. In recent years, naturalistic studies of college-level writing in the disciplines have been predominant, in part because quantitative

approaches yielded contradictory results in examining one of WAC's central tenets: that writing is a mode of learning. As a result of these naturalistic studies, we now know much more about how students approach writing in the various disciplines; yet these studies have not been systematically reviewed to suggest which pedagogical practices are sound and which may need to be changed or researched further. In "Where Do the Naturalistic Studies of WAC/WID Point? A Research Review" (Chapter 11), David R. Russell examines a number of qualitative studies, highlighting the complexity of what it means to both write to learn and learn to write in the disciplines.

Theorizing WAC

Writing-across-the-curriculum programs are grounded firmly in the theories of language and learning that have dominated the composition community during the last few decades. Cognitivist psychology has had a powerful influence on our conceptions of writing as a problem-solving process; psycholinguistics has also influenced our notions of the relationship between thought and language, and between language and learning. Poststructural theories and constructivist notions about the creation of knowledge, as well as anthropological notions about culture, have helped shape our understandings of academic discourse and discourse communities. Most recently, communication theories from sociology (on role representation, for example) are being emphasized as useful for the composition community. Further, WAC has flourished in part because program directors and researchers refused to stipulate careful definitions of what exactly we mean by "writing across the curriculum." The WAC tent is therefore large; programs are site specific and various, as local as each teacher's classroom. The theoretical challenge, then, is to find the center of WAC—or if there is no center, no orthodoxy, to examine the ramifications of such a diffuse and elusive concept.

What theories are on the horizon for WAC? In "Theory in WAC: Where Have We Been, Where Are We Going?" (Chapter 12), Christopher Thaiss ruminates on theory under the headings of "writing," "across," and "the curriculum," and speculates about how WAC's theoretical base may change as a result of pressures from some of the forces discussed in this volume.

A Changing Paradigm of Change

Having briefly discussed the opportunities for WAC that will be examined in this volume, we return now to the issue of change. The initiatives or forces now affecting higher education as well as WAC are symptomatic of the seismic changes we are facing in this new millennium. The thought of change on the scale predicted by those such as Peter Drucker (Lenzner and Johnson), mentioned earlier, may seem daunting, even threatening, to many of us in academe. Further, institutions of higher learning are conservative in both institutional structure and mission (e.g., the conservation of knowledge as well as the generation of new knowledge); retaining the status quo is much more likely than active response to change in educational systems, systems that are not set up to implement change quickly and efficiently. How should those of us involved or interested in WAC (in a larger sense, those of us interested in the quality of undergraduate education) respond in the face of changes that our academic institutions are in some ways built to resist? What should individuals, as well as institutions, do to plan for such change?

To answer these questions, it is important to understand the nature of educational change. First and foremost, such change is replete with variables (e.g., governmental policy changes, legislative funding whims, new technologies, shifts in immigration, changes in personnel and leadership). One writer about organizational change refers to such change as having "dynamic complexity"; unplanned factors routinely interfere, and cause and effect "are not close in time and space and obvious interventions do not produce expected outcomes" (Senge 365). Change in educational systems is therefore anything but predictable and linear. Yet institutions of higher education tend to respond to change as if it were, following a top-down model for vision-driven change (promulgated by Beckhard and Pritchard, among others): creating and setting the vision, communicating the vision, building commitment to it, and organizing personnel and processes to be aligned with that vision.

Writers on educational change have argued recently that we need a new paradigm of change, one modeled not on linear theories of cause and effect (e.g., mandate policy and thereby change teacher behavior) but on chaos theory. Chaos in a scientific sense is not disorder but a process by which complexities interact and coalesce into periodic patterns that are unknowable in advance (Gleick)—we might think of this as a postmodern paradigm of change. One researcher who studies organizational and educational change, Michael Fullan, has mapped out with his colleague Matt Miles what they call "Eight Basic Lessons for the New Paradigm of Change" for educational institutions to ponder (Fullan 21–22). Paraphrased for our purposes, these are:

Lesson One: *You can't mandate what matters* (the more complex the change, the less you can force it).

Lesson Two: *Change is a journey, not a blueprint* (change is nonlinear, loaded with uncertainty and excitement, and sometimes perverse).

Lesson Three: *Problems are our friends* (problems are inevitable and you can't learn without them).

Lesson Four: *Vision and strategic planning come later* (premature visions and planning blind us to other possibilities).

Lesson Five: *Individualism and collectivism must have equal power* (there are no one-sided solutions).

Lesson Six: *Neither centralization nor decentralization works alone* (both top-down and bottom-up strategies are necessary).

Lesson Seven: *Connection with the wider environment is critical for success* (the best organizations learn externally as well as internally).

Lesson Eight: *Every person is a change agent* (change is too important to leave to the experts).

Fullan elaborates on all eight lessons in his book *Change Forces*; although many of these lessons (such as combining top-down and bottom-up strategies) are familiar to WAC directors, it is the last one we wish to address here. One of us has written elsewhere about the concept of the "change agent" (McLeod, "Foreigner"). This concept grew out of the social activism of the 1960s, in particular out of a number of federal programs designed to improve public education through planned change. Under the sponsorship of the U.S. Office of Education, the Rand Corporation conducted a national study of 293 projects funded by four federal programs specifically intended to produce innovation in public schools—a four-year project that came to be known as the "Change Agent Study" (McLaughlin 11). What the Rand study (and a later examination of it) found was that there were a number of unexamined assumptions about change in schools, particularly about the local nature of change and the importance of involving teachers in implementing change. Policy, researchers found, did not change practice—in Fullan's terms, it did not mandate what mattered, which was what individual teachers did in the classroom. Instead, pedagogical and curricular change was a problem of the smallest unit, of local capacity and teacher motivation (12–13). The most effective change agents were not in fact outside consultants and external developers brought in for the various projects, but rather the teachers themselves.[5]

This research is congruent with one of Fullan's major points—change in organizations is brought about in large part at a very local level. Fullan argues that for educational change to be effective, all teachers must become change agents, which means being self-conscious about the nature of change and the change process. Institutions must pull teachers out of their isolation and work with them on (among other things) shared vision building and collaboration (12). One of the strengths of the WAC movement has been its work at that very level, with individual teachers, on their pedagogical practice, in collaborative workshop settings. One of the common outcomes of such workshops, the "conversion" experience described in the literature (Russell 295), is due in large measure, we would argue, to the fact that they involve shared vision building about the educational process itself. Over the past decades, many teachers who have attended WAC workshops have become more reflective about their teaching and more collaborative in their pedagogy (see Walvoord et al.)—they have become what may be defined as change agents. WAC programs have continued to grow in large measure because of their continued success and support at the local level.

By its very nature, then, WAC has been and continues to be a dynamic movement, one well suited to a postmodern paradigm of change in higher education. Change may be unsettling, but it also provides new opportunities for program development like those described in this volume. WAC programs could transform themselves so completely in the coming decades that the phrase "writing across the curriculum" might even disappear; but we trust that as long as there are teachers and administrators who care about effective teaching and student learning, the goals of WAC programs will continue to inform whatever new educational initiatives might appear on the horizon.

Notes

1. The first WAC faculty seminar was held in 1970 at Central College in Pella, Iowa, directed by Barbara Walvoord (see Russell 283; Walvoord 75).

2. For information about these conferences, contact Barbara Cambridge, Director, AAHE Assessment Forum, One Dupont Circle, Suite 360, Washington, DC 20036-1110.

3. For information on how to subscribe to the Service Learning and Writing Listserv, write to listmgr@lists.ncte.org.

4. The Immigration and Nationality Act of 1965 changed the old quota system for immigration, which favored immigrants from Europe, to a system that favors family members of people already in the United States. In the 1950s, the top three countries of origin for immigrants were Germany, Canada, and the United Kingdom. Today, about half of the legal immigrants to the United States come from seven developing nations: Mexico, the Philippines, Vietnam, the Dominican Republic, China and Taiwan, Korea, and India (see Cassidy 41).

5. An excellent example of how a single teacher can bring about enormous change is the Advancement Via Individual Determination (AVID) program, begun in 1980 by English teacher Mary Catherine Swanson of Clairemont High School in San Diego. Swanson combined rigorous

classes and a supportive environment to help at-risk students get ready for college. The program is now nationwide; nearly 95 percent of the students who experience it attend college (Freedman).

Works Cited

Abercrombie, M. L. J. *The Anatomy of Judgement: An Investigation into the Processes of Perception and Reasoning*. Harmondsworth, UK: Penguin, 1969.

Adler-Kassner, Linda, Robert Crooks, and Ann Watters. "Service-Learning and Composition at the Crossroads." *Writing the Community: Concepts and Models for Service-Learning in Composition*. Ed. Linda Adler-Kassner, Robert Crooks, and Ann Watters. Washington, DC: AAHE, 1997. 1–17.

Beckhard, Richard, and Wendy Pritchard. *Changing the Essence: The Art of Creating and Leading Fundamental Change in Organizations*. San Francisco: Jossey-Bass, 1992.

Birkerts, Sven. *The Gutenberg Elegies: The Fate of Reading in an Electronic Age*. Boston: Faber, 1994.

Blumenstyk, Goldie, and Denise K. Magner. "As Assessment Draws New Converts, Backers Gather to Ask 'What Works?'" *Chronicle of Higher Education* 11 July 1990: A11.

Bolter, J. David. *Writing Space: The Computer, Hypertext, and the History of Writing*. Hillsdale, NJ: Erlbaum, 1991.

Boquet, Elizabeth H. "'Our Little Secret': A History of Writing Centers, Pre- to Post-open Admissions." *College Composition and Communication* 50 (1999): 463–82.

Boyer Commission on Educating Undergraduates in the Research University. *Reinventing Undergraduate Education: A Blueprint for America's Research Universities*. SUNY Stony Brook for the Carnegie Foundation for the Advancement of Teaching, 1998.

Britton, James N. *Language and Learning*. London: Allen Lane, 1970.

Britton, James N., et al. *The Development of Writing Abilities (11–18)*. London: Macmillan, 1975.

Bruffee, Kenneth A. "Collaborative Learning and the 'Conversation of Mankind.'" *College English* 46 (1984): 635–53.

Burkland, Jill, and Diana Freisinger. "Talking about Writing: The Role of the Writing Lab." *Language Connections: Writing and Reading Across the Curriculum.* Ed. Toby Fulwiler and Art Young. Urbana: NCTE, 1982. 167–78.

Carino, Peter. "Open Admissions and the Construction of Writing Center History: A Tale of Three Models." *Writing Center Journal* 17 (1996): 30–48.

Cassidy, John. "The Melting-Pot Myth." *New Yorker* 14 July 1997: 40–43.

Conference on College Composition and Communication. "Students' Right to Their Own Language" [Special Issue]. *College Composition and Communication* 25 (1974): 1–32.

Emig, Janet. "Writing as a Mode of Learning." *College Composition and Communication* 28 (1977): 122–28.

Faigley, Lester. "After the Revolution." *College Composition and Communication* 48 (1997): 30–43.

Farris, Christine, and Raymond Smith. "Writing-Intensive Courses: Tools for Curricular Change." *Writing Across the Curriculum: A Guide to Developing Programs.* Ed. Susan H. McLeod and Margot Soven. Academic.Writing Landmark Publications in Writing Studies: http://aw.colostate.edu/books/mcleod_soven/ 2000. Originally published in print by Sage (Newbury Park, CA), 1992.

Finkel, Donald L., and G. Stephen Monk. "Teachers and Learning Groups: Dissolution of the Atlas Complex." *Learning in Groups.* New Directions for Teaching and Learning 14. Ed. Clark Bouton and Russell Y. Garth. San Francisco: Jossey-Bass, 1983. 83–97.

Finn, Chester E. Jr., and Brunno V. Manno. "Behind the Curtain." *Wilson Quarterly* 20 (1996): 44–57.

Freedman, Jonathan. *Wall of Fame.* San Diego: AVID Academic P with San Diego State UP, 2000.

Fullan, Michael. *Change Forces: Probing the Depth of Educational Reform.* New York: Falmer, 1993.

Gabelnick, Faith G., et al. *Learning Communities: Creating Connections among Students, Faculty, and Disciplines.* San Francisco: Jossey-Bass, 1990.

Gleick, James. *Chaos: Making a New Science.* New York: Penguin, 1987.

Gold, Steven D., and Sarah Ritchie. "How State Spending Patterns Have Been Changing." *Center for the Study of the States State Fiscal Brief.* Dec. 1995: 1–6.

Graff, Gerald. "Colleges Are Depriving Students of a Connected View of Scholarship." *Chronicle of Higher Education* 13 Feb. 1991: A48.

Haney, Walter. "Testing and Minorities." *Beyond Silenced Voices: Class, Race, and Gender in United States Schools.* Ed. Lois Weiss and Michelle Fine. Albany: SUNY P, 1993. 45–74.

Haworth, Karla. "Report Urges Colleges to Inspire Students and Improve Teaching." *Chronicle of Higher Education* 11 Apr. 1997: A14.

Heilker, Paul. "Rhetoric Made Real: Civic Discourse and Writing Beyond the Curriculum." Adler-Kassner, Crooks, and Watters 71–77.

Herrington, Anne, and Charles Moran. "Writing in the Disciplines: A Prospect." *Writing, Teaching, and Learning in the Disciplines.* Ed. Anne Herrington and Charles Moran. New York: MLA, 1992. 231–44.

Herzberg, Bruce. "Community Service and Critical Teaching." *Writing the Community: Concepts and Models for Service-Learning in Composition.* Ed. Linda Adler-Kassner, Robert Crooks, and Ann Watters. Washington, DC: AAHE, 1997. 57–69.

Jaschik, Scott. "Panel Seeks Common Assessment Method." *Chronicle of Higher Education* 2 Sept. 1992: A30.

Landow, George P. *Hypertext 2.0.* Rev. and amplified ed. Baltimore, MD: Johns Hopkins UP, 1997.

Lanham, Richard A. *The Electronic Word: Democracy, Technology, and the Arts.* Chicago: U of Chicago P, 1993.

Leatherman, Courtney. "Heavy Reliance on Low-Paid Lecturers Said to Produce 'Faceless Departments.'" *Chronicle of Higher Education* 28 Mar. 1997: A12–13.

Lenzner, Robert, and Stephen S. Johnson. "Seeing Things as They Really Are." *Forbes* 10 Mar. 1997: 122–27.

Lively, Kit. "Campus 'Accountability' Is Hot Again." *Chronicle of Higher Education* 2 Sept. 1992: A25.

Magner, Denise K. "Report Describes 'Revival of General Education.'" *Chronicle of Higher Education* 19 Jan. 1994: A20.

Magrath, C. Peter. "Eliminating Tenure without Destroying Academic Freedom." *Chronicle of Higher Education* 28 Feb. 1997: A60.

McLaughlin, Milbrey W. "The Rand Change Agent Study Revisited: Macro Perspectives and Micro Realities." *Educational Researcher* 19 (1990): 11–16.

McLeod, Susan H. "The Foreigner: WAC Directors as Agents of Change." *Resituating Writing: Constructing and Administering Writing Programs.* Ed. Joseph Janangelo and Kristine Hansen. Portsmouth, NH: Heinemann-Boynton/Cook, 1995. 108–16.

———. "Writing Across the Curriculum: The Second Stage, and Beyond." *College Composition and Communication* 40 (1989): 337–43.

Menad, Louis. "Everybody Else's College Education." *New York Times Magazine* 20 Apr. 1997: 48–49.

North, Stephen. "The Idea of a Writing Center." *College English* 46 (1984): 433–46.

Olson, Gary A. *Writing Centers: Theory and Administration.* Urbana, IL: NCTE, 1984.

Raimes, Ann. "Out of the Woods: Emerging Traditions in the Teaching of Writing." *TESOL Quarterly* 25 (1991): 407–30.

Reiss, Donna, Dickie Selfe, and Art Young, eds. *Electronic Communication Across the Curriculum.* Urbana, IL: NCTE, 1998.

Royster, Jacqueline Jones, and Jean C. Williams. "History in the Spaces Left: African American Presence and Narratives of Composition Studies." *College Composition and Communication* 50 (1999): 563–84.

Russell, David R. *Writing in the Academic Disciplines, 1870–1990: A Curricular History.* Carbondale: Southern Illinois UP, 1991.

Senge, Peter M. *The Fifth Discipline: The Art and Practice of the Learning Organization.* New York: Doubleday/Currency, 1990.

Silva, Tony, Ilona Leki, and Joan Carson. "Broadening the Perspective of Mainstream Composition Studies: Some Thoughts from the Disciplinary Margins." *Written Communication* 14 (1997): 398–428.

Sturnick, Judith. "Looking at Change in Higher Education." Writing Across the Curriculum Conference. Charleston, SC. 7 Feb. 1997.

Teaching/Learning Model. U of Phoenix. Aug. 1997 <http://www.uophx.edu/catalog/teaching.html>.

Thaiss, Christopher. "The Future of Writing Across the Curriculum Programs." *Strengthening Programs for Writing Across the Curriculum.* Ed. Susan H. McLeod. San Francisco: Jossey-Bass, 1988. 91–102.

Tierney, Rob. "Testing for the Greater Good: Social Injustice and the Conspiracy of the Proficiency Standards." *Council Chronicle* [Urbana, IL] Nov. 1998: 20, 16–17.

University of Colorado Online. Aug. 1997 <http://cuonline.edu/index.html>.

University of Phoenix. Aug. 1997 <http://www.uophx.edu>.

Villanueva, Victor. "On the Rhetoric and Precedents of Racism." *College Composition and Communication* 50 (1999): 645–61.

Walvoord, Barbara E. "The Future of WAC." *College English* 58 (Jan. 1996): 58–79.

Walvoord, Barbara, et al. *In the Long Run: A Study of Faculty in Three Writing-Across-the-Curriculum Programs.* Urbana, IL: NCTE, 1997.

Weimer, Maryellen. Foreword. *Engaging Ideas: The Professor's Guide to Integrating Writing, Critical Thinking, and Active Learning in the Classroom.* By John Bean. San Francisco: Jossey Bass, 1996.

Wolfe, Alan. "The Feudal Culture of the Postmodern University." *Wilson Quarterly* 20 (1996): 54–66.

Young, Jeffrey R. "Rethinking the Role of the Professor in an Age of High-Tech Tools." *Chronicle of Higher Education* 3 Oct. 1997: A26–28.

Zook, Jim. "Panel Asks Government to Measure College Learning." *Chronicle of Higher Education* 4 Aug. 1993: A20.

Chapter Two

Accommodating Complexity: WAC Program Evaluation in the Age of Accountability

William Condon
Washington State University

A ssessment. *Accountability.* These two closely related words are sufficient in and of themselves to chill the blood and roll the eyes of those who manage writing programs in general and writing-across-the-curriculum (WAC) programs in particular. Assessing writing is a complicated task made increasingly complex by teachers' desire for assessments that support instruction and, on the other end of the spectrum, the public's demand for *proof* of effective instruction. Once upon a time, the evaluation of writing seemed deceptively simple. Either a writing teacher in a single classroom applied what looked like his or her subjective judgment to each student's written products, or large numbers of students sat for multiple-choice-question (MCQ) tests that, the psychometricians assured us, measured verbal abilities indirectly, including the ability to write. Such assertions were always suspect since even the most basic common sense tells us that in order to assess writing ability, we must look at direct measures—at writing—rather than at bubbles filled in on an answer sheet. And so, over the years, writing teachers have led the way in establishing direct tests of writing (White; Morris) and, following the same impetus, portfolio-based writing assessment (Belanoff and Elbow; Belanoff and Dickson).

Each of these developments has accommodated the complexity involved in assessing writing ability, and each cycle of reform has produced a more complex, less positivist methodology for writing assessment—increasing the validity of the instrument while at the same time satisfying the psychometricians' criteria of reliability (Hamp-Lyons and Condon, *Assessing*; LeMahieu, Gitomer, and Eresh). Implicit in that evolution is the sense that writing itself seems more consistent with chaos theory than with the epistemology expressed in positivism. The idea of the "butterfly effect" perhaps best captures the impact of a given class or learning experience on a given student. Changes in writing ability depend, we know, on a dizzying array of factors—among others, the student's readiness, openness, and willingness; the teacher's careful planning, theoretical and pedagogical knowledge, good timing, and even showmanship; and careful design of and timing in the curriculum. Even then, even when these complicated factors come together in what we've come to call a "teachable moment," the effects may take years to manifest—at which point, they are hard to connect with any single class, teacher, or learning experience. In sum, the more we learn about the enterprise of writing and about the enterprise of *teaching* writing, the more complicated the task of teaching writing seems. And as difficult as the teaching of writing is, assessing writing involves yet another layer of difficulty.

How much more complicated, then, is the enterprise of assessing writing across the curriculum? How much more complex is the activity of evaluating WAC programs? I imagine here a set of nesting eggs, one inside the other. The expanding layers represent the stakeholders in writing—students as the center egg, then faculty, administrators, parents, politicians, the public at large. Each has a different set of questions. Each wants some return on investment. Each larger egg involves more people and therefore carries a broader context and an expanding set of stakes. Each larger egg represents one more level of difficulty above the difficulty of "simply" assessing writing ability. Thus, each larger egg comes with a worrisome combination of greater complexity and higher stakes.

In the face of these higher stakes, we are also hampered by the failure of traditional measurement tools and the emergent, experimental nature of newer and better tools. We may have come a long way since the development of direct tests of writing in the late 1960s and early 1970s, but the newer tools that have proven effective for measuring writing ability are still extremely limited in use and scope. Even the oldest of the improved methods, direct tests of writing—typically a timed writing holistically scored—are still only second to MCQ tests in frequency of use. Direct tests, of course, provide greater validity because they actually focus on a sample of what they purport to measure—writing. But their limitation to only one sample, collected under only one set of writing conditions—and that set itself the most constrained and unrealistic of all conditions under which people write—means that direct tests as well are able to answer only fairly simple, straightforward questions about a student's writing ability (such as whether that student is ready for the standard course in first-year composition or needs more practice first). Often, as Edward White points out, such questions depend on the most basic of writing skills—the ability to write consistently in complete sentences, or to use sentence-level punctuation correctly, or to arrange a short essay effectively into paragraphs (10–16).

Roberta Camp argues convincingly that we need more robust kinds of writing assessments, assessments that can answer more complicated and sophisticated questions about students' writing competencies ("Changing," "New Views"). Portfolios have begun to provide such assessments, but employing portfolios to provide reliable judgments involves levels of logistical and intellectual complication that sometimes stagger the teachers and administrators involved in the effort (Hamp-Lyons and Condon, "Questioning," *Assessing*). The experience can be so daunting that the group who developed Washington State's University Writing Portfolio assessment program compared their experience to "shooting Niagara" (Haswell, Wyche-Smith, and Johnson-Shull). Even strong advocates of the portfolio method have compared the experience to jumping off a cliff (Condon and Hamp-Lyons). Writing assessment, then, has become a much more complicated affair than it once was; in the attempt to measure more, and to make measures as fair and as accurate as possible, assessments themselves have become progressively more difficult to develop and to manage.

Emergent tools, greater complexity, higher risk. Each expansion of the audience outward raises the stakes, demands an accounting, affects the budget. Each audience for the evaluation comes to it from a different vantage point and looks for the evaluation to meet different needs. Inside the program, so to speak, students and faculty have needs closely related to instruction. As we move up the hierarchy, further away from the classroom, evaluation gradually but inexorably turns into accountability—into the ability to document a program's effectiveness, to lay out the benefits it offers to different stakeholders, and to justify a program's existence or continued growth.

Internal audiences—students and faculty—have perhaps the most direct need for information about performance. Students want to know how well they are doing, of course, and they want to know at times and in ways that often do not fit within the traditional course and grading agenda. What does a particular grade in a composition course or a writing intensive course mean in terms of overall writing ability? How does it predict the usefulness of that level of writing ability as students approach writing assignments in other courses— whether WAC or "regular"? Should they feel satisfied with their current level of ability, or should they devote significant amounts of time and tuition money to further development? What will the curriculum demand of their writing, and how well prepared are they to meet those demands? How will the lessons they learn about writing in their chosen fields help them after graduation? These are just a few of the easier questions students bring to this assessment arena. Some of these questions are shared by those who teach the students, both in writing courses and in other courses in the curriculum. Teachers—WAC faculty in particular—need to know what they can reasonably expect students to be able to do with and in writing, and they need to match those expectations with the level of expectations that are implicit in the teachers' own course objectives, objectives which, in turn, are determined by their location within the curriculum. Teachers need to know how to build more effective assignments—knowledge that involves both information about the writing students will do after taking a particular course (in careers or in subsequent courses) and information about the writing students have done to that point in the university's curriculum.

Audiences external to the WAC program want to know how well it works, but they want that information for varying reasons. University administrators, as Haswell and McLeod have pointed out, need information that can educate them about WAC in general and that can demonstrate the program's effectiveness, its impact on students, on faculty, and on learning in specific and in general. Beyond the academy, parents, legislators, employers, and the public in general want *results*—graduates who can write effectively as they enter their careers (our students, too, as they become our alumnae/i, share this need). At this level, evaluation works in the service of accountability, and as the scope for evaluation moves outward, evaluation becomes more and more involved with the overall accountability of the institution. Thus, WAC data can—and should—figure prominently in university accreditation; they should provide administrators with evidence that legislators can understand, evidence that documents the institution's efforts to provide more effective, more responsive learning opportunities for its students.

Each of these levels, each of these audiences, has complex needs that go far beyond the information we can gather by merely assessing students' writing. To date, WAC programs have done a poor job of addressing most of these audiences. Understandably, since WAC has been primarily a faculty development movement, program evaluation has focused on the effectiveness of those efforts. Even here, though, the results have been mixed. Fulwiler and Young admit that their early efforts at WAC evaluation led to the realization that they needed better assessment tools (2). As time passes, our efforts in this area are producing more useful results (Walvoord et al.). Still, the literature about WAC is only beginning to address questions that extend beyond the effectiveness of faculty seminars. In the latest—and to my mind the best—collection of essays about evaluating WAC, Kathleen Blake Yancey and Brian Huot's *Assessing Writing Across the Curriculum,* only two selections (Beason and Darrow; Kinkead) address student outcomes from WAC, and only two others (Morgan; Haswell and McLeod) address the administrative audience for WAC evaluation. The rest address the "same-old, same-old" issues that surround faculty development *qua* curriculum reform. We have to do more. We must do better.

As difficult as the problems are, as complex as they have become, the solutions involve, in effect, treating that complexity as an advantage. As long as we fall for the positivists' notion that the way to measure a complex construct is to reduce it to its simplest components and then measure each of those independently of the others, we will be unable to measure a construct as complicated as writing—and seriously at sea trying to measure the even more complex effects of a WAC program. If we make the complexity of the task clear to all, however, and if we resist the urge to oversimplify, we can open up space to explore new methods of assessment and evaluation, methods that promise to contribute to a fuller understanding of what happens throughout our WAC programs.

The very fact that we can frame the issue in these terms is an indication of how markedly assessment has changed in the last decade. For many years, Edward White's maxim, "Assess yourself, or others will do it for (to) you" represented not only good advice, but also current practice. Assessments were enforced from outside the instructional context; and those assessments were generally hostile to instruction—reducing learning to a set of questionable skills, ignoring local curricular goals and objectives in favor of some putative national norm, taking major amounts of time away from instruction so that students could learn effective test-taking strategies, and so forth (Smith and Rottenberg). In the face of such a threat, White's advice made sense. But the necessity of such advice is part of the reason we tend to dread assessment. It was the devil we knew, and we used it to fend off the devil we didn't know.

Changing the Paradigm for Assessment

Today, however, positivist models of assessment are giving way to constructivist models, local assessments based in inquiry and collaborative investigation rather than outside assessments delegated to national testing companies or experts in psychometrics. This newer model, pioneered by Guba and Lincoln, engages all the assessment stakeholders in designing the evaluation, carrying out the methodology, examining the results, and formulating responses to the findings. The constructivist model mirrors the research process that is already a fact of life for college faculty. As a result, assessment seems far less threatening and mysterious than it was in the days when psychometricians controlled the processes. Today, we have better reasons to assess, and we have tools for evaluation that are far more familiar to us, tools we can control. Thus, we can respond to the task of assessment without feeling defensive in the way White's maxim implies; instead, we can welcome assessment as a process that helps us achieve goals that are important to us.

The first step in a constructivist evaluation is to involve stakeholders in setting goals and objectives for the evaluation that are as close as possible to the goals and objectives for the activity being evaluated. If a WAC program seeks to increase the amount of writing students do as they move through the curriculum, then a constructivist evaluation would seek to discover whether, in fact, students write more than they did before the implementation of WAC. If the program objectives involve helping students become better writers, then the constructivist evaluation entails collaboratively defining "better" and determining the best ways of discovering whether students are better writers as a result of the program's efforts. (For an excellent example of how to document improvement in student writing, see Haswell, "Documenting.") Any and all measures in this process come out of the local context for the evaluation, and data collecting is designed to be as nonintrusive as possible. So, rather than require students in a course to sit for a timed writing that at best is only tenuously related to their curriculum, data collection would entail looking at the products of their class work—at the instructional outcomes they would have produced anyway. An added benefit, of course, is that these outcomes flow directly from the instructional objectives the teacher sets in designing the course in the first place, completing the constructivist cycle in such a way that the feedback from one iteration of the evaluation acts more as feed-*forward*, since its most immediate use is in improving instruction in the next iteration. This emphasis on engaging assessment with instruction in order to improve instruction first and *then* supply data for accountability to audiences outside the classroom fits well with learners' and teachers' needs—in addition, the priorities inherent in the process are more consistent with an educational process.

The proof of that last assertion lies in the literature that has grown out of the constructivist paradigm. Thomas Angelo and Patricia Cross's *Classroom Assessment Techniques,* for example, contains example after example of evaluations that grow out of and in turn support improvement in classroom instruction. Similarly, Banta's *Making a Difference: Outcomes of a Decade of Assessment in Higher Education* provides examples of program evaluations that examine instructional outcomes in order both to improve instruction and to provide data that are useful in establishing a program's accountability. Indeed, if programs are to survive the sheer weight of the demands for assessment and accountability, then programs must develop means of evaluation that focus first on improving learning and then, by extension, on being accountable to administrators, parents, the public, and the legislature. Washington State University's experience provides two useful examples of this kind of evaluation.[1]

Each year, incoming first-year students sit for the Writing Placement Exam (WPE), which determines whether a given student needs extra assistance in English 101, WSU's first-year composition course. Those who need help—about 14 percent of the incoming class—add a weekly small-group writing tutorial, English 102, to their English 101 enrollment. Later, as rising juniors, these students complete the University Writing Portfolio, a midcareer assessment of their writing. At that point, these students, whose WPE's placed them in the bottom third of entering students with regard to writing ability, perform almost identically to their classmates whose WPE's had indicated they did not need the extra assistance provided in English 102:

- ◆ Of 2,130 students who placed into English 101, 192 (9 percent) received a "Needs Work" rating on the Junior Writing Portfolio.

- ◆ Of 356 students who placed into English 101 + 102, 39 (11 percent) received a "Needs Work" rating on the Junior Writing Portfolio.

As these percentages demonstrate, the difference at the junior level is insignificant. Only 9 percent of the students who enter as competent writers evince a need for additional assistance as they enter their upper-division course (two of which will be Writing in the Major, or WID, courses). By comparison, only 11 percent of those who had been weaker writers at entry still occupy that niche. Does the peer-facilitated small-group tutorial help students improve their writing abilities? The figures indicate that the program works—feedback that was important to those involved in the instruction, but that proved equally impressive when cited to the provost, the Board of Regents, and the Higher Education Coordinating Board.

A second example also derives from the University Writing Portfolio. Ongoing assessment—in this case the biennial portfolio study for 1995–97—revealed a problem: among WSU's transfer students, more than 37 percent of non-native speakers (NNS) of English received a "Needs Work" rating on the portfolio—a rate more than three times higher than for the student body as a whole, which was 11 percent (Bonnema, Haswell, and Norris). Although we might expect students whose native language is not English to have a somewhat higher "Needs Work" rate than native speakers of English, 37 percent seemed far too high. Clearly, these students' needs were not being met. In examining the reasons for the high rate, we discovered that many of these students made poor selections of writing to include in their portfolios. Therefore, we changed how we work with these students so that they provide longer, more complex samples of their class work. In addition, the English department completely reformed its ESL offerings, building the portfolio process as a classroom assessment tool into English 105 (the equivalent of English 101 for non-native speakers) and changing that course so that it more completely parallels 101. Thus, more of our NNS transfer students take English 105 at WSU, rather than taking 101 elsewhere and transferring the credit. One result of these changes is that during the 1997–99 biennium, the rate at which NNS transfer students received a "Needs Work" rating dropped to 27 percent. We suspect this figure is still too high, but it represents good progress—and fast progress—in both formally and informally accommodating the instructional needs of these students.

These two examples lead to the next important reason that WAC programs should perform their own evaluations: we do it better. Indeed, in what Kathleen Yancey has called a "third wave" of assessment (491), all good assessment, like politics, is local. The constructivist paradigm takes advantage of access to local contexts—to curriculum, faculty, administrators, students, institutional values, etc.—in order to increase the evaluation's usefulness by increasing its relevance to the local context. Positivist methodologies tend to distance evaluation from the local context not only by employing outside experts to perform the evaluation, but also by using standard methodologies rather than developing methods that fit the context of the program being evaluated. The results are often disastrous, as even a casual perusal of Stephen Jay Gould's *The Mismeasure of Man* reveals. As I argued earlier, indirect tests of writing are prima facie invalid—lacking construct validity in particular—because they do not involve looking at even a small sample of the construct being assessed (writing). In such cases, mismeasurement is a foregone conclusion. Worse, since positivist models most often culminate in statistics, they report numerical measurements, which are too often subject to misuse. Both Educational Testing Service (ETS) and ACT administrators assert forcefully, for example, that the SAT and ACT should not be used for purposes of writing placement, yet these tests are routinely used for that purpose. Finally, indirect tests lack universal fairness. Again, the statistics and reports from the agencies themselves—from ACT and ETS—indicate unintended yet marked differences in performance by race, ethnicity, and culture. Put simply, these tests discriminate in favor of white, middle- and upper-class, urban and suburban students. By contrast, White and Thomas found that direct tests of writing resulted in fairer outcomes (186–87), and newer methods such as performance assessments clearly provide fairer opportunities for students to establish their competencies (Hamp-Lyons and Condon, *Assessing*). I will not argue that local assessments are free from problems, only that assessments designed locally to address local initiatives and contexts are more likely to portray those contexts accurately and treat the stakeholders fairly than are large-scale state, regional, or national assessments which are much more likely, of necessity, to use positivist methodologies.

Finally, by assessing locally we can develop strong ties with other units within our institutions whose missions affect WAC or whose philosophies are similar. The statistics on the success of WSU's English 102 program inspired the Student Advising and Learning Center (SALC) as that unit designed its Freshman Seminar Program—small, peer-facilitated courses that support students' learning and promote coherence among the students' classroom experiences. This program has proven highly effective (Henscheid), and the collaborations between SALC and the Campus Writing Programs continue to provide exciting opportunities for teaching and learning. Similarly, the Writing Programs' promotion of active learning, alternative assessments, and critical thinking has resulted in a natural partnership with WSU's Center for Teaching, Learning, and Technology (CTLT). CTLT, in turn, provides vital expertise as Writing Programs faculty search for better ways to measure the effectiveness of various programs. Most recently, students in a graduate seminar on writing assessment helped devise a rubric for measuring critical thinking. CTLT then "adopted" the rubric, conducting vital work in validating the rubric and giving it wider trials by encouraging faculty in general education courses to use it as a measure of instructional effectiveness. As a result, the director of general education, the senior fellow of CTLT (a faculty member), and the director of Campus Writing Programs just received a grant to do further work on the rubric—a grant that came from Washington's Higher Education Coordinating Board. Collaborations that grow out of evaluation activities lead to useful and beneficial relationships that reflect credit on all the partners to the collaboration. No positivist evaluation that I know of provides this kind of payoff.

In the end, what do these new methods mean for evaluating WAC programs? Clearly, no single form of assessment will give us all the information we seek. Just as clearly, collecting data will involve moving beyond traditional forms of writing assessment and research. The benefits of moving into new methods for evaluation, however, are substantial. Constructivist methods engage as wide a range of stakeholders as possible in order to frame questions, set goals, and devise methodologies—providing a context within which vital collaborative relationships are established and nourished. In addition, these evaluations yield richer sets of information and outcomes, so that improving WAC programs becomes easier, if only because the arguments for improvement are based on rich, convincing data. Finally, the constructivist paradigm recognizes that evaluation and improvement constitute a continual cycle—the bad news is that assessment becomes a constant, continuing activity, but the good news is that improvement also becomes a constant, continuing activity. By paying attention to the stakes and the stakeholders, by using multiple methodologies, by exploiting the relationships between WAC and other university initiatives, and by breaking down larger questions about effectiveness into smaller, more easily addressed questions, we can make significant progress toward accommodating the level of complexity that WAC programs inevitably face, not just in evaluation but in the very act of addressing their missions.

Implications

Accommodating complexity begins when we extend current efforts at WAC evaluation to include a wider range of stakeholders. While WAC has focused on faculty practice—on reforming pedagogy—its primary effect is on the students whose learning is affected by that pedagogy. We need to know more about the effects of WAC courses on students' writing. We can measure some of these effects by assessing the writing students do, of course. Measuring writing competencies at entry and at several points along students' college careers allows us to make some statements about the impact a WAC curriculum has on the quality of students' writing. Two examples suffice to demonstrate ways in which such assessments might prove useful as WAC evaluations.

The first example is drawn from Washington State University, where (as mentioned earlier) entering first-year students write two timed essays in a single two-hour sitting in order to help faculty place the students into the appropriate first-year composition course. Then, at the junior level, students sit for another timed writing, identical in format to the Writing Placement Exam, and this writing, along with three essays written in other classes, makes up a University Writing Portfolio, which serves as a qualifying exam for WSU's Writing in the Major courses. Thus, students entering their major concentrations receive feedback on their writing, and those who need additional assistance with writing are identified and guided into an appropriate level of assistance. One way in which these assessment experiences have proven useful is the comparisons we can make between the entry-level Writing Placement Exam and the junior-level Portfolio Timed Writing: in a preliminary study of students who, by chance, wrote on similar topics at the two levels, Rich Haswell discovered several areas in which students had gained ground in writing as they moved through WSU's writing-rich general education program. This "value-added" form of assessment allows us to document the fact that widespread learning is occurring in the curriculum, that students are becoming better writers in general and along specific dimensions such as organization, focus, use of support, style, mechanics, and so forth. The study also allows Haswell to argue that students become more *efficient* writers, since juniors wrote longer sentences, longer paragraphs, and more words on the same task they performed as first-year students, even though the juniors had half an hour less time to write than they did as first-year students (Haswell, "Preliminary Results"). This evidence proved extremely useful to the institution as it prepared for its ten-year accreditation process, and the final study has become part of WSU's reports to Washington's Higher Education Coordinating Board (HECB), the body that mediates between the universities and the legislature. Thus, a report which assures inside stakeholders that WSU's WAC program is having positive effects also serves to help WSU's administration argue in several critical venues that the institution is doing its job vis-à-vis writing instruction. (A fuller version of this study can be found in Haswell, "Documenting.")

The second example speaks more to external audiences and is happening as I write. In response to the legislature's call for "performance measures" that can be used to evaluate the effectiveness of Washington's six four-year universities, the six provosts asked the universities' assessment officers and writing programs staff to attempt to develop a writing assessment that could serve as an accountability measure—in other words, an assessment that the universities could ask the legislature to use in allocating state higher education funds. Obviously, if the plan works, this will be a high-stakes assessment for the institutions. They will be able to choose writing as a performance measure and to stake some portion of their state funding on being able to improve their students' performance on the assessment. The plan, as drawn up by Gerald Gillmore, the University of Washington's assessment officer, calls for collecting, at random, ten papers from each of ten senior-level classes (from ten different departments) on each of the six university campuses. These six hundred papers would be evaluated each summer by a combination of (1) writing programs faculty, (2) faculty in the disciplines from which the papers were selected, and (3) community members who are in careers in those disciplines. A university's performance would be measured by the proportion of students achieving a score of "Acceptable" in six categories of performance: Content, Organization, Reasoning, Rhetoric, Conventions, and Disciplinarity. In the pilot study conducted during the summer of 1998, an interdisciplinary team of writing specialists, assessment specialists, faculty from several other disciplines, and community members from those same disciplines was able to derive a scoring rubric and rate sample essays (see Gillmore). A second pilot in the summer of 1999 engaged a similar group of raters who evaluated approximately sixty essays and, using the rubric, achieved reliability of .79 on their overall scores.

This project needs further development before it can fulfill its promise as a fair, nonreductive, rigorous assessment of writing that can provide the major stakeholders (the universities and the legislature) with the information they need to make the decisions each must make. This feedback would be useful to the institutions as they focus their efforts on improvement: if their students do well in "Content" and "Conventions" but poorly in "Reasoning" and "Rhetoric," then they can focus their efforts on the latter two categories. If students perform well, for example, in all the categories except "Disciplinarity," then the university might enact some kind of WID program, along with examining the other ways in which departments prepare their majors to enter the discourse community of a given field. In turn, the legislature would tie some portion of the university's funding to the institution's ability to increase the proportion of students receiving scores of "Acceptable" in specific categories or across all the categories.

In both these examples, common assessment tools (performance assessments and direct tests of writing that use timed writings) are focused on particular questions that institutions must ask about WAC performance. From the far too general question, "Is WAC working?" we draw less often included questions: "Are students making progress as writers?" and "Are students able to perform satisfactorily as writers by the time they graduate?" These questions, together with others we might ask, begin to paint a more complete picture of students' progress and competencies as writers moving through the curriculum. In turn, that picture contributes to an overall understanding of how well the WAC program is working.

Clearly, evaluations of this sort cannot rely principally on assessments that are separated from the curriculum. For one thing, such assessments involve students in tasks in which they have no real stake. Even if we could require all students to complete a writing assessment task—say, a timed writing—what assurance can we have that students are motivated to do their best? Such tasks are typically barrier tests, requiring only a competent performance in order for the student to pass. If we are to gain an accurate picture of students' writing abilities, WAC measures need to come from high-stakes performances, from products of the students' degree work. Unless we collect samples of such high-stakes work, we cannot be certain that our portrait of abilities will be accurate or that it will serve us as we look to improve our performance as a whole.

Collecting actual classroom performances has another advantage, one so valuable that it is reason enough for collecting such samples. The opportunity to involve assessment with instruction provides many chances to examine students' progress, provide assistance to those who demonstrate a need for assistance, and target faculty development and curriculum reform wisely. In order to provide such rich and varied feedback and to perform the kinds of program evaluation that such data allow, we need to tap into instruction. To date, WAC evaluators' best and most prominent efforts have focused on what happens to faculty and to the courses and materials they design (Walvoord and McCarthy; Walvoord et al.). As important as that kind of evaluation is, its limits in today's context are clear: such evaluations stop far too short of outcomes, of the effects that a WAC curriculum has on students' development as writers. If we are to examine this crucial area, then we need to use performance assessments. We need to collect students' performances on the assignments they fulfill within the WAC curriculum, and we need to examine those performances in ways that help us identify the outcomes of our WAC programs.

To some extent, this kind of assessment is already being done at a handful of small liberal arts colleges around the country, the most prominent example of which is Alverno College in Milwaukee. Students at these schools keep what is being called a "developmental portfolio," a record of their progress toward the objectives the school sets in its curriculum. In smaller schools, the logistics of such assessments are less daunting than they are at large schools, and the lines of communication needed among faculty and students are easier to build and maintain. Yet this kind of performance assessment, in some form or another, is the only tool we have that allows us to collect the data we really need to examine. In the past—and still today in large-scale assessments such as ACT, SAT, NAEP, CAT, etc.—testing and evaluation have been separate from the curriculum. Tests and other tasks were set without regard to what happened in a particular school or a particular classroom. And, as often happened, if a school set curricular goals that were significantly different from the goals assumed by the test makers, that school's students would not perform well on the test. That is the stranglehold that large-scale assessment has on our K–12 school system. If we are to avoid a similar stranglehold on higher education, then we have to find ways to evaluate students' work as they try to achieve the goals our institutions set for them. We have to find ways, no matter the scale of our operations, to collect information on how well our curriculum is serving our students. Robust performance assessments, as the smaller schools have shown, can provide to outside stakeholders rich, credible, convincing data on performance; and it can provide, to internal stakeholders, evaluations of curriculum and pedagogy that can focus efforts to enhance and extend learning.

Performance assessments, however, are invasive assessments. They get into the curriculum and into the classroom in ways that standardized testing or even direct tests of writing do not. Unlike previous methods and tools for assessment, performance assessment looks directly at the responses students make to the tasks they are assigned in a class or set of classes. Therefore, these actual tasks are exposed to view, along with the teaching methods and practices that frame those tasks. Many faculty members find this prospect worrisome, for obvious reasons. Once the lens of an evaluation is focused on the classroom, how can the faculty member avoid losing control of the assessment and perhaps being unjustly taken to task by its results? The invasive quality of these assessments necessitates an evaluation mindset on the part of the institution that makes every effort to include as many stakeholders as possible. If we listen to external stakeholders, we must look at outcomes; we must be able to show and explain the effects our curricula are having on the learners in our classrooms. As important as these external audiences are, however, we cannot focus on them alone. We must also see to the needs of internal stakeholders—primarily faculty and students—if the evaluation of anything as complex as a WAC program is to be effective. Evaluation cannot be something done *to* faculty and students; it must be something in which they participate—knowingly, at least, if not always willingly.

One way to recruit faculty and students as willing participants is to involve WAC with larger learning outcomes. On an institutional level, this can mean integrating WAC with assessment programs, for example, or developing WAC within the context of a writing-rich general education program. Both these strategies have benefited WAC at WSU, where the University Writing Portfolio, a junior-level assessment, provides data that help evaluate the university's newly revised general education curriculum. The portfolio also acts as a qualifying exam for the two upper-division Writing in the Major (M) courses that each student must take. The position of the portfolio serves WAC in two significant ways: (1) because students must have writing to incorporate into a portfolio, assessment provides an incentive to create and maintain a writing-rich general education curriculum; and (2) because the portfolio identifies students who need further assistance with writing—and because it requires that they get that extra assistance—the portfolio acts as a strong support for the upper-division writing-in-the-disciplines curriculum. Portfolio raters are drawn from faculty who teach M courses since these faculty are the ones setting expectations for students' writing at that level. Thus, these programs serve larger agendas—curriculum reform, faculty development, definition of standards, etc.—and so WAC can participate in the evaluations of these other programs. When the Writing Assessment Office carries out its biennial self-study, it provides information, for example, about students' writing experiences in general education and M courses, about the number of faculty who are assigning writing, and about particular populations such as non-native speakers of English or students in different programs or departments. This information in turn acts as one component of WAC evaluation. Similarly, when general education undergoes its regular evaluations, it yields data about WAC at the lower-division level. In other words, much of the process of evaluating WAC at WSU takes place in ongoing evaluations of programs with which WAC is imbricated. To an extent, then, WAC evaluation involves refocusing and reinterpreting portions of these other programs' data. And, in true symbiotic fashion, the data generated in evaluations focused directly on WAC are useful to these other programs as well.

WAC can also serve individual faculty agendas. For example, results from surveys of WSU faculty who have taken an online version of Angelo and Cross's teaching goals inventory and their students who have taken a corresponding learning goals inventory indicate that faculty and students set a high priority on improving higher-order thinking skills. We know, too, that writing assignments promote higher-order thinking skills (see the preliminary report of the National Center for Higher Education Management Systems). Therefore, the results from the teaching goals and learning goals inventories allow us to join our WAC efforts to a goal that both faculty and students have identified as one of their most important. In this simple example, the WAC program can be framed as serving objectives that are important to both faculty and students. By turning the lens of performance assessment on course curricula and writing assignments (which we might describe as faculty outcomes in a WAC course), we can help faculty improve their course performances by helping them develop assignments that more closely address course goals and objectives (or, in an earlier step, by prompting faculty to develop explicit course goals and objectives).

In a related example, many schools—WSU among them— are busily developing a variety of online learning environments that can serve as extensions of onsite courses and as the environment for distance education. To the extent that these environments allow interaction between students and between students and teachers, they also create a context within which WAC can flourish (see Reiss and Young, Chapter 3, this volume). Online learning environments that foster interaction between students and faculty are, as I have argued elsewhere, *written* classrooms (Condon). Because the primary means for interaction is writing, these environments incorporate writing into the learning experience more thoroughly than any purely onsite classroom can hope to do. As institutions across the country move online, WAC programs need to engage in that effort and participate in the kinds of evaluation that will of necessity accompany these new initiatives (Bober). WAC programs can save money, effort, and time by incorporating WAC into these new environments so that when the environments are evaluated, so is WAC—at least to the extent of its presence in the online environment.

The efforts mentioned in this essay by no means exhaust the possibilities for WAC evaluation. They do, however, begin to lay out an agenda that can lead us productively beyond the current state of the art, which focuses almost solely on faculty development. If we are to demonstrate the ways in which WAC serves its many stakeholders, we must move evaluation beyond current efforts, and in ways already being suggested by Gail Hughes (170–73) and Kathleen Yancey and Brian Huot (7–15). That is, we must begin to employ multiple measures, some quantitative and some qualitative; and we must engage more of WAC's stakeholders both as planners of the evaluation and as audiences for it. Basically, I want to suggest three major directions for WAC evaluation:

1. Using Guba and Lincoln's *Fourth Generation Evaluation* as a touchstone, we need to ask our stakeholders—both within

and outside the university—what outcomes we ought to evaluate when we look at our WAC programs and what interests such an evaluation needs to serve. We also need to involve those stakeholders—students, faculty, administrators, parents, higher education coordinating boards, the public in general—in designing the methods and the specific strategies and tactics we will use to evaluate our programs. This process helps ensure that our WAC curricula serve students' interests, that WAC supports the teaching and learning goals that faculty and students hold in our institution, and that the outcomes of college writing, broadly conceived, prepare students to embark on their careers ready to produce the kinds of writing that will help them perform at a high level.

2. We need to tie evaluation to actual performances—to the concrete outcomes of our WAC programs. In other words, we need to examine WAC course syllabi and assignments, and students' performances in those courses and on those tasks. Separating evaluation from the classroom context results in poorer data and less direct—and hence less useful—evaluations. If faculty are to invest in this kind of intrusive evaluation, the results need to serve the faculty's agendas—results need to figure into faculty development in positive ways, helping faculty satisfy the institution's demand for evidence of strong teaching performance. In addition, such an evaluation needs to serve other agendas that faculty identify as important: promoting higher-order thinking, for example, or maintaining high standards.

3. Evaluating WAC must be a continual effort. In part, WAC evaluation must be continual for reasons of self-preservation. WAC's very complexity demands complex forms of assessment. Continual evaluation allows us to spread the various evaluations out in ways that make them manageable. In addition, continual evaluation allows WAC directors to provide frequent "mini-reports" to stakeholders about the effectiveness of some aspects of the program and the need for reform in others. Thus, continual evaluation creates a context in which WAC evaluation will be perceived as re-

sponsive and responsible; continual evaluation also keeps the WAC program visible to central administrators, who receive the reports the evaluation generates. All these outcomes help the WAC program be a "good scout" within the institution.

The overall purpose of this kind of evaluation, of course, is to maintain the WAC program's health and effectiveness. Evaluation involves far more than protecting the program or providing statistics for their own sake. WAC evaluation ultimately must focus on improving the program, an objective that demands measures that will reveal weakness as well as strength. Over time, the weaknesses can be eliminated and the evaluations can document improvement—hence the need for long-range evaluations. And to the extent that the program is strong and effective—or to the extent that it can demonstrate improvement—the information gathered in these assessments feeds directly into accountability. Thus, WAC evaluation serves multiple needs, helping the program thrive, helping the institution evolve, and helping explain one way in which the university's curriculum serves important aspects of the public's agenda for higher education.

Note

1.   For a complete discussion of writing assessment and instruction at Washington State University, see *Beyond Outcomes: Assessment and Instruction within a University Writing Program*, edited by Richard Haswell (Westport, CT: Ablex, 2001).

Works Cited

Angelo, Thomas A., and Patricia Cross. *Classroom Assessment Techniques*. 2nd ed. San Francisco: Jossey-Bass, 1993.

Banta, Trudy W. *Making a Difference: Outcomes of a Decade of Assessment in Higher Education*. San Francisco: Jossey-Bass, 1993.

Beason, Larry, and Laurel Darrow. "Listening as Assessment." *Assessing Writing Across the Curriculum: Diverse Approaches and Prac-*

tices. Ed. Kathleen Blake Yancey and Brian Huot. Greenwich, CT: Ablex, 1997.

Belanoff, Pat, and Marcia Dickson, eds. *Portfolios: Process and Product*. Portsmouth, NH: Boynton/Cook, 1991.

Belanoff, Patricia, and Peter Elbow. "Using Portfolios to Increase Collaboration and Community in a Writing Program." *WPA: Writing Program Administration* 9 (1986): 27–39.

Bober, Marcie. "Online Course Delivery: Is Meaningful Evaluation Possible?" *Distance Education Report* 2.11 (1998): 1–3.

Bonnema, Doug, Richard Haswell, and Joel Norris. *The Washington State University Writing Portfolio: Second Findings, June 1995–May 1997*. Pullman, WA: WSU Office of Writing Assessment, 1997.

Camp, Roberta. "Changing the Model for the Direct Assessment of Writing." *Validating Holistic Scoring for Writing Assessment: Theoretical and Empirical Foundations*. Ed. Michael M. Williamson and Brian A. Huot. Cresskill, NJ: Hampton, 1993.

———. "New Views of Measurement and New Models for Writing Assessment." *Assessment of Writing: Politics, Policies, Practices*. Ed. Edward M. White, William Lutz, and Sandra Kamusikiri. New York: MLA, 1996.

Condon, William. "Virtual Space, Real Participation: Dimensions and Dynamics of a Virtual Classroom." *The Online Writing Classroom*. Ed. Susanmarie Harrington, Rebecca Rickly, and Michael Day. Cresskill, NJ: Hampton, 2000.

Condon, William, and Liz Hamp-Lyons. "Introducing a Portfolio-Based Writing Assessment: Progress through Problems." *Portfolios: Process and Product*. Ed. Patricia Belanoff and Marcia Dickson. Portsmouth, NH: Boynton/Cook, 1991. 231–47.

Fulwiler, Toby, and Art Young. "Preface—The WAC Archives Revisited." *Assessing Writing Across the Curriculum: Diverse Approaches and Practices*. Ed. Kathleen Blake Yancey and Brian A. Huot. Greenwich, CT: Ablex, 1997.

Gillmore, Gerald M. "UW OEA: Research and Assessment." University of Washington, Office of Educational Assessment. 9 Nov. 1997 <http://www.washington.edu/oea/asessen.htm>.

Gould, Stephen Jay. *The Mismeasure of Man*. Rev. ed. New York: Norton, 1996.

Guba, Egon G., and Yvonna S. Lincoln. *Fourth Generation Evaluation.* Newbury Park, CA: Sage, 1989.

Hamp-Lyons, Liz, and William Condon. *Assessing the Portfolio: Principles for Practice, Theory, and Research.* Cresskill, NJ: Hampton, 1999.

———. "Questioning Assumptions about Portfolio-Based Assessment." *College Composition and Communication* 44 (1993): 176–90.

Haswell, Richard. "Documenting Improvement in College Writing: A Longitudinal Approach." *Written Communication* 17 (2000): 307–52.

———. "Preliminary Results from a Value-Added Study of WSU Undergraduate Writing." Washington State University Writing Assessment Office Internal Report. 21 June 1996.

Haswell, Richard, and Susan McLeod. "WAC Assessment and Internal Audiences: A Dialogue." *Assessing Writing Across the Curriculum: Diverse Approaches and Practices.* Ed. Kathleen Blake Yancey and Brian A. Huot. Greenwich, CT: Ablex, 1997. 217–36.

Haswell, Richard, Susan Wyche-Smith, and Lisa Johnson-Shull. "Shooting Niagara: Making Assessment Serve Instruction at a State University." *WPA: Writing Program Administration* 18.1 (1995): 44–53.

Henscheid, Jean. "Preparing Freshmen to Excel." *Bridges to Student Success: Exemplary Programs 1998.* NASPA/Student Affairs Administrators in Higher Education, 1998. 34–41.

Hughes, Gail M. "The Need for Clear Purposes and New Approaches to the Evaluation of Writing-Across-the-Curriculum Programs." *Assessment of Writing: Politics, Policies, Practices.* Ed. Edward M. White, William Lutz, and Sandra Kamusikiri. New York: MLA, 1996.

Kinkead, Joyce. "Documenting Excellence in Teaching and Learning in WAC Programs." *Assessing Writing Across the Curriculum: Diverse Approaches and Practices.* Ed. Kathleen Blake Yancey and Brian A. Huot. Greenwich, CT: Ablex, 1997.

LeMahieu, Paul G., Drew H. Gitomer, and JoAnne T. Eresh. *Portfolios beyond the Classroom: Data Quality and Qualities.* Princeton, NJ: Educational Testing Service, 1995.

Morgan, Meg. "The Crazy Quilt of Writing Across the Curriculum: Achieving WAC Program Assessment." *Assessing Writing Across the Curriculum: Diverse Approaches and Practices.* Ed. Kathleen Blake Yancey and Brian A. Huot. Greenwich, CT: Ablex, 1997.

Morris, Barbra S. "The English Composition Board at the University of Michigan." *Literacy for Life: The Demand for Reading and Writing.* Ed. Richard W. Bailey and Robin Melanie Fosheim. New York: MLA, 1983. 265–68.

National Center for Higher Education Management Systems. *A Preliminary Study of the Feasibility and Utility for National Policy of Instructional "Good Practice" Indicators in Undergraduate Education.* Washington, DC: National Center for Education Statistics, U.S. Department of Education, Office of Educational Research and Improvement, 1994. 94–437.

Smith, Mary L. and Cart Rottenberg. "Unintended Consequences of External Testing in Elementary Schools." *Educational Measurement: Issues and Practice* 10 (1991): 7–11.

Walvoord, Barbara E., and Lucille P. McCarthy. *Thinking and Writing in College: A Naturalistic Study of Students in Four Disciplines.* Urbana, IL: NCTE, 1990.

Walvoord, Barbara E., et al. *In the Long Run: A Study of Faculty in Three Writing-Across-the-Curriculum Programs.* Urbana, IL: NCTE, 1997.

White, Edward M. *Teaching and Assessing Writing: Recent Advances in Understanding, Evaluating, and Improving Student Performance.* Rev. ed. San Francisco: Jossey-Bass, 1994.

White, Edward M., and Leon L. Thomas. "Racial Minorities and Writing Skills Assessment in the California State University and Colleges." *College English* 43 (1981): 267–83.

Yancey, Kathleen Blake. "Looking Back as We Look Forward: Historicizing Writing Assessment." *College Composition and Communication* 50 (1999): 483–503.

Yancey, Kathleen Blake, and Brian A. Huot, eds. *Assessing Writing Across the Curriculum: Diverse Approaches and Practices.* Greenwich, CT: Ablex, 1997.

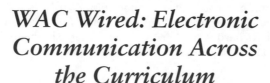

CHAPTER THREE

WAC Wired: Electronic Communication Across the Curriculum

DONNA REISS
Tidewater Community College

ART YOUNG
Clemson University

As a new century begins, educators are giving special attention to the future of higher education in general and of communication and literacy in particular. New technologies figure significantly in these deliberations either directly or indirectly, as illustrated in this example from faculty at a recent writing-across-the-curriculum workshop at a regional university. Writing in their journals and then brainstorming together, teachers generated a list of expectations from constituencies beyond the campus for universities in the twenty-first century:

◆ increased emphasis on undergraduate education

◆ interdisciplinary cooperation and communication

◆ better integrated levels of education: K–12 and two- and four-year colleges; general education and professional education

◆ decentralization of project-based education, co-ops, internships, reality-based education: distance learning, videoconferencing, site-based course packaging

◆ *service* as a good word: outreach to communities, schools, industries, nonprofits, government

◆ transfer of knowledge more quickly from researchers to users

- quick adaptation to rapidly changing contexts

- computers integrated to help students participate fully in the global information age

- total quality management: team-based projects, client service, continuous improvement

- wise resource management: do more with less

- accountability: conduct regular assessments of all activities and all personnel, including tenured faculty

- more curriculum buzzwords: *communication skills, international, multicultural, computers, interdisciplinary, service learning, collaborative learning, learning communities, lifelong learning, critical thinking,* and *creativity*

Workshop participants paused only briefly to point out some of the apparent contradictions in their list and to comment that legislators, businesspeople, alumni, parents, and educational commissions don't always understand the traditional and important role of universities in developing knowledge and passing that knowledge on to newcomers in specialized disciplinary fields. Participants also realized that the charge to create the "university of the future" was a pointed challenge to "higher education as usual," in which individuals and departments are rewarded for disciplinary specialization but not for service to other constituencies. Most faculty at the workshop wanted to embrace this challenge, evidenced by their attendance. Writing across the curriculum (WAC) and communication across the curriculum (CAC) represent one consequential way, in theory and in practice, for college faculty to respond to the broad educational and political issues of the new millennium. Additionally, as society and our definitions of literacy are transformed by information technology, we are reexamining our perceptions of language and learning in relation to electronic media. As McLeod and Miraglia point out in their introduction to this volume, a new acronym, ECAC—electronic communication across the curriculum (Reiss, Selfe, and Young)—can be added to WAC and CAC as another approach to literacy, communication, collaboration, and community outreach for educational programs and institutions.

The literacy spaces we inhabit now are located both in physical space and in cyberspace and more than ever across classrooms, campuses, countries, and continents. Barbara Walvoord invited us in 1996 to explore new media in a WAC context when she wrote that with information technology, "lines blur between writing and other forms of communication and between classrooms and other learning spaces" (72). In fact, this blurring of boundaries has long been characteristic of WAC, even though the name "Writing Across the Curriculum" never sufficiently recognized the broader initiatives that WAC has spearheaded or supported: oral and visual communication, creative and critical thinking, interactive and collaborative learning, and informal and formal communication with audiences within and beyond the classroom. Addressing the 1997 international Writing Across the Curriculum Conference in Charleston, South Carolina, Elaine Maimon reminded us that WAC really means "active learning across the curriculum," encompassing a variety of ways to help faculty and students make connections with each other and to effect curricular reform. A number of WAC programs have changed their names or institutional structures to reflect this wider scope, becoming CAC programs or participating in variously named centers for teaching and learning, and we can comfortably predict further expansion to incorporate ECAC. Although WAC programs will not necessarily change their names, an expanded focus to include information technology as an instructional tool in classrooms and in physical and cyberspaces beyond classrooms is inevitable, as well as opportune for transforming the culture of learning. In a no-longer-surprising reversal, information technology is encouraging disciplines across the university to work with WAC in an interdisciplinary quest for the effective educational use of electronic mail, hypertext, the World Wide Web, and multimedia.[1]

Information technology is transforming almost every area of our culture, especially higher education and the professional workplace. Some educators are adapting comfortably to the changes; others are resisting for reasons financial, pedagogical, and personal. Many administrators, legislators, scholars, and classroom teachers remain cautious about investing in infrastructure, bandwidth, intranets, and Internet 2. Fortunately, WAC/ CAC program directors and teachers have an opportunity to take leadership roles in these transitions because communication is fundamental to the new computer technologies and because rethinking teaching and learning has long been the foundation of WAC/CAC. In this volume, many contributors address the impact of computer-mediated communication on WAC and CAC. Chris Thaiss emphasizes the ways our definitions of writing itself are being challenged by new media as increasingly "the act of writing means choosing among a huge array of images and forms, only some of which are 'words'" (p. 307). Susan McLeod and Eric Miraglia write, "In addition to shaping the integration of new learning technologies within the proximal world of the traditional university classroom, the WAC community must now look to apply its profound transformational strategies to new models of student-teacher and student-student interaction" (p. 8).

And these new models are the strength of electronic communication across the curriculum. ECAC at its best is student centered and supports the development of an individual's academic and communication abilities for both personal and professional objectives. We began this chapter with a list of broad issues facing higher education, but often the personal meets the professional for students in the very singular process of securing employment. And so the broad issues proclaimed by prestigious educational commissions might be compared with the sparse wording in the "Help Wanted" section of Donna's local newspaper:

- Legal secretary: "excellent computer and communication skills"

- Senior accountant: "good computer skills, excellent oral/written communication skills"

- Sales and marketing assistant: "prepare/edit technical proposals and reports. Must be computer literate"

In the twin context of broad national issues and local student-centered issues, this chapter describes some of the ways WAC/ CAC has changed and is changing in the digital age. Not included here are the thousands of courses and hundreds of programs that use the Internet for instruction, many of which either accidentally or intentionally provide students with one or more language-rich activities that would win the praise of communication-across-the-curriculum specialists. Instead, we focus on those projects that consciously incorporate a computer-supported WAC/CAC dynamic into their classes and programs. Recognizing that some models of information technology on campuses and some distance learning courses will simply transfer drill-and-practice approaches to computers, the digital age's equivalent to multiple-choice scanning sheets, we believe WAC/CAC people in an ECAC environment will advocate (1) an increase in information technology to support the activities of WAC/CAC programs, (2) an increase in alliances between instructional technology programs and WAC/CAC programs, and (3) additional emphasis on communication-intensive uses of technology, or ECAC, among teachers and institutions that emphasize active learning and the development of communication competence in all their students.

WAC/CAC activities at our campuses are certain to have a direct connection to technology. The nature of that connection will vary considerably, just as our technological infrastructures and organizational structures vary. Use of computer-supported information delivery and collaborative writing tools is sometimes institutional, sometimes programmatic, and sometimes the project of a couple of enthusiasts who set up a few computers or a simple internal network or who take advantage of Internet connections to establish e-mail exchanges among students in their own classes or with other audiences. More elaborate models include Web-based classes and multimedia projects that communicate verbally, visually, aurally, and interactively within and between classes and into the community. Some are funded generously, others meagerly. To place the future of WAC/CAC and communication technology in context, "WAC Wired" presents a short history plus descriptions of a range of approaches to ECAC currently in use even as technologies and our related pedagogies continue to change. And so at the new century's beginning, we revisit, this time online, writing and learning across the curriculum.

A Short History of Electronic Communication Across the Curriculum (ECAC)

The computers that transmit information within and among organizations are increasingly important on college campuses. In *The Campus Computing Project,* his annual survey of information technology in higher education, Kenneth C. Green of the Center for Educational Studies of the Claremont Graduate University states, "Students of all ages and across all fields come to campus expecting to learn about and also to learn *with* technology" ("1998 National Survey"; emphasis added). [2] His survey reports significant increase in the use of e-mail and of World Wide Web pages "for class materials and resources." Administrators cite faculty development and technological support for faculty as among their most pressing concerns. Clearly, WAC/CAC programs must and in many cases already do respond to the faculty development needs with ECAC workshops and resources for using new media to communicate effectively.

Increased numbers of and upgrades to computer labs in campus buildings and dormitories, along with increased personal computing as the price of equipment goes down and the use of the Internet becomes more prevalent in the home as well as the workplace, suggest opportunities for WAC/CAC programs to expand their activities and audiences to include new technologies. Significantly, because the use of e-mail and most Internet resources still involves primarily text, people using these resources are always writing, always reading. Even when using the World Wide Web, with its increasingly glitzy graphics and growing commercialization, students and others are reading, conducting research, making critical choices, and, if there's a feedback form or a threaded discussion, writing, perhaps even joining an interactive discussion. As a result, students are writing for their classes across the curriculum even when they are not formally enrolled in a writing intensive course. They are also writing to their grandparents and to friends and to cyberpals in chat rooms, corresponding with audiences who take their writing seriously.

Many of the key elements of WAC/CAC in the 1970s and the computers-and-composition movement of the 1980s intersect today as ECAC. WAC encourages all teachers to value their students' writing and to respond to it with guidance for improvement rather than with discouragement or punitive remarks. The incorporation of multiple drafts, peer response, and draft conferences into classes across the curriculum, and the establishment of writing centers that support students from every area of a college, are among the ways WAC/CAC has influenced teachers whose primary interest is generating "better writing" on student tests and papers. In his chapter on research in this volume, David R. Russell reports that by studying writing themselves, faculty "critically reflect on their practice and change that practice" (p. 291), a WAC/CAC outcome that our programs can extend to critical reflection on computer-mediated communication across the curriculum. Teachers across the curriculum are also aware of employers' demands for better writing. Russell has written elsewhere that "one characteristic of our post-industrial society is a recognition that competitive advantages come through more effective communication, often written, among workers in all levels and roles" ("Writing Across the Curriculum" 68).

The business world and writing instruction met comfortably around the computer keyboard in the late 1970s and 1980s as writing teachers discovered the benefits of word processing for editing and revising and, by the end of that decade, for text sharing over computer networks. Writing teachers, already the leaders of communication across the curriculum on many campuses, thus became early promoters of computers across the curriculum through their writing centers, WAC/CAC programs, or informal conversations with colleagues. Nonetheless, as Cynthia L. Selfe writes, most faculty "seemed prone in those early years to want to use computers to address surface-level correctness rather than to encourage writing as a way of thinking." In the 1990s, however, as the personal computer became more widely used and as faculty desktops became connected to college networks and the Internet, "WAC faculty in a range of disciplines began to experiment with writing-intensive learning activities" (Selfe xii–xiii).

Recognizing this trend, Barbara Walvoord emphasizes the need for WAC programs—traditionally strong builders of alliances—to develop partnerships with instructional technology specialists (72). After all, at many colleges around the country, WAC/CAC leaders, writing center directors, and writing teachers have been early users of information technology and have participated in institutional technology initiatives, in some cases administering those initiatives, as Karen Schwalm does at Glendale Community College, as Leslie Harris does at Goucher College, and as Trent Batson did for nearly twenty years at Gallaudet University. The director of one national instructional technology project—Steven W. Gilbert of the Teaching, Learning, and Technology Group (TLT Group) affiliated with the American Association for Higher Education—regularly highlights the pedagogical groundwork of faculty in computers and composition. The TLT program also was allied with the Annenberg-PBS grant-funded Epiphany Project, directed by Trent Batson and Judy Williamson, a national professional development initiative directed primarily at writing teachers but always with an ECAC presence because several of the project leaders also were associated with WAC/CAC at their campuses.

That writing teachers and WAC/CAC program heads have become institutional leaders of ECAC is not surprising, for WAC and computers-and-composition grew up almost side by side at Michigan Technological University, where Toby Fulwiler and Robert Jones of the Department of Humanities (chaired by Art Young) led workshops for faculty beginning in 1977. Also at Michigan Tech, Cynthia L. Selfe and Dickie Selfe began building the Center for Computer-Assisted Language Instruction in the 1980s, now the laboratory for the summer workshop on computers in the writing intensive classroom, as well as the center for writing to support students in engineering and other disciplines. In his chronicle of the early conjunctions of WAC with technology, Mike Palmquist dates the first recorded activity as 1983, when Kate Kiefer and Charles Smith used Writer's Workbench with engineering students, a project expanded by Muriel Harris and Madelon Cheek. According to Harris and Cheek: "This can lead to a stronger interest in writing instruction within their [engineering] classrooms, drawing them into the writing-across-the-curriculum movement via the computer" (qtd. in Palmquist 380; Harris and Cheek 5). A few years later, Nicholas Gordon and Susan Mansfield wrote that "it makes sense to expand a writing-across-the-curriculum project into a computers-across-the-curriculum project" (qtd. in Palmquist 380; Gordon and Mansfield 11).

In her chapter on writing centers in this volume, Joan Mullin describes the impact of technology on writing centers and WAC, where "the connection between instructor, student, and WAC and writing centers provides generative feedback through continual reflective assessment about the learning process" (p. 190). At least two books now connect writing centers with computer-mediated communication. In *Wiring the Writing Center* (Hobson), the chapter "WAC on the Web: Writing Center Outreach to Teachers of Writing Intensive Courses" (Kimball) deals directly with the relationship between writing centers, WAC, and technology, while other chapters do so less directly; after all, the mission of most writing centers includes outreach across the disciplines. According to *Taking Flight with OWLS: Examining Electronic Writing Center Work* (Inman and Sewell), at the end of the 1990s, many teachers across the curriculum were using WAC/CAC online in their individual classes or in collaborations with teachers in their own or other disciplines, and growing numbers of schools and colleges have incorporated technology into their WAC/CAC or writing programs or have included WAC/CAC as partners in their technology professional development programs. In selecting its four Colleges of the Year for 2001, Time Inc. and the Princeton Review focused on writing across the curriculum, naming Sarah Lawrence College, Cornell University, Longview Community College (Lee's Summit, Missouri), and Clemson University. Integration of electronic communication was one of the noteworthy characteristics of Clemson's program, and electronic communication at Tidewater Community College was mentioned as "in the running" ("College of the Year").

The Middle Ground: Writing to Learn and Learning to Write Online

WAC encourages the instructional use of various functions of written language for learning and communication in the belief that such practices strengthen students' language and critical thinking abilities. Although perhaps we overgeneralize, we sometimes say that the primary function of writing in classrooms has been for testing, evaluation, and demonstration of skills mastered, content learned, problems solved, or homework completed. WAC asks us to use writing for other not mutually exclusive purposes such as "writing to learn," in which emphasis is placed on using written language to learn new and unfamiliar content or to develop analytical or creative habits of mind, rather than to demonstrate how much has been learned. In other words, in writing to learn, mistakes, false starts, hallelujahs, connections, and misconceptions all are viewed as part of the process by which learners learn. Most WAC proponents believe that these two functions should be integral to all writing intensive courses and often label them informal and formal writing, or writing to learn and writing to communicate, or expressive and transactional writing. These two functions have never been viewed as totally distinct, but rather as existing on a continuum on which some of the writing we do in classrooms falls somewhere in the middle. With the advent of ECAC, this middle ground has gained a more prominent focus. At California State Polytechnic University, Pomona, for instance, where Carol Holder served for many years as director of both faculty development and writing in the disciplines, WAC has been integrating information technology for more than a decade, recently emphasizing "electronic kinds of informal writing for an audience (an interesting hybrid of expressive and transactional modes), and radical changes in the features of 'text' with the possibilities that hypertext/web publishing allows" (Holder).

The chart in Figure 3.1 helps us consider further the "interesting hybrid" of "conversational learning" and ways that electronic communication tools can support active and engaged learning. We view this chart as a starting place and a heuristic; it is not meant to construct a universe of discourse but rather to suggest the fertile ground for the development of an interactive discourse that lies between personal discourse and public discourse. On the left side of the chart, personal discourse exhibits the familiar characteristics of informal, expressive writing. This is the discovery writing that writers do for themselves in places such as journals and notebooks, and that word processing and e-mail preserve in electronic journals or word-processed freewrites. On the right side of the chart, public discourse exhibits the familiar characteristics of transactional, formal writing, often composed in the form of essays and reports written to a distant audience.[3] In college classrooms, public discourse is often referred to as academic discourse, the language of the academy in general, or more specifically, the language of the intended audience—for example, the discourse of physics, or the discourse of political science—and a generally agreed-on goal of most college composition courses is to teach students to write this academic discourse. For students, one challenge is to figure out how to write like an academic or like a physicist or a political scientist before actually becoming an academic or a physicist—that is, before knowing what a physicist knows and before acquiring the habits of mind and discourse conventions of physics that come with knowledge and experience in that discipline. Such a rhetorical situation sometimes leads students to "fake" writing like an academic and thereby produce texts that teachers over the years have referred to as dummy runs, pretend writing, or "Engfish."

Our chart visualizes in the center column the actual and virtual space of the classroom, the "middle ground," where students gain knowledge, develop scholarly habits of mind, and acquire rhetorical and communication competence in a variety of public and academic contexts. It is that interactive social space where writers can combine their existing knowledge of content and inquiry with the new knowledge and experience they are acquiring in a particular course in order to generate texts for a "real" audience of classmates. In the process of such an interchange, knowledge is generated collaboratively, and a discourse, in some ways unique to those participants, is created that we situate in the middle ground. Electronic media have been facilitating such discourse in networked environments where students write to and for each other in a place where it is safe to practice the language of a discipline. E-mail discussion lists (listservs), class or Internet newsgroups, and threaded Web discussion forums promote collaborative writing in the language of the learner and do not require students to be in the same place at the same time to engage in these conversations. This discourse activity of the middle ground combines the writer's existing language and

	Personal Discourse	Classroom Discourse	Public Discourse
Function	*Expressive Writing* ■ Self-discovery ■ Inner speech	*Interactive Writing* ■ Conversational ■ Dialectical	*Transactional Writing* ■ Informative ■ Persuasive
Purpose	Explains to Oneself	Explains to Classroom Colleagues	Explains to Distant Others
Audience	*Self and Trusted Others* ■ Privileges language of learner ■ Accountability to self	*Classroom Community: Familiar and Known* ■ Privileges language of classroom community ■ Accountability to classmates	*Distant and Other: Unknown* ■ Privileges language of critical audiences ■ Accountability to public
Genre	■ Journals ■ Diaries ■ Logs ■ Notebooks ■ Freewrites ■ Braindumps	■ Letters ■ Notes ■ Questions ■ Poems ■ Parodies ■ E-mail ■ Dialogue journals	■ Essays ■ Articles ■ Reports ■ Proposals ■ Memos ■ Multimedia ■ Web publications
Response Time	Immediate: Shaping at Point of Utterance	Quick: from "Real" Audience—Visible and Tactile	Lengthy: to Publication or Presentation

Classroom Environment
■ Social and collaborative
■ Respects diversity and risk taking
■ Active learning and interactive teaching
■ Motivation for reading and writing

Developing Knowledge That Is Personally and Professionally Useful

FIGURE 3.1. *Classroom discourse and writing across the curriculum.*

rhetorical practices with those of the academy under the tutelage of the teacher, in most cases the more experienced academic practitioner. The goal becomes not to pretend to know and to communicate but actually to do so within the context of being a novice writing to a known "real" audience of other learners on- or offline within a new course or field of study.

This chart on classroom discourse and writing across the curriculum is speculative and dynamic. The three columns should be imagined as on a continuum; most genres can fall in any column or between columns or in more than one column. E-mail, poems, essays, or letters can be written to fulfill any of the three purposes or a combination of them. All writing, in some sense, is personal, and all writing, when read by others, is public. Further, our chart suggests that ECAC does not create new rhetorical forms nor represent a major paradigm shift, but rather represents a useful way to view written, oral, and visual language in both traditional and computer classrooms. Viewed this way, this visualization assists us in "reading" student writing in the context of "conversational learning"—what many of us are doing for the first time with the advent of the Internet, e-mail, and computer conferencing. And it suggests a powerful pedagogy for the development of students' language and critical thinking abilities. It formulates for teachers and students a recursive and dialectical language process in which the cognitive and social inform each other in the development of writers and thinkers. It helps us understand the learning that occurs as teachers across the nation experiment with ECAC activities in courses within and across disciplines.

Teachers are discovering or rediscovering "middle ground" pedagogies as they implement projects that use new technologies to aid student learning and to improve communication with their students and between students in their classes. For example, WAC/CAC principles informed the use of newsgroups in educational psychology classes when Lawrence Sherman at Miami University designed activities for extending communication and collaboration in response to articles in the journal *Teaching of Psychology*. Finding that students read, reflected on, and responded to each other's electronic postings in ways that led by the end of the term to more complex thinking, Sherman concluded, "While the strategies . . . obviously take up more instructor time in reading, responding and evaluating, . . . the gains in student writing abilities and critical thinking (rhetoric), and the motivating stimulation of the class discussions are worth the efforts."

At the University of North Carolina at Charlotte, Deborah Langsam introduced "biochallenges, . . . questions that asked for applications of the material under study," to her nonmajor biology students, who responded sometimes with applications and sometimes with additional questions, which Langsam considered to be a success in ways that WAC advocates will recognize: "Even for those students who simply had questions—and there were many—the e-mail was instructive; it provided (1) a place to try to articulate them, (2) a person who would respond, and (3) an opportunity to learn just in the putting of the question" (Langsam and Yancey 236).

In her literature classes for engineering students, Paula Gillespie of Marquette University found that e-mail journal exchanges led resistant students (resistant to literature, not computers) to discuss fiction enthusiastically and "not only allowed students to write to learn, but . . . allowed them to see how others wrote to learn" (230). After using a read-write-respond approach for an online southern literature class at Loyola University, Barbara Ewell wrote, "The high quality of student engagement and learning that resulted more than convinced me that this kind of structured electronic discussion certainly can substitute for the classroom discussions that many teachers most fear losing in delivering their courses electronically." Featured in *Learning Literature in an Era of Change: Innovations in Teaching* are chapters on incorporating electronic communication—in particular, multimedia—into the teaching of both undergraduate and graduate literature and literary theory courses (Hickey and Reiss).

Many projects incorporate a variety of informal and formal writing tasks in various combinations of print and electronic media, thus reflecting the reality most professionals encounter in their workday lives. For example, Teresa M. Redd of Howard University taught an all-black composition class of engineering students that was linked with a predominately white graphic design class at Montana State University taught by Stephanie Newman-James. E-mail enabled these two classes, 1,600 miles apart, to produce a print publication about racism, with essays by Howard students, graphics by MSU students, and reprints of e-mail exchanges from both groups. Just as important as the development of students' rhetorical and electronic abilities was the knowledge gained by both groups about the difficult social issue of racism. In her essay describing this project, Redd concludes with the words of an MSU student: "The experiences you and your friends have gone through is something I don't have to think about very often and they are startling and painful to read. . . . I truly hope that being able to work together on this project will result in some new understanding and breaking down of barriers" (Redd 146). Another approach that involves the interplay of the visual and the verbal is June Woest's e-art field trips for her online art appreciation courses at Houston Community College. After their visits to art Web sites, students report to a class bulletin board in one of five designated "writing styles" that include making up a story, describing design elements, and using adjectives. She observes that "the quality of the student's written communication skills improve while understanding and interpretation of the visual arts deepen" as a result of their online work.

Electronic communication also helps establish connections beyond classes, colleges, and countries. For instance, formal debate across international borders links business students from the University of Rhode Island with counterparts in Turkey and Germany for a project called International E-mail Debate, guiding students "to understand the constructed nature of each debate position and to appreciate the differences of perspective rooted in divergent cultural experience" (Shamoon 158).

These examples illustrate the benefits for teachers across the curriculum that communication-rich uses of computers have long brought to writing teachers. They also demonstrate the direction that new technologies can take within WAC/CAC programs that incorporate ECAC. With e-mail at their fingertips, teachers across the curriculum can use writing-to-learn online to encourage participation in the writing-as-thinking process, to build communication confidence and competence, to establish authentic peer audiences, and to provide a printable record of the exchanges that subsequently can be used as study guides and resources for planning formal papers. Students learn to use the discourse of the disciplines informally and to ask questions either privately with e-mail to the professor or more publicly with e-mail to class groups, learning even as they frame the questions for their readers.

Collaborative Learning and Writing Online

Nearly a decade has passed since Thomas Barker and Fred Kemp described the still-new concept of the collaborative, networked writing classroom as "enfranchising, open, and egalitarian," and its theory as "an application of postmodern pedagogy to classroom needs" (23). The same year Lisa Ede and Andrea Lunsford wrote:

> Nowhere are the competing and disparate definitions of selfhood and collaboration more apparent than in the technological revolution. . . . [W]e must find ways of describing—and valuing—forms of collective or collaboratively generated and electronically disseminated knowledge, knowledge that will not easily fit into our old forms of individual intellectual property. (viii–ix)

Although they were concerned primarily with writing and the teaching of writing, these two collaborative pairs anticipated with their social constructivist perspectives on technology those concerns that would soon confront teachers from every discipline in what we now call ECAC.

Information technology offers a range of tools that make collaborative learning easier and perhaps inevitable. The sharing of quantities of information across distances at a speed more like a telephone message than a telegraph, and the ease of editing even text-based electronic mail messages—for example, writing in ALL CAPS between the lines to distinguish commentary typographically from the original message—gave writers new ways to collaborate faster and at a detailed interlinear level that soon would be developed further as word processors incorporated comment features and text comparison markings similar to those used by professional editors. Pop-up windows, colored type, and yellow highlight swashes superimposed on drafts in progress could pass back and forth between writers, editors, and collaborators to clarify who had changed what.

Writing teachers were quick to adopt these word-processing enhancements that were developed for the business world. The ability to save and compare multiple drafts was a perfect adjunct to process writing. Copy- or cut-and-paste techniques supported revision well. Writing teachers also were early adopters of the groupware that businesses had been using; early "real time" conferencing tools such as the ENFI project, Real-Time Writer, Daedalus InterChange, Connect, Aspects, and CommonSpace were designed by or in collaboration with educators to take advantage of the writing-to-learn capabilities of these shared writing environments. Internet-based MOOs (multi-user domains, object oriented), chat rooms, forums, and new whiteboard technologies that allow people to write synchronously or asynchronously on the same document are extending this capability even further.

The conversational aspects of synchronous shared writing spaces provide alternative discussion media for any subject, as evidenced by the use of these platforms outside of writing classes. At Virginia Tech, for example, collaborative writing software has been used by teachers in history, biology, and art history. It is not surprising that English-as-a-second-language or foreign-language instructors were early adopters of the tools that encouraged students to write to each other online either in networked writing environments or with Internet connections to students in other countries.

The Internet has expanded opportunities for writing online in elementary, middle, and secondary schools as well. Pamela Childers, director of the Caldwell Writing Center at the McCallie School, Chattanooga, Tennessee, collaborates with faculty across the disciplines not only to use writing for learning but also to use the World Wide Web and e-mail to support instruction. She sees the advantages of using "the visuals of technology to help students learn, think and verbalize their thought," but cautions that "people contact needs to be made at the point where students and faculty should encourage appropriate interaction for intellectual, social, spiritual, and physical growth." The George School, a private secondary school in Pennsylvania, incorporates computer conferencing in history, science, foreign language, ESL, and English instruction (McBride). And at Pioneer High School in Michigan, history teacher Robin Wax uses synchronous computer conferences to provide

> the multicultural classroom environment my students so desperately need. The use of Writing-to-Learn methods with the history curriculum has pulled together ideas rather than separated them. . . . The format of computerized instruction makes access to ideas and to other learners and to means of expression easy, fun, and permanent.

Efforts to establish links between classes in the same and different disciplines, in the past restricted by complex exchange logistics, have been made easier by Internet chat rooms and MOOs, where students can meet online from computers anywhere on campus, anywhere in the world. Online pals became the pen pals of the 1980s and 1990s. Same-time conversations with the immediacy of telephone calls and the reflective and archival advantages of text were especially appealing in classrooms where a single computer could provide a connection to students on other continents. Many World Wide Web sites now provide gateways for matching classes at every school level.

Learning communities also are well served by computer communication. At the University of South Florida, for example, a FIPSE grant project under the direction of Joseph Moxley is supporting the integration of both WAC and technology into USF's Learning Community Initiative, and its 1999 conference, Creating and Sustaining Learning Communities: Connections, Collaboration, and Crossing Borders, focused on the use of technology to support learning communities ("Learning Communities"). Members of the English department are collaborating with colleagues in social science, history, non-Western perspectives, and art to teach and grade collaboratively, working with the same fifty students over a two-year period. This initiative, says Christian R. Weisser, was a direct response to WAC and to the university's need for "assessment, organization, and integrated assignments." Through listservs, MOOs, and student Web pages that link students and teachers across the curriculum, technology can "facilitate and 'bridge the gaps'" while strengthening writing for thinking and learning as well as writing for academic success. Computer communication also plays an important role in the George Mason New Century College learning community model described in this volume (Zawacki and Williams, Chapter 5).

Programs: ECAC and WAC, Writing Centers, and Centers for Teaching and Learning

At present, few collegewide programs formally identify themselves as Electronic Communication Across the Curriculum or by a similar name. Programs within a wide range of departments and initiatives do exist, however, many of them shared ventures among writing or WAC/CAC programs, writing centers, technology centers, and centers for teaching and learning. The need for such explicit connections has been apparent to many WAC leaders (Walvoord; Thaiss). In her travels to campuses throughout the country, Cynthia L. Selfe reports that one of the most frequent questions from faculty is, "How are other teachers using computers to support writing across the curriculum?" (xiii). Centers for teaching and learning have been in the forefront of recognizing that communication-intensive pedagogies best serve students as their teachers incorporate new technologies into instruction.

At the University of Illinois at Urbana-Champaign, Gail E. Hawisher of the Center for Writing Studies, which houses the WAC program, has been active in the engineering department's asynchronous learning network (ALN) project. "Both WAC and ALN," Hawisher and Pemberton (formerly part of the program) report, "are capable of reshaping the social contexts of classes if we bring to them the necessary kinds of critical thinking and pedagogical values that successful educational innovations require." Reflecting on the electronic messages of an engineering class, they conclude that "in good WAC fashion the students often come upon the answers to the problems they pose after they have been able to articulate the problem and after they write (or talk) it through with classmates" (27–28).

In another WAC-influenced technology program, the Mellon Multimedia Courses project at Spelman College in Atlanta, a division of their Comprehensive Writing Program, has electronic communication as its core (Hocks and Bascelli). Psychology, art, Spanish, and French faculty have been active in Spelman's initial projects to use electronic communication.

Some of the connections between WAC/CAC and information technology are piecemeal, some are still in the form of initial steps, and a few already combine to comprise full-fledged programs. In 1996, Patricia Williams, director of the Across-the-University Writing Program at Sam Houston State University,[4] wrote to the WAC-L listserv that the program's workshops and newsletter have featured writing using technology; "I think we are making progress in learning how technology can enhance both student and faculty writing." Writing centers and WAC/CAC programs around the country have been making similar progress a few classes and workshops at a time. One comprehensive initiative is the University of Missouri–Columbia's Institute for Instructional Technology (MUIIT),[5] a group of faculty and staff organized by the Program for Excellence in Teaching to facilitate use of educational technology to enhance teaching and learning. MUIIT has strong ties to the distinguished campus writing program directed by Martha A. Townsend. With its extensive and clearly organized links to resources under the headings Enhancing Traditional Teaching, Changing Pedagogy, and Changing Content or Epistemology, along with examples of projects at the university and elsewhere, MUIIT hosts institutes that use an online daily journaling form. It also features discussion lists for making learning active. The writing program has its own direct ECAC initiative in "Expressive Media: Composing with Technology," developed by Andy White of the writing program with Peter Campbell and Marsha Lyon. In an e-mail message to WAC-L, Townsend emphasized that "writing to learn" in the disciplines includes the use of multimedia.

The Virginia Tech professional development program[6] designed to train faculty to incorporate technology into their courses in meaningful ways has generated communication-rich approaches that include a history professor using networked synchronous conferencing to stimulate interaction in a classroom; a philosophy professor incorporating threaded discussion forums into Web-enhanced classes; and a professor of veterinary medicine having students author multimedia presentations for their classes. Carol A. Bailey, director of the Virginia Tech University writing program, writes that her office has close ties to both the Center for Excellence in Undergraduate Teaching and Educational Technologies and the online courses at their cyberschool. These programs are visible through their Web site, which includes Peter Shires's reflections on the effort and time involved in retooling his veterinary medicine course, a process that "does focus faculty attention and results in improvements to course content that would not otherwise be accomplished. . . . As our specialties involve considerable visual and audible evaluation of problems, this methodology of teaching is well suited to our needs."

For many faculty who attend workshops to learn how well-chosen technology applications can enhance their teaching, the response is similar to Shires's and familiar to those who conduct WAC/CAC/ECAC workshops: the focus on rethinking their courses and curricula is as important as learning new pedagogical and technological strategies. Intrigued by the possibilities of WAC/CAC/ECAC, educators look for ways in which freewriting, journaling, multiple drafts, and collaborative problem solving might guide their students' learning. In other words, WAC/CAC does indeed drive course and curricular change.

So too does information technology, despite claims that the pedagogy should drive the technology. Influenced by the editing opportunities of word processing, writing teachers sought ways to bring these tools to their students. Before long, their colleagues also wanted their students' papers spell checked and printed in Times Roman. Impressed with the information exchanges facilitated by e-mail, teachers looked for ways this platform could serve students, and thus developed discussion groups and paper exchanges. Encouraged by the universality of HTML and the dynamic communication combination of text, graphics, sound, and video, teachers taught themselves and their students the discourse of Web pages, a precursor to Web portfolios.

Before the widespread availability of e-mail and Internet computer conferencing, internal synchronous environments made possible reflective learning communities within classrooms fortunate enough to have networked computers. WAC/CAC teachers who participated in such communities introduced their colleagues in other fields to the benefits of WAC's write-to-learn emphasis through informal freewriting and other methods of prewriting, collaborative planning and exploration of topics, peer response, and multiple drafts. WAC became wired.

Reflections on the Future of Electronic Communication Across the Curriculum

We cannot predict the future of WAC/CAC/ECAC in relation to technologies that are changing so rapidly. Not included in this chapter but on the near horizon for expanding ECAC, for example, are desktop videoconferencing and speech-generated text production. We can predict, however, that such changes will continue to bring new energy to WAC/CAC programs as they consider their place in the academy of the twenty-first century. We anticipate increasing alliances between WAC and other departments as pedagogies promoted by communication across the curriculum offer some of the best instructional uses of information technology. When she wrote the following statement in 1996, Reiss was thinking of then-innovative uses of computers in her own college's initial projects: "What is e-mail but the epistolary pedagogy so often used by WAC advocates? Now students use writing-to-learn letter exchanges not only across classes and campuses but across the world. What are newsgroups and chat rooms but tools for the kinds of collaborative conversation and composition WAC has modeled?" (722). Today these approaches are commonplace.

Students whose intellectual lives sometimes seem isolated or fragmented might find that the immediacy of electronic media helps them connect, as did students in Mary Beth Oliver's Introduction to Communication Research course at Virginia Tech. One student responded to an anonymous class evaluation that e-mail "makes a large class seem smaller and the teacher more accessible" and provides a "self-evaluation process of what we understand or don't understand." Such self-assessment online resembles the familiar WAC activities on paper of freewrites, microthemes, question-and-answer pairs, one-minute essays, five-minute responses, and journals. With an optional e-mail listserv, students can get timely feedback from classmates and professors in the "middle ground" of WAC/CAC/ECAC activities that new technologies generate almost automatically. With teacher guidance, such e-mail lists can also support more structured write-to-learn activities such as required daily or weekly messages, small-group problem solving, and posted focused freewrites.

Electronic portfolios are likely to become more widespread, perhaps driven by employer demand. Multimedia résumés can enhance job searches and graduate school applications; they might even become the standard for the future. A first-year writing class, or a general education core course, or a student orientation class might be the first step in creating a Web site that presents selected student projects to represent their work in a variety of courses. Most of these projects are likely to involve substantial writing and other forms of communication, and their public nature on the Web might lead the teachers who "approve" these projects for publication to become more directly involved with WAC/CAC/ECAC. For in some ways, electronic portfolios may lead to a natural but public performance assessment for both students and teachers. At least one college has initiated such a requirement beginning with the class of 2000, according to a report in the *Chronicle of Higher Education*. The academic use of the Web "is meant to enhance the academic-advising process by helping students to reflect on the whirlwind of their college experiences and to articulate what they're getting out of Kalamazoo's offerings" (Young, "A New Graduation" A23).

Portfolios are not a new concept in writing classes; electronic portfolios were featured in a 1996 special issue of *Computers and Composition* (Yancey) and constitute one of the four perspectives of *Situating Portfolios: Four Perspectives* (Yancey and Weiser). The implications for broad professional use are suggested by Kristine L. Blair and Pamela Takayoshi, one of whose students used Hypercard to build a writing portfolio "not unlike the construction of a prospective employee portfolio. It opens with an introductory welcome to her portfolio, followed with a copy of her resume, and then particular samples of her design work" (362). When such portfolios are posted on the Web for all to read, one of the perceived gaps between personal writing, classroom writing, and public writing will have been bridged, for such writing will serve the purposes of the individual student, of classroom instruction, and of formal public communication.

David R. Russell ends his historical overview of college and university writing with this insight:

> With WAC, the old battles between access and exclusion, excellence and equity, scientific and humanist worldviews, liberal and professional education, all come down to very specific questions of responsibility for curriculum and teaching. WAC ultimately asks: in what ways will graduates of our institutions use language, and how shall we teach them to use it in those ways? (*Writing in the Academic Disciplines* 307)

"WAC Wired" suggests that future graduates increasingly will use computer technology to communicate and to learn, and that educators will increasingly use computer technology to teach students to communicate and to learn. We consider traditional WAC/CAC pedagogy to be among the most effective and available ways to carry out this task. But we are aware of the dangers in doing so and the major hurdles to overcome.

In 1990, before the rise of ECAC, Art Young and Toby Fulwiler delineated what they called "the enemies of WAC," that is, those attitudes and practices that subvert WAC's efforts to transform education: resistance from faculty, resistance from students, resistance from English departments, compartmentalized academic administration, faculty reward systems, departmental priorities, unstable leadership, and testing mania. This litany is familiar to WAC/CAC practitioners, and we might update it for the electronic age simply by adding computer phobia. But there are at least four areas of concern we should pause to consider further: issues of access, of the faculty reward system, of copyright and intellectual property, and of academic freedom.

Of particular importance for ECAC are the access and equity concerns incumbent upon such expensive tools as computer networks. One major concern is that the pedagogical benefits of information technology will benefit a new elite with access to powerful computers and networks, thereby creating a new information gap and widening the existing economic gaps between wealthy and poor school districts, poor and middle-class students, and native-language speakers and international users with little or no English-language proficiency. Still, this peril is accompanied by the enormous promise of such technology that leads faculty to advocate for improved general student access in higher education and that leads community members themselves to wire their local public schools, libraries, and community centers on Net Days. At one time, books, televisions, and ballpoint pens were out of the reach of nonwealthy citizens; free libraries, less expensive televisions, and disposable pens have made these technologies widely available. Educators must continue to press for universal access to information and tools for communication at all economic and educational levels.

When Chris Thaiss described "interactive language-rich technology techniques" as the "single biggest influence on ways we define writing and thinking about the curriculum and across the curriculum" ("Reliving"), the word *thinking* clearly paralleled *writing*. Thaiss also acknowledged the impact of distance learning on WAC, asserting that "in on-line curricula there's no escaping writing and no teacher thinks of it as an 'extra responsibility'" ("When WAC" 8). We also should recognize, however, that such time-intensive literacy instruction often does involve "extra" work for teachers, work that deserves appropriate recognition and compensation. Currently, the most interactive distance learning pedagogies are constructed around writing, reading, and responding, the responding element providing the socially constructed dynamic and student-centered learning that WAC/CAC/ECAC promotes. ECAC advocates can and should assume a leadership role in distance education projects to speak for communication-intensive communities of learners rather than a correspondence course model of distance learning.

In response to their members' concerns that teaching innovations in general and experimentation with new technologies in particular will interfere with and even damage promotion and tenure opportunities, professional organizations such as the College Art Association, the Conference on College Composition and Communication, and the Modern Language Association, among others, are drafting policy statements regarding ownership of electronic media, institutional support for the time-intensive training and development teachers need to use new media, and revision of promotion and tenure policies to reflect faculty innovations and contributions with new media. Academic conventions now feature sessions on the impact of technology on the discipline and on teaching the discipline. ECAC, we trust, will play an important role in changing many college cultures that devalue undergraduate teaching in the interest of encouraging research, publications, and grants.

Nobody can deny that information production and distribution has changed radically in the past decade now that most major publications put their archives online. After a little time online, people remember URLs as they do oft-dialed telephone numbers: even if they've never bought a book there, educators know www.amazon.com; even if they've never taken the tour, they know about www.whitehouse.gov; if they're looking for academic jobs, they certainly know www.chronicle.com. And they know how to cut and paste and forward and download and file. Issues on how to cite sources, verify sources, copy sources, revise sources, and republish sources are all in the process of being negotiated for electronic media, and the media itself are changing much more rapidly than our laws and accepted publication practices. For example, the *Chronicle of Higher Education* reported that a "former University of Nebraska student has sued the university and a professor for posting on the Internet a personal essay the student had written in class several years earlier" ("Former U. of Nebraska Student"). What are the legal and ethical implications when a student or faculty member "publishes" a Web page or electronic portfolio on the college's Web site?

New technologies add new issues and exacerbate familiar challenges to WAC/CAC. Among these are the role of the professor—in particular, the talented lecturers in higher education reluctant to relinquish the stage to student collaborative projects, and also the teachers in professional fields obligated to prepare students for mastery of material that will meet the criteria of board certification exams. Not to be overlooked is the uncertain impact on promotion and tenure for faculty who invest time and energy in instructional innovations, nor the administrative mandate for larger classes. In the October 3, 1997, issue of the *Chronicle of Higher Education,* for example, the Information Technology section headlines read, "Rethinking the Role of the Professor in an Age of High-Tech Tools" and "Canadian University Promises It Won't Require Professors to Use Technology." Despite the potential of technology to foster the interaction that stimulates learning and prepares students for the contemporary workplace, Phil Agre, associate professor of communication at the University of California, San Diego, warns that "there will be an economic incentive to reduce the interactive components to reduce the labor cost" (Young, "Rethinking" A26). Thus, the struggle to integrate technology into instruction meets an economic reality: it is expensive. Further, the educational uses of technologies that promote active learning and the interactive development of communication abilities are more expensive than those uses that offer only a one-way transfer of information. While administrators sometimes use technology to increase class sizes, outsource instruction, or increase the use of television, video, and computer packages in order to make institutions more efficient, proponents of quality over quantity continue to advocate for instruction that utilizes and emphasizes the higher-order communication and problem-solving skills that citizens, scholars, and workers need to succeed in this information age. Some chief academic officers clearly appreciate the Internet for its active learning capabilities. Despite reservations that "electronic communication will always lack critical elements of 'real' conversation," Neil L. Rudenstine, former president of Harvard, affirmed the power of "conversational learning" from online discussions and the opportunities for faculty and students to reconsider the teaching-learning process. He could have been an ECAC program director when he wrote that the Internet "calls upon the user to be active and engaged: following leads, distinguishing the substantial from the trivial, synthesizing insights drawn from different sources, formulating new questions. Seated before the computer, a student is challenged to make something happen, to act or pursue, rather than merely react or absorb" (A48). It is not the computer, of course, that challenges the student, but the computer-supported activity designed and guided by an instructor whose "prompts" lead students to fruitful inquiry, research, synthesis, and collaborative writing. Therefore, the professional development workshops that have characterized WAC/CAC for a quarter of a century must broaden to include ECAC as active learning with computer-mediated communication. As we demonstrate to teaching colleagues and administrators the potential for such learning, we provide an enlightened response to challengers such as Sven Birkerts and David Noble.

Thus, issues of access, intellectual property, budget and administration, and academic freedom are interrelated. With the advent of distance learning and online courses, who makes key decisions about whether to include a course in a college's online offerings? Or what the course will include? Or whether a course must be taught online? Or who will be able to enroll? Many teachers fear outside interference with course objectives and instructional methods for nonacademic reasons by enthusiastic proponents of the new media or by administrators looking to cut budgets, or sell products, or win legislative support. They fear a college requirement that all course instructors must maintain a Web page, without first conducting an inquiry into whether all courses will benefit from such a tool. They question whether all students should be required to purchase a particular laptop computer. They fear that distance learning might be set up as skill-and-drill, an exercise in dissemination and regurgitation. They lament the megadollars and time and effort spent on technology that might better serve academic purposes such as smaller class sizes. And for such good reasons, we need to proceed with caution, but proceed nonetheless.

As we write this chapter, another educational commission has issued a national report: the Boyer Commission on Educating Undergraduates in the Research University's *Reinventing Undergraduate Education: A Blueprint for America's Research Universities.*[7] Among its ten recommendations are these four: remove barriers to interdisciplinary education, link communication skills and course work, use information technology creatively, and cultivate a sense of community. Hawisher and Selfe also suggest the way forward: "A major project for English teachers will be to develop a responsible professional vision—a vision grounded in sound composition theory and practice, and tempered by critical, informed, and humanistic perspectives on technology and reading" (312). Indeed, teachers across the curriculum might take on this responsibility through ECAC programs or committees. To accept such a responsibility, to be educational activists, WAC/CAC and ECAC faculty and program administrators can exercise wise and informed leadership for the electronic age on their campuses. And while the vision for each campus should be unique to that campus, we can see an outline for a national vision when we combine the list of faculty concerns with which this chapter began with the ECAC projects described throughout: communication, computers, active learning, collaboration, interdisciplinary, international, multicultural, across educational levels, interactive, reaching out to the public, reality-based, research into practice, adapting quickly to rapidly changing contexts. These issues are the basis of WAC/CAC/ECAC, key components of the evolving WAC vision since the 1970s, and a strong foundation for significant cultural change in higher education in the twenty-first century.

Notes

1. The ECAC resources Web site—http://onlinelearning.tc.cc.va.us/faculty/tcreisd/projects/ecac/—lists many of these collaborations as well as WAC classic programs and gateways, WAC programs with an ECAC emphasis, and WAC/CAC programs and resources for computer-mediated communication across the curriculum. WAC now has its own online journal and resource, established in 1999 by Mike Palmquist of Colorado State University. *Academic.writing: Interdisciplinary Perspectives on Communication Across the Curriculum* takes advantage of the many communication options of electronic communication to publish refereed texts and hypertexts, links to WAC programs and publications online, columns about WAC and CAC activities, reviews of conferences of interest to WAC, reissues of out-of-print publications, and a new book first published entirely online.

2. Along with the current survey and report, previous surveys are linked to this site.

3. The terms "expressive" and "transactional" come from the work of James Britton et al., *The Development of Writing Abilities (11–18)*, London: Macmillan Education, 1975. We gratefully acknowledge their influence on our thinking, even though we realize they would probably quarrel with aspects of our chart.

4. See http://www.shsu.edu/~edu_paw/.

5. Check out the Educational Technologies at Missouri Web site at http://www.etatmo.missouri.edu/.

6. The Virginia Polytechnic Institute and State University (Virginia Tech) Instructional Development Initiative Web site is http://www.edtech.vt.edu/idi.html.

7. The full text of the Boyer report is online and available in print through the Web site: http://notes.cc.sunysb.edu/Pres/boyer.nsf.

Works Cited

Academic.writing: Interdisciplinary Perspectives on Communication Across the Curriculum. <http://aw.colostate.edu/>.

Bailey, Carol A. E-mail to Donna Reiss. 3 Jan. 1998.

Barker, Thomas, and Fred Kemp. "Network Theory: A Post-Modern Pedagogy for the Writing Classroom." *Computers and Community: Teaching Composition in the Twenty-First Century.* Ed. Carolyn Handa. Portsmouth, NH: Boynton/Cook, 1990. 1–29.

Blair, Kristine L., and Pamela Takayoshi. "Reflections on Reading and Evaluating Electronic Portfolios." *Situating Portfolios: Four Perspectives.* Ed. Kathleen Blake Yancey and Irwin Weiser. Logan: Utah State UP, 1997. 357–69.

Boyer Commission on Educating Undergraduates in the Research University. *Reinventing Undergraduate Education: A Blueprint for America's Research Universities.* SUNY Stony Brook for the Carnegie Foundation for the Advancement of Teaching, 1998.

Britton, James N., et al. *The Development of Writing Abilities (11–18).* London: Macmillan, 1975.

Childers, Pamela. E-mail to Donna Reiss. 27 Oct. 1997.

"College of the Year: But Can They Write?" *The Best College for You, 2000.* New York: Time/Princeton Review, 2000. 63–74.

Ede, Lisa, and Andrea Lunsford. *Singular Texts/Plural Authors: Perspectives on Collaborative Writing.* Carbondale: Southern Illinois UP, 1992.

Ewell, Barbara. E-mail to Donna Reiss. 6 Oct. 1997.

"Former U. of Nebraska Student Sues over Posting of Personal Essay." *Chronicle of Higher Education* 20 Feb. 1998. 11 June 1998 <http://chronicle.com>.

Gillespie, Paula. "E-Journals: Writing to Learn in the Literature Classroom." Reiss, Selfe, and Young 207–30.

Gordon, Nicholas, and Susan Mansfield. "Computers Across the Curriculum: A Confluence of Ideas." *Computers and Composition* 6.1 (1988): 9–13.

Green, Kenneth C. *The Campus Computing Project*. Claremont, CA: Claremont Graduate University, 1997.

———. "The 1998 National Survey of Information Technology in Higher Education." *The Campus Computing Project*. 23 June 1999 <http://www.campuscomputing.net/>.

Harris, Muriel, and Madelon Cheek. "Computers Across the Curriculum: Using Writer's Workbench for Supplementary Instruction." *Computers and Composition* 1.2 (1984): 3–5.

Hawisher, Gail E., and Cynthia L. Selfe. "Wedding the Technologies of Writing Portfolios and Computers: The Challenges of Electronic Classrooms." *Situating Portfolios: Four Perspectives*. Ed. Kathleen Blake Yancey and Irwin Weiser. Logan: Utah State UP, 1997. 305–21.

Hawisher, Gail E., and Michael A. Pemberton. "Writing Across the Curriculum Encounters Asynchronous Learning Networks." Reiss, Selfe, and Young 17–39. 4 July 1999 <http://www.english.uiuc.edu/cws/ and http://w3.scale. uiuc.edu/scale/>.

"Help Wanted." Business News. *Virginian-Pilot* [Norfolk]. 15 Mar. 1998: D17–19.

Hickey, Dona J., and Donna Reiss. *Learning Literature in an Era of Change: Innovations in Teaching*. Sterling, VA: Stylus, 2000.

Hobson, Eric H., ed. *Wiring the Writing Center*. Logan: Utah State UP, 1998.

Hocks, Mary E., and Daniele Bascelli. "Building a Writing-Intensive Multimedia Curriculum." Reiss, Selfe, and Young 40–56. 1 Jan. 1998 <http://www.wcenter.spelman.edu/courses.html>.

Holder, Carol. E-mail to Donna Reiss. 7 Oct. 1997. 4 Jan. 1998 <http://www.faculty.csupomona.edu/center/>.

Inman, James A., and Donna N. Sewell. *Taking Flight with OWLS: Examining Electronic Writing Center Work*. Mahwah, NJ: Erlbaum, 2000.

Kimball, Sara. "WAC on the Web: Writing Center Outreach to Teachers of Writing Intensive Courses." *Wiring the Writing Center*. Ed. Eric H. Hobson. Logan: Utah State UP, 1998. 62–74.

Langsam, Deborah M., and Kathleen Blake Yancey. "E-mailing Biology: Facing the Biochallenge." Reiss, Selfe, and Young 231–41.

"Learning Communities at University of South Florida." 4 July 1999 <http://www.usf.edu/~lc/ and http://www.usf.edu/~lc/conf/>.

Maimon, Elaine. "Time Future Contained in Time Past." Writing Across the Curriculum Third National Conference. Charleston, SC. 5–8 Feb. 1997.

McBride, Stephanie. *Testimonials . . . Instructors Have the Last Word.* 26 Dec. 1997 <http://www.daedalus.com/info/testimny.html>.

Oliver, Mary Beth. "Incorporating Technology in the Classroom: Introduction to Communication Research." 3 Jan. 1998 <http://www.edtech.vt.edu/innovations/oliver.html>.

Palmquist, Mike. "Notes on the Evolution of Network Support for Writing Across the Curriculum." *Inventing a Discipline: Rhetoric Scholarship in Honor of Richard E. Young.* Ed. Maureen Daly Goggin. Urbana, IL : NCTE, 2000. 373–402.

Redd, Teresa M. "Accommodation and Resistance on (the Color) Line: Black Writers Meet White Artists on the Internet." Reiss, Selfe, and Young 139–50.

Reiss, Donna. "A Comment on 'The Future of WAC.'" *College English* 58 (1996): 722–23.

Reiss, Donna, Dickie Selfe, and Art Young. *Electronic Communication Across the Curriculum.* Urbana, IL: NCTE, 1998.

Rudenstine, Neil L. "The Internet and Education: A Close Fit." *Chronicle of Higher Education* 21 Feb. 1997: A48.

Russell, David R. "Writing Across the Curriculum in Historical Perspective: Toward a Social Interpretation." *College English* 52 (1990): 52–73.

———. *Writing in the Academic Disciplines, 1870–1990: A Curricular History.* Carbondale: Southern Illinois UP, 1991.

Selfe, Cynthia L. Foreword. Reiss, Selfe, and Young ix–xiv.

Shamoon, Linda K. "International E-mail Debate." Reiss, Selfe, and Young 151–61.

Sherman, Lawrence W. "A Postmodern, Constructivist Pedagogy for Teaching Educational Psychology, Assisted by Computer Mediated Communications." CSCL95 Conference. Bloomington, IN. 17–20 Oct. 1995. 4 July 1999 <http://www.muohio.edu/~lwsherman/cscl95.html>.

Shires, Peter. "Integrating Technology into Veterinary Medicine." 5 July 1999 <http://www.edtech.vt.edu/innovations/shires.html>.

Thaiss, Chris. "Reliving the History of WAC—Every Day." Writing Across the Curriculum Third National Conference. Charleston, SC. 5–8 Feb. 1997.

———. "When WAC Becomes WE." *Composition Chronicle* 9.6 (1996): 8–9.

Townsend, Martha A. "Re: reading and . . ." E-mail to WAC-L @postoffice.cso.uiuc.edu. 30 Apr. 1997. 1 Jan. 1998 (Campus Writing Program http://www.missouri.edu/~writcwp/); (Expressive Media www.missouri.edu/~witsml/); (MUIIT http://www.missouri.edu/~muiit).

Walvoord, Barbara E. "The Future of WAC." *College English* 58 (1996): 58–79.

Wax, Robin. "University-High School Collaboration: Writing-to-Learn, Student-Centered Learning, and Computer Technology." *Wings* 2.1 (1994). 26 Dec. 1997 <http://www.daedalus.com/wings/wax.2.1.html>.

Weisser, Christian R. E-mail to Donna Reiss. 12 Oct. 1997. 5 Jan. 1998 <http://chuma.usf.edu/~cweisser>.

Williams, Patricia. "Writing/Technology." E-mail to WAC-L @postoffice.cso.uiuc.edu. 22 May 1997.

Woest, E. June. "Welcome to eArt Field Trips." 1997. 4 July 1999 <http://www.hccs.cc.tx.us/JWoest/jw_trips.htm> and "Using the Internet for Art and Writing" <http://www.hccs.cc.tx.us/JWoest/MyProjects/jw_proj.htm>.

Yancey, Kathleen Blake, ed. *Electronic Portfolios*. Spec. issue of *Computers and Composition* 13.2 (1996).

Yancey, Kathleen Blake, and Irwin Weiser, eds. *Situating Portfolios: Four Perspectives*. Logan: Utah State UP, 1997.

Young, Art, and Toby Fulwiler. "The Enemies of Writing Across the Curriculum." *Programs That Work: Models and Methods for Writing Across the Curriculum*. Ed. Toby Fulwiler and Art Young. Portsmouth NH: Heinemann-Boynton/Cook, 1990. 287–94.

Young, Jeffrey R. "Canadian University Promises It Won't Require Professors to Use Technology." *Chronicle of Higher Education* 3 Oct. 1997: A26–A28.

———. "A New Graduation Requirement at Kalamazoo: Create a Web Page." *Chronicle of Higher Education* 23 May 1997: A23.

———. "Rethinking the Role of the Professor in an Age of High-Tech Tools." *Chronicle of Higher Education* 3 Oct. 1997: A26–A28.

CHAPTER FOUR

Writing Across the Curriculum and Service Learning: Kairos, Genre, and Collaboration

DAVID A. JOLLIFFE
DePaul University

At a university where I used to teach, a dean was fond of using the phrase "every boat on its own bottom," meaning that every academic program had to be responsible for keeping its enrollments, faculty "productivity," and student approval ratings high, and every academic program would in turn reap financial rewards commensurate with its performance on those measures. Needless to say, there was not a lot of interdisciplinary, interdepartmental, or interprogrammatic cooperation at this university. If every boat had to be on its own bottom, it was difficult to get two people in the same boat.

Writing across the curriculum (WAC) and service learning (SL) have the power to subvert this unproductive ideology. While administrators and faculty of WAC and SL programs could choose to see their movements as two boats, each bobbing along on its own bottom, WAC and SL are actually natural allies. The two movements clearly share some important features: they are both writing intensive in a variety of ways, and they both represent alternatives, sometimes contested but often energizing and invigorating, to traditional patterns of teaching, research, and service in higher education. Given this common ground, WAC and SL should find ways to cooperate, with each movement strengthening the other; this chapter offers guidance that might foster this connection. For WAC and SL to get into the same boat, or even for each to help the other's boat sail better, proponents of both movements must think clearly about what each can contribute to the other. WAC faculty and administrators can tap into the ample energy SL has generated in colleges and universities as a result of the latter movement's responses to an array of political, social, and economic issues in higher education. SL faculty and administrators can benefit from WAC by considering, with the assistance of writing specialists, how the genres they ask students to work with in SL courses and projects help to shape the students as thinkers, writers, and citizens.

Definitions and Origins

SL is built on the deceptively simple, apparently self-evident, two-word phrase that names the movement. In SL courses, students engage in some kind of service, usually in a community or campus organization, that allows them to apply in "real life" settings the principles and practices they learn in their courses. For example, students in a political science course studying immigration policies and practices might spend time with neighborhood immigrant organizations helping members prepare to take U.S. citizenship tests. Students in a management course might put together organizational plans for not-for-profit agencies. Students in an art history class could assemble, install, and curate an exhibition in a home for the elderly.

At some institutions, SL operates solely within traditional curricular units, such as colleges and departments, and service activities are integrated and required in course syllabi. At other institutions, SL is co-curricular, with the service activities organized by a supporting office on campus. Students can then choose to perform service that is related to the course content, but they may not be required to do so.

One of SL's leading proponents, Edward Zlotkowski, offers the following definition: service learning is "meaningful community service that is linked to students' academic experience through related course materials and reflective activities" ("A New Model" 3). A more intricate definition comes from the Commission on National and Community Service. According to this organization, a service learning program

- provides educational experiences in which students learn by participating in carefully organized service activities that meet actual community needs and are coordinated collaboratively by school and community-based personnel;

- is integrated into the students' academic curriculum and provides the opportunity for them to think, discuss, or write about what they learned during the service activities;

- provides students with occasions to use their newly acquired perspectives and knowledge in situations in their own communities; and

- enhances the school-based curriculum by extending learning beyond the classroom and helping to foster a sense of caring for others. (Kraft and Krug 200)

Although the term "service learning" may invite deceptively simple definitions, SL programs are complex entities, and their development has entailed untold hours of discussion and deliberation at colleges and universities that have instituted SL options or requirements. The issues that faculty and administrators must haggle over are embedded in two major questions: First, what is "service" in SL? That is, what kinds of activities must students engage in for their work to qualify for SL credit? What kinds of agencies, organizations, or individuals must they serve? And for how long and at what intervals? Second, what is "learning" in SL? That is, what must students do in order to demonstrate that they have learned something from the service? How must students document their work in order to receive SL credit? To whom must students present evidence of their service work, and how will it be assessed, evaluated, and graded?

Taking up the issues embedded in the first question, as interesting as they are, goes beyond the bounds of the present chapter. (I cannot resist, however, offering a fascinating scenario under the first rubric: Suppose a student in a political science SL course proposes for his service to organize and participate in pickets at an abortion clinic and thereby runs afoul of the law. Does that count as service?) Two important issues embedded in the second major question, however, are precisely the focus of this chapter: What kinds of writing, what genres, should students produce in SL courses and projects, and why? What is the connection between the genres students are asked to work in and the things they learn—about the content of the SL course, about the organization or individuals they are serving, about writing in and beyond academia, and about themselves as citizens?

As David Russell illustrates in his history of writing in academic disciplines, writing across the curriculum was in place at some colleges and universities long before a movement known as WAC coalesced (*Writing*). The same is true for SL. Faculty, students, and campus life professionals were sponsoring community service projects long before the SL movement came together as a recognizable entity. If we propose, as the editors of this volume do, that WAC faculty development workshops in the early 1970s were one spark that led eventually to the birth of the WAC movement, then we can see that WAC and SL have had roughly the same gestation period. According to Allen J. Wutzdorff and Dwight E. Giles Jr., while SL emerged from many traditions in U.S. higher education, "The term *service-learning* first arose in 1964 in connection with the community service programs developed by the Oak Ridge Associated Universities in Tennessee" (107). Wutzdorff and Giles list several "service-learning milestones in higher education" following that date:

- In 1972 the federally funded University Year for Action program "involved students from campuses across the country in serving their communities." Several SL programs still in operation—for example, those at the University of Vermont, Michigan State University, and the University of Southern California—were established under this program.

- In the early 1970s, the federal government established the National Center for Service Learning.

- In 1982 the National Society for Experiential Education, still a national leader in the SL movement, created its Service Learning Special Interest Group, now one of the most active SIGs in the organization.

- In 1985, under the sponsorship of the Education Commission of the States, "a consortium of college and university presidents who support the educational value of service and make a commitment to foster public service on their campuses" formed Campus Compact: The Project for Public and Community Service.

◆ In 1990 the National and Community Service Act was signed by President George Bush, and in 1993, the National and Community Service Trust Act was signed by President Bill Clinton. The latter established the Corporation for Public Service, a national organization headed by retired General Colin Powell and former U.S. Senator Harris Wofford.

◆ In 1995 the American Association for Higher Education chose "The Engaged Campus" as the theme of its annual national conference, fostering discussion and SL program planning on its members' campuses.

◆ In 1996 SL was included for the first time as a strand at the American Educational Research Association conference (Wutzdorff and Giles 107–8).

Potential Connections

Given that the two movements emerged in roughly the same milieu in higher education, it is surprising that, so far, SL and WAC in general have remained nearly separate entities at both the national and the local, institutional level. There has been, however, considerable convergence of SL proponents and general, first-year college composition programs and some hints of a melding of SL and WAC. The inaugural book published in the American Association for Higher Education's projected eighteen-volume service-learning-in-the-disciplines series was *Writing the Community: Concepts and Models for Service Learning in Composition*, edited by Linda Adler-Kassner, Robert Crooks, and Ann Watters. In addition, a major organizational effort to bring together service learning–oriented composition specialists was launched at the 1998 Conference on College Composition and Communication.

One of the prime movers behind this effort was Thomas Deans, whose book, *Writing Partnerships: Service-Learning in Composition*, describes a wide range of college composition programs that have incorporated a community-service component. Deans creates a taxonomy of purpose, classifying programs according to whether their courses embody "writing *for* the community," "writing *about* the community," or "writing *with* the community." Though Deans's title suggests his book focuses solely on college composition courses, he exemplifies two of his three emphases with descriptions of courses that might be seen as WAC offerings.

Indeed, in another document Deans explicitly conjectures about a possible WAC-SL linkage. Writing in the AAHE volume cited earlier, he sees the following potential connections between WAC and SL:

♦ Both movements aim to embody pedagogical modes that help students learn course material more effectively rather than simply report what they learn.

♦ Both represent "a significant departure from traditional teaching and learning in college courses" ("Writing Across" 29). As a consequence, both have the potential to benefit professionally faculty who teach at institutions that encourage effective pedagogical innovation, or to impede professionally those who teach at places where change is not rewarded.

♦ Both are potentially cross-disciplinary, allowing instructors to import whatever disciplinary knowledge seems appropriate into the WAC or SL context.

♦ "Both can prompt faculty to adopt new perspectives on the values and conventions of their home disciplines" (30).

♦ Both are valued by select faculty and are lauded as worthwhile by administrators, students, parents, and society beyond the university, yet both are devalued within the traditional higher education reward hierarchy.

♦ Both are perceived to take time away from content and to lower standards.

♦ Both have gained footholds in secondary and postsecondary settings. (29–30)

♦ Finally, both movements, Deans notes, are innovating cautiously, perhaps because their pedagogies can be seen as threats to customary and established postsecondary teaching and because higher education has not seen fit to reward innovation readily. "Service-learning seems to be . . . slowly and incrementally building on the personal commitment of early adopters interested in exploring new forms of pedagogy, " Deans writes, "while steering clear of reform that would threaten disciplinary formations or insist on radical critique. This approach of 'service-learning in the disciplines' rather than a pan-curricular reform effort is a strategic (even if not consciously plotted) and, I think, wise one" (32).

I believe that WAC and SL can combine their strengths to produce a reform effort that would be, if not pan-curricular, at least broader—and eventually healthier for higher education in general—than either movement could generate on its own. Each movement can look to the other for a source of strength.

The Energy of Service Learning

As Deans's work makes clear, SL is not uncontested territory. Faculty and administrators are approaching SL cautiously for the reasons mentioned earlier—curricular and pedagogical innovation is potentially threatening and often not rewarded—plus two more. First, SL usually involves what some educators characterize as "applied knowledge" and therefore may be perceived as anti-intellectual, inimical to the liberal arts tradition. Second, SL can be seen as embodying a variety of vocationalism, one which some faculty are wont to characterize as an unreflective, thousand-points-of-light do-goodism. At many colleges and universities, however, these misgivings are being overcome. SL is both creating and thriving on the good vibrations it produces within almost all populations connected to higher education—students, faculty, administrators, boards of trustees, parents, potential employers of students, and external funding agents. How has SL managed not only to establish itself as a legitimate entity in higher education but also to secure such a luster? What is the source of SL's positive energy?

Service learning is not just a visible curricular and pedagogical movement in U.S. higher education today; it is also a discourse, a set of statements about curricular, intercurricular, and co-curricular practices that coalesced into an identifiable entity in the mid-1990s. SL is, in other words, the product of what Michel Foucault calls a "discursive formation," the set of tacit "rules of formation" that actually produce the "objects" that people in discourse communities talk and write about (31–39). Students and faculty were engaging in academically oriented community service projects well before 1990, but it was only in the middle of that decade that "service learning" became the unmistakable label for what they were talking about when they referred to these projects.

What social, political, and economic forces from the mid-1990s to the present have enabled service learning to emerge as a definable movement? Or, to put the question in terms of classical rhetorical theory, what has been the *kairos*—the sense of the opportune moment, the right time and place—that the discourse of service learning has capitalized on? Let me outline five forces—five sites where the politics and economics of U.S. culture influence higher education—that service learning advocates have used to legitimize and energize their movement.

Let us call the first force "higher education faculty bashing," the trend among conservative critics in government, the media, and occasionally within the academy itself to fault faculty for living cushy lives inside the ivory tower. It has been more than ten years since Charles Sykes lobbed the first major salvo in this attack with *ProfScam: Professors and the Demise of Higher Education*, and the assault has intensified since then. A more recent compendium of the attacks can be found in William H. Honan's *New York Times* article, "The Ivory Tower under Siege: Everyone Else Downsized; Why Not the Academy?" Though initially focusing on the faculty-bashing efforts of James Carlin, chair of the Massachusetts Board of Higher Education, Honan's essay effectively draws together critics' views from across the country on the academy's overemphasis on arcane research and specialized publication instead of teaching, the apparently light workload of the faculty, the professoriate's seeming abuse of the tenure system, and its role in contributing to the escalating cost of getting a college degree. Honan quotes James Purley, president of the American Association of University Professors, who senses that faculty are under fire for poor performance in all three of their traditional activities—scholarship, teaching, and service. "It's 360-degree bashing," says Purley (qtd. in Honan 33).

The second force emerged partly as a reaction to faculty bashing and partly as a proactive effort to reconnect the academy's research and teaching to its service mission. Let us call this force "the New American Scholar/New American College movement," adopting the phraseology of its progenitor, the late Ernest L. Boyer, president of the Carnegie Foundation for the Advancement of Teaching. Boyer's 1990 book, *Scholarship Reconsidered: Priorities of the Professoriate*, gained considerable national attention for its attempt to reorient the academy's emphases from the traditional triumvirate of research, teaching, and service to a new, four-part view of faculty scholarship: the scholarship of discovery, or what was traditionally referred to as research; the scholarship of integration, or activities that foster inter- or multidisciplinary approaches to inquiries; the scholarship of application, or efforts that specifically aim to point scholarly agendas toward solving consequential, social problems; and the scholarship of teaching. In a series of later articles, Boyer called on colleges and universities to weigh these four emphases equally. He envisioned an institution that "celebrates teaching and selectively supports research, while also taking special pride in its capacity to connect thought to action, theory to practice" ("Creating" A48).

The third, fourth, and fifth forces that have energized SL and allowed it to coalesce as a distinct movement are all implicit in Boyer's calls for a "new American scholar" and "new American college." Let us call the third the "redefinition/integration of service movement." At scattered colleges and universities across the country, efforts are underway both to integrate community service in the institutions' mission statements and to describe explicitly how a faculty member's community-service efforts should be rewarded in salary, promotion, and tenure deliberations. A highly visible leader in this movement is Portland State University, which has moved to fully integrate community service in its mission statement; organizational structure; and hiring, promotion, and tenure processes, and has worked explicitly to involve student organizations, campus publications, faculty governance, and the Portland community into its service orientation (Holland). The fourth force is the general movement in intellectual and academic circles around the world toward "inter- or multidisciplinary inquiry," a movement that Boyer aimed to encourage in his "scholarship of integration." A highly visible proponent of this movement is Jerry Gaff, a senior staff member for the American Association of Colleges and Universities. In a 1991 study of colleges and universities undergoing general-education curricular change, Gaff found that most of the institutions whose academic leaders perceived that their curriculum had improved significantly required students to take a core of interdisciplinary courses. The fifth force that has energized service learning is the desire among the "clientele" of colleges and universities—students, parents, and vocal employers of college graduates—for higher education to be more strongly "experiential." An experience at Hobart and William Smith Colleges in Geneva, New York, reveals an interesting manifestation of this force. When the administration of this institution surveyed employers of their graduates, asking them what recommendations they would offer to make the education offered by Hobart and William Smith more valuable, the respondents did not find fault with any of the traditional liberal arts emphases of the curriculum, but they almost all called for students to participate in more internships in their undergraduate years (Cooke).

Clearly, each of these forces helped the discourse of SL secure a foothold, both within U.S. colleges and universities and among that portion of the population that pays attention to higher education. SL visibly involves faculty and students in projects that both they and outside observers view as significant to the public good. SL links the academy to the community and to the society at large. If SL is made integral to the mission of a college or university, its faculty will be rewarded for engaging in academic service projects. As Zlotkowski ("Service-Learning Colloquium") points out, SL courses and projects are among the very few productive avenues for interdisciplinary cooperation on college and university campuses. By their very nature, SL projects are experiential. In short, SL is doing what the critics of higher education are asking colleges and universities to do.

Genres of Writing in Service Learning

WAC and SL programs could easily cooperate because extensive writing sits at the center of each movement. SL courses could be labeled as writing intensive at institutions where such labels denote the WAC requirement; likewise, if WAC courses involved students performing extensive and useful community service, the courses could be designated as SL. But for the WAC-SL connection to be productive—that is, if faculty teaching courses throughout the curriculum hope their students will comprehend the course content, apply the course material and principles in valuable service projects, and learn something about the nature of effective writing—then faculty teaching SL courses might think in more sophisticated, more pedagogically focused ways about the genres they ask students to work in as they write about their service experiences and how those genres embody different kinds of learning.

Those scholars who have investigated possible linkages between SL and college composition—for example, Deans and Paul Heilker, whose work is described later—have seen the connections in terms of the *purposes* of student writing in a service-oriented course. I want to suggest that *genre* offers a more productive perspective for faculty and administrators who are designing writing intensive SL courses—in other words, for those who are looking for how SL and WAC might collaborate. As the final section of this chapter argues, genre theory holds great potential for explaining how students learn to "behave" as functioning, intellectual adults in the discourse communities they encounter in college and beyond it. When instructors decide to require students to produce writing in a certain genre, they are making a decision, perhaps unconsciously, about the scope and range of rhetorical activity they want the students to engage in and the type of discourse community in which they want students to gain experience as writers. I hope that instructors of SL courses would make these decisions consciously and that WAC specialists could provide theoretically sound guidance to help them.

Students in SL courses at colleges and universities throughout the country are currently producing writing in many of the traditional genres of academic writing. The most frequently assigned genre in SL courses, and that which most explicitly embodies the student reflection that most SL definitions call for, is the journal entry, in which students write a variety of personal responses to their service experiences. A subgenre of the journal entry is the reflective paper, which emerges from conflating and adapting several journal entries. A typical use of the personal journal and reflective writing in an SL course can be found in the syllabus for Political Science 536, Public Human Resource

Administration, at the University of Utah. Administrators of the Lowell L. Bennion Community Service Center at the university awarded this course an SL designation because students could, in lieu of taking one examination, work for three hours a week at LifeCare Services for the Elderly in Salt Lake City and then complete two writing projects: "a regular journal of one's experiences and impressions" and "a 6–8 page paper about the nature of your service, what you learned from the experience, and implications for public administration as you see it" (DiPadova 3–4).

Clearly, the personal journal and any reflective papers that might be produced by fleshing out the journal entries represent adequate genres through which students can ponder their service experience in writing. But some faculty members who have worked to connect SL and first-year college composition question whether these genres necessarily elicit critical reflection on the part of students, and their caution about the personal journal and reflective essays are worth noting in the WAC arena as well. In groundbreaking work involving first-year writing students doing service with Boston's poor, Bruce Herzberg's students at Bentley College would regularly write journal entries, reflecting on their service activities. In these compositions, according to Herzberg, students would report that "homelessness and poverty were just abstractions before they met the homeless and the poor, but now they see that the homeless are people 'just like themselves'" (58). The inherent problem of the personal journal entry as genre, says Herzberg, is that it does not encourage students to view poverty or homelessness (or whatever social phenomenon is the focus of their service) in a larger perspective. "Here, perhaps ironically, is a danger," Herzberg writes. "If our students regard social problems as chiefly or only personal," as the genres of the personal journal entry and reflective paper tacitly encourage them to do, "then they will not search beyond the personal for a systemic explanation. . . . Writing personal responses to community service experiences is an important part of processing the experience, but it is not sufficient to raise critical or cultural consciousness" (58–59). Similarly, Linda Adler-Kassner reports that students writing about SL experiences as part of a first-year writing course in the University of Minnesota's General College (an academic unit that admits underprepared students and helps them succeed in college) produced journals that were "often dominated by students' complaints about their sites or client communities or their realization that 'this could happen to me'" (552; also qtd. in Heilker 74).

The personal journal and reflective essay are certainly not the only genres of academic writing that students in SL courses are producing. A recent essay by Paul Heilker that urges connections between SL and general, first-year composition implies a taxonomy of additional genres intrinsic to such projects. Heilker proposes a hierarchy of five purposes for student writing projects, and one can readily detect genres of writing in current SL courses implied by each of the purposes. The first, again, is the personal journal and the related reflective paper. Heilker rehearses the problems inherent in this approach that Herzberg and Adler-Kassner raise. A second genre would be the academic research paper. Such a paper, Heilker explains, "construes the experience of doing community work as *research*—research to be used as a work consulted or a work cited for a term paper or as a basis for criticizing an author's treatment of a given topic" (74). Third, students could write analytic essays, papers that critique "the systemic inequities and injustices that make service work necessary in the first place" (74). The genre inherent in Heilker's fourth option actually comes from Adler-Kassner's teaching at Minnesota's General College. Heilker cites Adler-Kassner's call for SL writing courses to elicit stance or position papers in different disciplines. These projects, Adler-Kassner maintains, would "'concentrate on developing students' acumen with academic writing' and see service-learning experiences as good places 'to start helping [them] frame their ideas in a form that is more acceptable to the academy'" (qtd in Heilker 74). Heilker saves his strongest recommendation for "a fifth form of service-learning in composition, one that enables students to understand writing as social action. In this version," Heilker writes, "the students actually complete essential writing tasks for the nonprofit agencies in which they are placed" (74). I refer to these papers as "working documents" in the communities beyond academia.

An informal survey of syllabi for upper-division writing intensive courses, both in English departments and throughout the curriculum, suggests that SL courses are already incorporating projects that elicit all of these genres. Examples of researched writing, drawing on both traditional "library" research and field studies, are abundant. For example, Ruth Overman Fischer and Victoria Rader of George Mason University created linked courses involving first-year composition and introductory sociology. As part of the course, GMU students worked as tutors in an elementary magnet school, which enrolled primarily African American and Hispanic students, for two hours each week. At the end of each day, according to Fischer,

> students wrote field notes of the day's experiences. They noted their observations of what had gone on in the classroom, their reflections on and analysis of these observations, and questions arising out of these observations and reflections. The field notes thus provided a context for students to instantiate sociological concepts and reflect critically on their experiences in the elementary classroom. . . . Their questions ultimately led to topics for their research papers dealing with some aspect of education as a social institution.

At Indiana University, Joan Pong Linton, in a sophomore-level English course called Writing for a Better Society, had students do a minimum of two hours a week of community service, then complete a series of assignments "leading up to a research paper that extends traditional library research to the practical world of service." The research paper was to "focus on a social issue (e.g., promoting the arts in the community) or a problem (e.g., implementing inclusion practices in the public schools). In addition to [consulting] published work, the students do interviews and, in some cases, surveys." In Linda Simmons's political science SL course at Northern Virginia Community College, students wrote dialogues involving characters, "imaginary or real," who converse about "how government impacts the site where students serve, how the site is governed, and [what] problems or solutions [the students perceive] at the site. The dialogues are documented as an essay would be. They usually show an awareness of different points of view—and some real creativity on the parts of the authors." A fascinating example of analytic writing embodying a systemic social critique in an upper-division SL writing course can be found in the work of Deborah Minter, Anne Ruggles Gere, and Deborah Keller-Cohen, whose students undertook careful critical analyses of the social conditions underlying the lives of students they were tutoring in an after-school literacy program. In addition to reading widely in both literacy theory and literary representations of literacy acquisition, the students wrote weekly, integrative journal assignments and, ultimately, a "research paper of their own design . . . that directly engaged with the topics or issues raised in their reading, writing, tutoring, or class discussions for this literacy course" (670).

Although SL courses can provide students with ample opportunities to produce writing in academic genres such as the journal, the research paper, and the analytic essay, I believe the most distinctive and effective melding of SL and WAC occurs when students undertake "real world" writing projects that address the needs of agencies or individuals they are serving. In these projects, which I refer to simply as "working documents," students go beyond writing about service—certainly a good end in itself—by actually doing service with their writing. As the following section of this chapter makes clear, because genres emerge in response to rhetorical situations, such projects can teach students how to produce the kinds of writing that "do business" in settings outside the university and, in some cases, how to create innovative, hybrid genres for new rhetorical situations.

Three examples of working documents from different SL courses show the potential of these genres to introduce students to rhetorical activity beyond the boundaries of the university. In Civil Engineering 420 (Traffic Engineering) at the University of Utah, another Bennion Center–approved course, students conduct actual studies of traffic congestion in Salt Lake City and then learn to write technical reports that they then submit to governmental bodies and local organizations that are petitioning for new roadways and traffic patterns (Martin). In a course entitled Writing Nature: Thinking and Writing about Nature and Identity, sponsored by the Haas Center for Public Service at Stanford University, students at two points in the course have the option of writing "academic essays," based on interviews or library research, or "comparable Community Service Writing projects"—actual documents produced for the not-for-profit agencies where students were doing their service work (Ross). At

DePaul University, I regularly teach an upper-division writing intensive course, primarily serving education and English majors, called Topics in Writing: Tutoring in City Schools. In this course, students spend two intensive weeks learning to conduct writing tutorials and run writing groups, then tutor for three hours a week for the remainder of the term at a Chicago public high school. Their major written work is a sequence of four papers, each on the same subject, called an Inquiry Contract, which I have described elsewhere (Jolliffe, "Discourse," *Inquiry and Genre*). Students keep a journal throughout the experience, and the first paper in the contract is reflective. The second involves research and is primarily informative in purpose. The third involves a systemic critique and is exploratory. The final paper is a working document—a text that addresses an audience beyond the academic community, dealing with a real problem involving urban education that the students have uncovered in their work as a tutor. For this final project, I have had students produce written work ranging from a parent's manual for establishing a summer reading program for high school students, to a teacher's guide for working with hearing-impaired students, to a Web page for parents of teenage girls who have psychologically influenced eating disorders.

One innovative SL program immerses student writers in situations in which the real-world genres of working documents need adapting to meet challenging rhetorical goals. Courses offered by Carnegie Mellon University at the Community Literacy Center in Pittsburgh establish working teams consisting of CMU students, staff members of the literacy center, and center clients ranging from troubled, inner-city high school students, to single parents, to underemployed workers (Peck, Flower, and Higgins). Because the center proposes to help its clients learn to use literacy to inquire critically into the dynamics of the conflicted situations they find themselves in, to work for social justice, and to foster "genuine, intercultural conversation" (205), CMU students have collaborated in producing hybrid genres that give voice to the different stakeholders in these situations. For example, a group of teenagers at the center believed they were subjected to an overly rigid suspension policy at their high school and were concerned about "the rising rate of out-of-school suspension among African-American males" (210). The CMU students served as mentors to these teens in the Whassup with Suspension project that allowed students to write about their frustrations with the suspension policy, and then brought in teachers and administrators to respond to the students' writing. Eventually, after considerable conversation through "uncharted territory" (211), the teenagers, aided by CMU students, produced a "hybrid text": "an eight-page newsletter which denounced mindless authoritarianism by adults, illustrated feelings of both students and teachers involved in suspension disputes, and gave a series of dramatic scenarios for understanding how suspensions occur" (212). The Whassup with Suspension newsletter eventually became required reading for teachers and students at an inner-city Pittsburgh high school. The CMU students and their partners at the center learned a valuable lesson about the ways genres not only emerge from the rhetorical demands of a situation but also give shape to the action of the situation itself.

Genre Theory: What WAC Can Contribute to SL

As do many faculty members experienced in the WAC movement, I frequently conduct instructional development seminars, either for new teachers of college writing courses or for faculty members across the curriculum who want to incorporate more writing in their courses. If WAC and SL move toward more cooperative ventures, I imagine WAC specialists will be increasingly called on to lead such events. I sometimes try to stimulate a discussion in these seminars by taking an overly simplistic view of the teaching of writing: All we do as writing teachers, I suggest demurely, is (a) give students something to write about, (b) tell them what kinds of papers to produce as they write about this content, (c) teach them appropriate writing processes, (d) help them understand how they did, and (e) set them to work on the next task. *Voilà!* As simple as that! Each of these tasks, of course, requires great professional savvy, and the not-so-hidden complexity of, and interrelations between, these five goals and responsibilities are what motivates vigorous discussion in the seminars.

The WAC movement has made great progress toward leading faculty in a wide range of disciplines to see the connections between these five tasks and unpack their curricular and pedagogical implications. WAC professionals have helped their colleagues understand that what they ask their students to write about is influenced by the type of papers they teach them to write; likewise, how they teach students effective writing processes, assess their products, and set them to work on other projects is also constrained by this interaction of their discipline's domain of subject matters and its conventional written products. As David Russell's essay in this volume points out, dozens of naturalistic studies show that the "most crucial choice of tools" for students learning to write in courses across the curriculum and within the disciplines "is that of genre." Effective WAC/WID faculty should, according to Russell, direct students to write in genres that "bring students into contact with the uses of facts and concepts in their (students' and professors' and professionals') worlds." The choice of genres, he suggests, governs, at least in part, the students' motivations for writing, the identities they form through writing, and the processes they employ to write successfully (p. 287).

As the previous sections of this chapter make clear, faculty teaching SL courses can draw from a broad menu of genre options in creating writing projects for their students. But it would help SL come together as a rigorous academic movement if its faculty and administrators would think carefully and consciously about *why* they ask students to produce writing in some genres and not others. Just as WAC can benefit from the energy and good vibrations of SL's timely emergence in higher education, so SL can benefit from WAC's developing expertise in genre theory.

First of all, of course, SL faculty and administrators must recognize a principle of genre that some WAC movement theorists have been promulgating for the past two decades—that genres are not simply empty shells into which "contents" can be poured willy-nilly. Instead, genres are psychological and social meaning-making templates that help writers understand rhetorical situations and that give shape to their intellectual work within them. Carolyn Miller first affirmed this principle in her 1983 article, "Genre as Social Action": "A rhetorically sound definition of genre must be centered not on the substance or form of the discourse but on the action it is used to accomplish" (151). In a more recent review of genre theory, I have elaborated on the principle somewhat:

> [T]he concept of genre forms a kind of linchpin in an intellectual community's processes of generating and disseminating information. As she investigates a subject matter appropriate to her field, a scholar typifies and recognizes a recurrent rhetorical situation, and she produces a text that instantiates one of the field's preferred genres, a textual form that requires her to invoke certain *topoi*, create an exigence, effect an appropriate style, and achieve a recognizable purpose. In turn, the genre not only allows the scholar to report her research, but its conventions and constraints also give structure to the actual investigation she is reporting. (Jolliffe, "Genre" 283)

I maintain that this dual thrust of genre—its ability to help writers recognize recurrent rhetorical situations and its power to shape and constrain knowledge work—holds as true for student writers performing community service as it does for scholars writing articles for academic publication.

Russell's important 1997 article "Rethinking Genre in School and Society" supports this position and offers a rich perspective on how genre affects student writing and learning, a perspective that could profitably inform the growing SL movement. Drawing on activity theory, Russell develops a framework, which he calls an *activity system*, for analyzing writing and learning situations (such as a WAC course). He displays his exemplary activity system as a triangle, with "subject(s)," or the "agent(s) whose behavior" is being analyzed, at the lower left juncture; "object/ motive, followed by outcome," or the "raw material or problem space" that is "changed and shaped over time," at the lower right; and "mediational means," or "tools in use" (including textual tools such as genres), at the apex (510–11). In a WAC course, to use Russell's framework, the students would be the subjects, the subject matters and knowledge work of the discipline would be the object/motive followed by outcome, and the genres students learn to write in would be one of the mediational means, part of the tools they are using to change and shape the disciplinary content. Drawing on the work of Charles Bazerman, Russell characterizes genres as "forms of life" that "regularize and stabilize" an activity through "routinized tool use within and among (sub)groups" (513). In other words, regular use of genres helps writers both establish their own identities and clarify the knowledge work they are engaging in.

Russell proceeds to describe how activity-system analysis can explain the phenomenon of students learning to write in academic contexts such as WAC or SL courses. An initial phase of learning involves what Russell calls *appropriation*. When newcomers to an activity system—such as students learning to write in a new genre in a new discipline or profession (to them)—the new ways they use these tools called words are encountered at the level of conscious actions. Through continued interaction with others in the activity system, the ways of using the tools (say, the introduction, methods, results, discussion [IMRD] structure in science writing) become a routine operation, often unconscious (516). Russell adds that as they learn to appropriate the discipline's genres, some students may also "appropriate the object/motive and subjectivity (identity) of the collective, of a new activity system" (516).

In a university, Russell continues, a student's "[e]xpanding involvement" leads him or her to become "an active participant in one or more activity systems, to maintain and perhaps transform that activity system" (528). The student positions himself or herself to "make a difference," "to recognize, appropriate, participate in—and perhaps transform, in ways large or small— the genres that operationalize some of these disciplinary/professional activity systems, the kinds of writing that help make these forms of life (and, eventually, the student's life) work" (529). When students become so inscribed, so enrolled, in such an activity system, Russell maintains, they "throw them*selves* into it through the reading/writing of its genres, to make a difference as well as make a grade" (534).

Here certainly is brain food for faculty and administrators developing SL courses and programs. The individuals, organizations, and agencies that students encounter in SL are distinct activity systems comprising agents, objects, motives, and outcomes of action, and mediational means, including relatively system-specific genres. How do the faculty and administrators planning

SL programs hope that students will *inscribe themselves* in the SL activity systems? Do SL faculty and administrators hope that students will observe these activity systems and simply reflect on what they perceive? Do SL faculty and administrators want students to see these activity systems as sources of objective, relatively distanced research and study? Do SL faculty and administrators want students actually to *participate* in the activity system? Any of these would be justifiable goals for an SL course or program, but they should be goals that SL faculty and administrators consciously and explicitly agree on. WAC-oriented genre theory would help SL faculty, administrators, and their students address these goals consciously and purposefully.

Works Cited

Adler-Kassner, Linda. "Digging a Groundwork for Writing: Underprepared Students and Community Service Courses." *College Composition and Communication* 46 (1995): 552–55.

Adler-Kassner, Linda, Robert Crooks, and Ann Watters, eds. *Writing the Community: Concepts and Models for Service-Learning in Composition*. Washington, DC: American Association for Higher Education, 1997.

Boyer, Ernest L. "Creating the New American College." *Chronicle of Higher Education* 9 Mar. 1994: A48.

———. *Scholarship Reconsidered: Priorities of the Professoriate*. Princeton, NJ: Carnegie Foundation for the Advancement of Teaching, 1990.

Cooke, Dana. "Life's Ups and Downs." *Pulteney Street Survey* (Spring 1997). 19 July 1999 <http://www.hws.edu/new/pss/Careers.html>.

Deans, Thomas. "Writing Across the Curriculum and Community Service Learning: Correspondences, Cautions, and Futures." *Writing the Community: Concepts and Models for Service-Learning in Composition*. Ed. Linda Adler-Kassner, Robert Crooks, and Ann Watters. Washington, DC: American Association for Higher Education, 1997. 29–38.

———. *Writing Partnerships: Service-Learning in Composition*. Urbana, IL: NCTE, 2000.

DiPadova, Laurie. "Syllabus for University of Utah, Political Science 536, Public Human Resource Administration." 12 Jan. 1998 <http://csf.Colorado.edu/sl/syllabi/poly-sci/dipadova536.html>.

Fischer, Ruth Overman. "WAC/Service Learning Project." E-mail to the author. 14 Jan. 1999.

Foucault, Michel. *The Archaeology of Knowledge*. London: Tavistock, 1972.

Gaff, Jerry G. *New Life for the College Curriculum: Assessing Achievements and Furthering Progress in the Reform of General Education*. San Francisco: Jossey-Bass, 1991.

Heilker, Paul. "Rhetoric Made Real: Civic Discourse and Writing beyond the Classroom." *Writing the Community: Concepts and Models for Service-Learning in Composition*. Ed. Linda Adler-Kassner, Robert Crooks, and Ann Watters. Washington, DC: American Association for Higher Education, 1997. 71–78.

Herzberg, Bruce. "Community Service and Critical Teaching." *College Composition and Communication* 45 (1994): 307–19. Rpt. in *Writing the Community: Concepts and Models for Service-Learning in Composition*. Ed. Linda Adler-Kassner, Robert Crooks, and Ann Watters. Washington, DC: American Association for Higher Education, 1997. 57–70.

Holland, Barbara. "Analyzing Institutional Commitment to Service: A Model of Key Organizational Factors." *Michigan Journal of Community Service Learning* 4 (1997): 30–41.

Honan, William N. "The Ivory Tower under Siege: Everyone Else Downsized; Why Not the Academy?" *New York Times* 4 Jan. 1998, spec. sec. 4: 33+.

Jolliffe, David A. "Discourse, Interdiscursivity, and Composition Instruction." *Reconceiving Writing, Rethinking Writing Instruction*. Ed. Joseph Petraglia. Mahwah, NJ: Erlbaum, 1995. 197–216.

———. "Genre." *Encyclopedia of Rhetoric and Composition: Communication from Ancient Times to the Information Age*. Ed. Theresa Enos. New York: Garland, 1996. 279–84.

———. *Inquiry and Genre: Writing to Learn in College*. Boston: Allyn & Bacon, 1999.

Kraft, Richard, and James Krug. "Review of Research and Evaluation on Service Learning in Public and Higher Education." *Building*

Community: Service Learning in the Academic Disciplines. Ed. Richard J. Kraft and Marc Swadener. Denver: Colorado Campus Compact, 1994. 199–213.

Linton, Joan Pong. "Query about Types of Writing in Service-Learning Courses." E-mail to author. 18 Nov. 1997.

Martin, Peter. "Syllabus for University of Utah, Civil and Environmental Engineering 420." 12 Jan. 1998 <http://csf.Colorado.edu/sl/ syllabi/ engineering/martin420.html>.

Miller, Carolyn R. "Genre as Social Action." *Quarterly Journal of Speech* 70 (1984): 151–67.

Minter, Deborah Williams, Anne Ruggles Gere, and Deborah Keller-Cohen. "Learning Literacies." *College English* 57 (1995): 669–87.

Peck, Wayne Campbell, Linda Flower, and Lorraine Higgins. "Community Literacy." *College Composition and Communication* 46 (May 1995): 199–222.

Ross, Carolyn. "Community Service Writing: Providing a Missing Link in the Composition Classroom." 1996. 12 Jan. 1998 <http:// www-leland.stanford.edu/class/wct3b-04/WNHaasNews Article.html>.

Russell, David R. "Rethinking Genre in School and Society: An Activity Theory Analysis." *Written Communication* 14 (1997): 504–54.

———. *Writing in the Academic Disciplines, 1870–1990: A Curricular History*. Carbondale: Southern Illinois UP, 1991.

Simmons, Linda J. "Query about Types of Writing in Service-Learning Courses." E-mail to author. 17 Nov. 1997.

Sykes, Charles J. *ProfScam: Professors and the Demise of Higher Education*. Washington, DC: Regnery Gateway, 1988.

Wutzdorff, Allen J., and Dwight E. Giles Jr. "Service-Learning in Higher Education." *Service Learning. Ninety-sixth Yearbook of the National Society for the Study of Education*. Ed. Joan Schine. Chicago: National Society for the Study of Education, 1997. 105–17.

Zlotkowski, Edward A. "A New Model for Excellence." *Successful Service-Learning Programs: New Models of Excellence in Higher Education*. Ed. Edward Zlotkowski. Bolton, MA: Anker, 1998. 1–14.

———. "Service-Learning Colloquium." American Association for Higher Education Conference on Faculty Roles and Rewards. Orlando. 29 Jan. 1998.

CHAPTER FIVE

Is It Still WAC? Writing within Interdisciplinary Learning Communities

TERRY MYERS ZAWACKI
George Mason University

ASHLEY TALIAFERRO WILLIAMS
George Mason University

I t's almost a cycle—every several months or so, someone just starting a learning community program at his or her institution queries the writing listservs about how WAC and, in most cases, first-year composition fit into this new model. Besides all the helpful advice, what is perhaps most interesting to the two of us are the new voices that respond each time around, as more and more institutions design learning community (LC) programs in an effort to reform curriculum and pedagogy, particularly as these relate to the first-year experience. The most commonly used definition of a learning community, as well as descriptions of an array of LC models, comes from the pioneering work of Faith Gabelnick, Jean MacGregor, Roberta Matthews, and Barbara Leigh Smith (Gabelnick et al.). In brief, learning communities are curriculum change initiatives that link, cluster, or integrate two or more courses during a given term, often around an interdisciplinary theme, and involve a common cohort of students. Although LC structures are quite variable, they all have the common goal of fostering greater academic coherence and more explicit intellectual connections among students, between students and their faculty, and among disciplines.[1] With LC rapidly becoming a paradigm for curricular reform, the time seems right for an examination of how both WAC and first-year composition (FYC) are being transformed by their inclusion in these communities.

In "The Future of WAC," Barbara Walvoord suggests that we reexamine WAC within the frame of other educational reform movements—assessment, critical thinking, cross-curricular initiatives—in order to think more creatively about "its characteristics, strengths, and problems" (61). We also need to work within these movements in order to accomplish our goals. WAC must "dive in or die" (70), Walvoord argues, a process that involves locating WAC "skillfully, powerfully, visibly or invisibly, among the complex forces and discourses of the academy" (74). This process has not been one-sided for the LC movement, which from the outset has not only pointed to WAC as a valuable model for pedagogical reform, but has also seen writing as foundational to its cross-disciplinary aims. As we will show in this chapter, however, when WAC is incorporated into LC models, it can be transformed in complex, sometimes unrecognizable, ways.[2] To illustrate, we describe our experiences with WAC in two LC models—the Linked Courses Program[3] and the New Century College at George Mason University. In examining these new sites for WAC—a program and a college—we argue that WAC has become a much more reciprocal process, with writing faculty and faculty in the disciplines engaged in a sustained conversation about writing processes and products. In the case of New Century College, where writing is infused in the interdisciplinary curriculum, we suggest we may need new terminology to describe writing within innovative curricula.

We begin by discussing the robust tradition of WAC and its influence on curricular and pedagogical innovation at George Mason University, including the learning communities that are the focus of this chapter. As various contributors have observed on the electronic listserv for writing program administrators (WPA-L@asu.edu), learning communities tend to reflect the individual campus cultures. Similarly, the richness and complexity of the two LC programs we discuss reflect our campus culture—the willingness of our faculty to take risks, cooperation across disciplines encouraged by WAC, and, not least, institutional flexibility. Next, each of us discusses how writing occurs in her particular learning community and the complex issues that tend to surface, including the issue of assessment—of writing, of learning communities, and of WAC in learning communities: the egg inside the egg inside the egg, to paraphrase Bill Condon (Chapter 2, this volume). Condon's metaphor is particularly apt because, as he notes, "each larger egg is one more level of difficulty above the difficulty of 'simply' assessing writing ability" (p. 29). We suggest that the work of the American Association for Higher Education (AAHE) Flashlight Project on evaluating the relatively new technology-across-the-curriculum movement can provide some useful guidelines for assessing WAC in learning communities. We close with a vision of WAC for the new millennium as Writing Across Curricular Cultures, a good description, we think, of what happens to writing instruction and, more important, writing practices in learning communities when new alliances are formed—among faculty, students, and other campus professionals—and disciplinary genres merge and expand.

Robust Tradition of WAC

WAC enjoys a robust tradition at George Mason dating back to 1977, when a faculty task force, concerned about student writing, called for workshops to help faculty across the disciplines learn to use writing as a tool of teaching. Early WAC activities included workshops conducted by Elaine Maimon and others. The presence of the Northern Virginia Writing Project on campus also encouraged WAC activities, in particular through faculty institutes during the summers of 1980 and 1981. One result of this effort was the publication of *Writing to Learn: Essays and Reflections on Writing Across the Curriculum,* edited by Chris Thaiss, in 1983. By 1990, when the faculty senate mandated a writing intensive requirement, the university's experience with WAC, marked by these and other developments, was fairly typical of a number of WAC programs nationally (see Griffin; McLeod, "Writing"). Significantly, for much of its history at George Mason, WAC provided virtually the only organized forum for conversation about teaching across department lines, conducted mainly through workshops and brown-bag discussions.

Closely intertwined with the history of WAC at George Mason is the history of curricular revision, particularly in general education, which includes the creation of a number of interdisciplinary initiatives in the 1980s and 1990s. Not surprisingly, faculty involved in WAC have also frequently been involved in curricular reform in general education. The cornerstone of these reform efforts was the establishment in 1982 of the Plan for Alternative General Education (PAGE), later revised into an honors program, which offers a forty-five-hour comprehensive, interdisciplinary, writing intensive program for approximately two hundred students. At about the same time that PAGE was being pioneered, the College of Arts and Sciences (CAS)—where general education resides—was also experimenting with a small cluster-course program, offering a limited number of first-year students and sophomores "clusters," which linked two or three courses from different disciplines and included a monthly integrative seminar. This program was supplanted after two years by a pilot of a general education core curriculum, funded by the Fund for the Improvement of Postsecondary Education (FIPSE), offering limited opportunity for cross-disciplinary connections. In this program, the first two courses for first-year students were linked, so that five composition faculty members worked as a group to link up with humanities faculty teaching a Western culture course. Assessment of the core pilot showed higher student and faculty satisfaction with the two linked courses than with the stand-alone courses. Armed with these assessment data, composition faculty in the pilot proposed to the CAS dean that the linked arrangement be continued between existing introductory courses and the composition course even though faculty rejected the core initiative as a model for general education. We comp teachers were convinced that our students were more invested in writing courses when they were asked to write about ideas and texts they were studying in another course. Perhaps even more persuasive was our own sense that we were no longer teaching writing skills in isolation; we were creating enhanced communities for our students and for ourselves. In the next section, Terry describes the Linked Courses Program more fully.

Linked Courses Program

While we in the core pilot believed we had created a new model, when I took over direction of the Linked Courses Program, I discovered the extent to which other institutions had also created linked or clustered courses within general education programs. Typically, the clusters are aimed at first-year students and include a first-year composition course as an integral part of the learning community, the space in which students can process the information they are learning in the other course(s). This is the case partly because first-year composition is usually the only small class first-year students will have in their first semester and partly because of its flexible content, as writing teachers tend to be more concerned with the "how" of learning than the "what." For this reason, as Tim McLaughlin points out, writing teachers often play key roles "not only as learning community organizers but as creators of connective tissue between courses" (7).

From its inception in 1992, Mason's Linked Courses Program has been fully endorsed and supported by the College of Arts and Sciences, which is now actively seeking to expand the program beyond the students' first semester. A sample of linked courses includes first-year composition linked variously to introductory courses in psychology, sociology, anthropology, philosophy, engineering, government, history, and so on. The more ambitious links, three of which I will discuss in this section, include a third course in the link: first-year composition (FYC), government, and philosophy; an e-mail mentoring link designed for psychology majors, which includes FYC, psychology, and a peer-mentoring component; and FYC, sociology, and a one-credit community service course. Before I turn to a discussion of writing within these linked courses, however, I want to explore the way the traditional first-year composition course has been influenced by the linked program.

In his 1997 WAC conference presentation, "A 'Linked-Courses' Initiative within a Multi-faceted WAC Program: Administrative Problems and Solutions," Chris Thaiss discussed the pressure that a linked writing course puts on the writing program director to reexamine the content and "integrity" of first-year composition. To what extent, he asked, can unlinked composition courses "effectively prepare students for other environments," and, conversely, what "separable content" must be maintained? These questions about FYC—whether linked or unlinked—have been the focus of numerous articles and presentations in WAC and composition journals and conferences. Many of us in comp are familiar with the "new abolitionism," one term used to describe the movement to eliminate required composition courses. Proponents of abolishing required writing courses typically see a strong WAC program as the best alternative (see, for example, Connors and Crowley, among others). Faculty in other disciplines, even those most committed to WAC aims, do not, however, necessarily support the elimination of the first-year writing requirement. Joan Mullin, in "WAC and the Restructuring of First Year Composition," a 1995 WAC conference talk, discussed some faculty objections: their belief, for example, that the writing skills we "should be" teaching in writing courses can be decontextualized. Furthermore, Mullin pointed out, faculty in other disciplines, while understanding that they employ a specific disciplinary discourse, are reluctant to acknowledge themselves as "teachers of language." One solution, according to Mullin, is an arrangement whereby writing and content teachers collaborate as mentors and resources on writing in the disciplines.

It is this kind of collaboration and mentoring I see occurring in the Linked Courses Program where, in the best arrangements, the writing teacher retains the integrity of the composition course and also works proactively as a "WAC change agent," a term Thaiss used in his talk to mean teaching writing and rhetorical skills within the context of another course yet also showing how those skills can transcend specific disciplinary discourses. When I say in the "best arrangements," I am referring to links in which there is a one-to-one correspondence in class size, making it possible for all of the teachers in the link to assign, talk about, and be responsible for writing. In George Mason's linked program, however, as well as in most of the LC programs I am familiar with, the correspondence among classes (in all senses of the word) varies. In the remainder of this section, I describe three linked variations, showing how the composition course functions in each variation and how responsibility for writing—from creating to evaluating assignments—gets allocated.

Variation One—Sections of FYC Linked to a Large Lecture Course

One of the dean's main objectives in funding the Linked Courses Program is to increase first-year student retention by creating a comfortable, less isolating learning environment. For this reason, over half of the thirty or so linked packages offered each fall semester are made up of FYC and a large introductory general education course (150 to 300 students), such as psychology, sociology, and anthropology, in which there is no writing assigned and Scantron tests are the norm. In these links, all responsibility for writing falls to the composition faculty, who teach, in two sections, 44 of the students enrolled in the lecture course. While this is not an ideal WAC situation, students are writing in the context of a discipline and there is an exchange of ideas and methods between the two teachers (one reason it is especially important to employ experienced writing teachers). In this exchange, then, both teachers stand to gain. The noncomposition teacher engages in discussions about writing and writing assignments. At the same time, the FYC instructor gains valuable WAC experience, something that is not generally a feature of traditional programs, in which FYC is disconnected from WAC (see Christopher Thaiss, Chapter 12, this volume).

In a presemester workshop, the linked-course teachers work together to coordinate their syllabi. Though there may not be much flexibility on the part of the lecture teachers, they often see ways they might incorporate writing-to-learn strategies in the lecture class, or they may visit the writing class to talk about a particular assignment. Sometimes they redesign assignments based on their discussions with a writing professional. An anthropology teacher, for example, who had stopped using a micro-ethnography assignment because he was disappointed with the results, worked with his composition partner to redesign his assignment instructions and to articulate criteria for evaluation. He began using the revised assignment, giving it to students as an alternative to one of his multiple-choice tests. As David Russell points out in his review of WAC/WID research (Chapter 11, this volume), we know that the "very process of studying writing in conjunction with faculty helps faculty to critically reflect on their practice and change that practice" (pp. 290–91). I see these kinds of changes occurring again and again in linked planning sessions and in collaborative work throughout the semester.

In another iteration of the large lecture/small FYC link, we have experimented with assigning first-year writers who are also enrolled in Introduction to Psychology to e-mail mentors, upper-level psychology honors students who receive internship credit in psychology for their participation. When I originally designed this link, I was most interested in its e-mail aspect. I anticipated that the FYC students, who had declared psych as a major, would learn the conventions of e-mail communication, increase their writing output, and learn more about writing in their major. In turn, the upper-level mentors would be engaging in a writing-to-learn review of the discipline, a useful preparation for taking the Graduate Record Exam (almost all were headed to grad school); I also speculated that they would gain by becoming more reflective writers themselves. The mentors performed as expected, writing volumes in response to their mentees' rather short questions. To encourage her first-year students to write at greater length, FYC instructor Mary Kruck began requiring them to send paper drafts to their mentors for comments and suggestions. She also held a short online "workshop" for the mentors to discuss some ways they might respond to their mentees' drafts. Interestingly, Kruck—a very student-centered, well-liked teacher—noticed that once her students began sending drafts to their mentors, they seemed to transfer allegiance from her to the mentors, questioning her comments and grades. Some of the mentors also questioned her, wondering why she didn't comment on all of the surface errors each time. Why wasn't she, for example, teaching them subject-verb agreement and simple punctuation rules? In the process of working out the intricacies of this particular link, the psychology professor, the writing instructor, the mentors, and the first-year students all became involved in discussions about writing. Among other observations, the psychology mentors reported that they gained invaluable knowledge about themselves as writers and learners in their chosen field as well as about the writing and learning processes of less experienced students.

Variation Two—Fully Linked Sections of Two or More Courses

Perhaps the most typical LC models are those in which students are enrolled together in two or more courses with teachers who have created overlapping syllabi and reading and writing assignments. In the most successful versions of fully linked courses, the faculty members meet often to plan, rethink, and revise their assignments in light of the students' learning needs. Engaging in this kind of collaborative process, beginning with the presemester planning workshop, tends to make all of the teachers in the link much more conscious of how they approach student writing. "Every time I teach in a link I learn more about how to teach writing," a history professor tells me enthusiastically whenever he sees me. He has high praise for the two writing teachers he has linked with; he has always assigned lots of writing, he says, but now he understands the importance of building in a processing component even in his courses that are not linked. If a WAC aim is for teachers in other disciplines to help their students "process" writing, then fully linked courses help achieve that aim. Once again it is worth noting that WAC aims are also achieved in the composition course. As Dennis Young (an experienced composition teacher) reported at the 1997 WAC conference, teaching collaboratively in a three-way link with Social and Political Philosophy and Introduction to American Government courses helped him realize the importance of students having "a frame of reference, a sense of one's place in the dialogue of disciplines, a ground for discussion in any writing course."

Yet Young's course was far from a service course designed to accommodate the philosophy and government teachers' course materials. Rather, all of the teachers benefited as they struggled to create assignments in which, as Young emphasizes, rhetorical choices are integrally related to political and ethical choices. One such assignment, for example, asked students to appeal to Socrates, Machiavelli, Hobbes, Locke, and Jefferson to sign the

Declaration of Independence and support the suffrage movement. The government teacher, who had always instructed students *not* to use "I" in their writing because it "encourages them to rely too much on personal opinion," was persuaded by Young and the philosophy teacher that the personal must always be an aspect of the political and philosophical debate. Instead of forbidding the use of "I," she began talking with students about how to position the "I" in their writing. Not surprisingly, this particular linked package produced some fascinating hybrid assignments—that is, assignments calling for papers that crossed disciplinary ways of thinking and challenged the teachers to formulate different evaluative criteria.

Assignments like these, as Young pointed out, would not be possible in stand-alone courses, not only because they require a great deal of shared context but also because they rely on mutually formulated expectations and criteria for writing. The three teachers had decided, for reasons of expediency, to read the papers independent of the others, and each gave his or her own grade; they found, however, that they each had to explain their evaluative processes to the students. Explaining meant that the individual teachers needed to be aware not only of their own disciplinary assumptions and expectations for writing but also of their personal likes and dislikes and how these might differ from the other teachers' personal preferences. To their satisfaction, the teachers reported only minor discrepancies in their grades. All was not perfect, however, as Young is quick to acknowledge; too often, he was cast as the "grammar cop" by the philosophy and government teachers, who were happy to discuss matters of content and structure with students but wanted him to work on the intricacies of grammar, punctuation, and sentence structure. "I got them to try their hand at conferencing and allowing early drafts and the chance for revision," Young noted, but it was much harder to convince them that "helping students to improve their communicative style is our work, not just the work of the English teacher."

As writing teachers involved in WAC know all too well, the perception that our job is primarily "dealing with" grammar and mechanics is difficult to overcome. After all, if we have no "real" content and we expect teachers in other disciplines to assign, process, and grade writing, what is left for us to do? This question, for me, is at the heart of discussions about required FYC and its role in a strong WAC program. Do students need a required writing course when teachers in other disciplines are committed to and knowledgeable about working with student writers? What specific kinds of expertise and understanding do writing teachers and writing courses provide? The next linked-course variation I describe provides some partial answers to these questions.

Variation Three—Fully Linked Sections with a Service Learning Component

In the linked courses described earlier, students are using writing to engage with the discipline content. While they may be asked to include the personal, ultimately they are still writing to display their knowledge and their ability to analyze and synthesize information, whether from experience or from sources. They are not, in other words, philosophizing, constructing histories, or making policy statements. But when linked courses or fully integrated learning communities—like a number of New Century College classes—include an experiential learning component, students often have the opportunity to write "the real thing"—that is, the kind of writing practitioners in the field might be doing. In the linked cluster with FYC, Introduction to Sociology, and a one-credit service learning course, the students are not only enhancing their own literacy, but they are also helping others become literate and then analyzing that process through the lens of a discipline. The sociology course is taught by a faculty member deeply committed to social action agendas and experienced in using writing-to-learn strategies in her courses. In addition to a similar commitment to community service, composition teacher Ruth Fischer brings her background in ethnographic research to the writing course and to the experiential component she also teaches, which consists of students working twenty hours a semester in a racially and ethnically diverse magnet school close to Washington, D.C. Together the two teachers plan a series of writing assignments framed by sociological concepts and based on field research in the magnet school; in turn, the students' reading and writing serve to frame their volunteer experiences.

Underlying most experiential learning theory, according to its practitioners, is a basic process: action-reflection-action. In this cyclical process, each action is transformed as a result of observations and reflections on previous actions (Eyler and Giles). The writing process is integral to service learning because writing captures the reflection and also leads to more and deeper reflection. Yet, as David Jolliffe points out (Chapter 4, this volume), keeping a journal and/or writing a reflective paper does not necessarily entail critical thought on the part of the student. Fischer's expertise in teaching composition, then, is an important component in this particular link. Central to all of the work Fischer's students do are their field notes. In a presentation on writing in this linked cluster at the 1997 WAC conference, Fischer explained that the field notes—submitted to both teachers—were an essential tool for teaching writing skills. The notes required students to be careful observers, write factual descriptions of what they observed, reflect on and analyze these observations, and pose questions arising out of their observations and reflections. Their questions ultimately led to topics for their research papers, which were focused on some aspect of education as a social institution; students were then encouraged to "test out" these topics in their community service experience. "We found," Fischer said, "that because of the support students received in their writing class and our ongoing faculty interaction and subsequent negotiation of writing assignments, students were able to write effectively about highly complex sociologically oriented topics." As we have learned in the Linked Courses Program and as Ashley will show in her discussion of New Century College, this kind of faculty interaction and negotiation around writing and writing assignments is critical if students are to be successful writers in learning communities.

New Century College: An Integrated Studies Baccalaureate Degree Program

As the description of learning community models (see note 1) suggests, the coordinated/integrated studies structure creates an intensive learning environment and a changed dynamic between students and teachers. In turn, this new and different learning situation suggests interesting possibilities for examining how WAC continues to evolve. Because much about New Century College is highly innovative, it is necessary to provide some background and description before considering the writing environment.

New Century College (NCC), which belongs to the genre of the experimental college, was established at George Mason University in 1995 in response to a state mandate for new initiatives in higher education. NCC currently houses several interdisciplinary baccalaureate programs, the largest being integrative studies, on which I focus here. All classes offered by this program are set up as learning communities, many taught by two or more faculty from different disciplines. The structure of the general education learning communities is distinctive. Students who enroll in NCC as first-year students take a sequence of four interdisciplinary team-taught learning communities (based on the coordinated studies model) and thus complete virtually all general education requirements in one year. Each of these first-year LC courses lasts seven weeks and conveys eight credit hours; for most students, this one course constitutes a full academic load. The titles of these courses are informative: Community of Learners, The Natural World, The Socially Constructed World, and Self as Citizen. Each course is team-taught by eight to ten faculty members drawn from various disciplines and faculty ranks, including teaching assistants, all of whom work together to create the writing requirements for the course. (For the online writing guide for integrative studies students, see http://classweb.gmu.edu/nccwg/index.html.)

After completing general education courses, integrative studies students have a wide variety of courses from which to choose, including upper-division NCC learning communities and traditional courses offered by other university programs. Students must complete twelve credit hours in experiential learning, choosing among service learning, internship, and study abroad options. In conjunction with faculty and academic advisors, integrative studies students construct interdisciplinary concentrations (majors), many of which clearly reflect the changing world of work. Not surprisingly, a number of these concentrations include significant technology components.

A description of the first course in the general education sequence, Community of Learners, suggests the scope of the first-
year learning communities. This course is about college habits of
mind, notes John O'Connor, founding dean of NCC and a former
director of composition with expertise in computers and writing.
Successful completion of this course conveys full credit for first-
year composition and additional credits in communication, computer science, and analytical reasoning. In addition, this learning
community incorporates elements of a first-year success course,
with student services professionals facilitating sessions on intercultural communication and student life issues. As many as two
hundred students at a time are enrolled in this learning community. Most mornings they meet in groups of approximately twenty
with their seminar instructors in inquiry-based discussion, finding connections and disjunctions among and between assigned
readings (for example, from Plato, Frederick Douglass, and Jane
Goodall) and other course experiences (such as workshops in
information literacy and collaborative problem solving). In the
afternoon, students may meet in the full cohort of two hundred
to hear a faculty panel discuss changes in higher education. The
next day students may make group presentations to their seminar sections in the morning and spend the afternoon in a writing
workshop. In all phases of the course, the key grouping is the
five-person study group, assigned for the duration of the course;
in each of the three subsequent general education learning communities, students will likewise be assigned to study groups.

Though logistically and thematically complex, with many
components, Community of Learners is only one course in the
sequence. Three elements help students create coherence out of
the complexity: the small seminar section (in which the instructor is mentor and facilitator), membership in the study group,
and writing. Kenneth Bruffee says, "Writing is not ancillary to
teaching with collaborative learning, as it is to traditional teaching. It is central" (53). Writing, he explains, helps create the in-
terdependent conversation in which knowledge is constructed and
provides a means of acculturation, enabling students to become
part of the academic community. While the course syllabus calls
for several "formal" writing projects (including a sequence of
assignments related to the year-long research project described

later), the daily writing assignments—e.g., response journal entries, abstracts, e-mail, and integrative logs—take on a major role in helping students construct meaning from course content and activities. Writing to learn and to speculate helps students analyze, synthesize, and make connections across multiple perspectives and get their minds around big ideas. This kind of writing, which is assigned almost every day the seminar meets, prepares students for their roles as seminar participants and nourishes the conversation of the course. Students refer to or read from their daily writing in study groups and seminar discussions and often revise portions of this work into longer assignments. In turn, seminar instructors read and respond to this daily writing, asking questions and making brief comments—optimally in the manner of the teacher-facilitator/empathic mentor Susan McLeod describes ("Pygmalion"). Although the motive for assigning this writing is to help students navigate through complex ideas in a way they find intellectually, ethically, or practically important, the writing also serves a transactional purpose, giving students practice in communicating their ideas. Additionally, in a course with little or no conventional testing, this writing functions as an accountability measure.

Writing-to-learn activities are highly valued in WAC practice. What is striking in the NCC experience, however, is the degree to which writing to learn, speculate, and integrate is crucial to meaning making. The central role of this kind of writing and the multiple purposes it serves suggest the need for a more robust understanding of writing to learn and also new thinking about how such work can be categorized. The expressivist-transactional dichotomy that emerged as an unintended oversimplification of complex discussions in composition (see Christopher Thaiss, Chapter 12, this volume) is inadequate to describe student writing in learning communities such as those in NCC. In the changing social and power dynamics created by collaborative and experiential learning and by "wired" writing, our students' work occupies a different space. In their examination of electronic communication and WAC in Chapter 3, Donna Reiss and Art Young speculate about how student writing might be charted along a continuum from personal/expressive to public/transactional. They describe a middle ground of "classroom discourse" in which students "gain knowledge, develop scholarly habits of mind, and acquire rhetorical and communication competence in a variety of public and academic contexts." This concept of "classroom discourse" in which students "combine their existing knowledge of content and inquiry with new knowledge and experience" aptly describes the writing that students do in NCC learning communities. As Reiss and Young explain, in this middle ground students combine their own discourse with that of the academy (p. 62).

Although successful completion of this first learning community fulfills the FYC requirement, students enrolled in NCC will encounter a diverse array of writing assignments in the three succeeding general education learning communities, each of which is writing intensive. During these courses, they will write in a number of genres, some fairly typical of academic writing and others less so. Students will conduct and summarize interviews, write advocacy letters, annotate bibliographies, participate in an online asynchronous conferencing environment, and write versions of the three- or four-minute essay suggested by classroom assessment strategies (Angelo and Cross). They will compose a poem, write lab reports and essays, create posters for poster presentations, and collaborate in researching and writing press kits for a mock press briefing on a public policy issue. They will also create several portfolios during the year.

Any analysis of such a rich writing environment must acknowledge the challenging discursive scenes and rhetorical situations students face (and which faculty need to take into account in evaluating student work). Some writing assignments in the first-year learning communities are explicitly disciplinary in nature (e.g., lab reports and literary analysis). Others are created to cross (or even transcend) disciplinary lines. Most assignments, however, are graded by individual seminar instructors who, despite their commitment to the integrative gestalt of the course, are nevertheless informed by their respective disciplinary traditions. While faculty are encouraged (for example, in WAC discussions) to articulate their expectations for student writing (and to explain why they hold these expectations), students are sometimes baffled about "what the teacher wants." As students negotiate this complicated terrain, where they sometimes believe every teacher has a different set of expectations, many must feel like strangers in a strange land. No doubt some students might identify with Dave, the general education student who struggled with the demands of writing in three courses (and in three versions of academic discourse) as documented in Lucille Parkinson McCarthy's study. In contrast, integrative studies students in their first year of college are faced with writing across and at the intersections of multiple and sometimes competing discourses in a writing intensive course lasting only seven (packed) weeks.

Although NCC students face formidable challenges as first-year college writers, many seem highly motivated by active learning and close collaboration with peers and teachers. Most develop fluency and flexibility in dealing with varied writing contexts, and when faculty come together to read portfolios in year-end evaluation sessions, they often see significant growth in student writing across the year. In an essay on genre in the writing class, Charles Bazerman says: "Once students learn what it is to engage deeply and write well in any particular circumstance, they have a sense of the possibilities of literate participation in any arena" (26). What is most important in assigning genres, he believes, is finding those that give students a site where they can engage with and solve problems that are important to them. I would suggest that the central role of writing-to-learn activities—in several genres—may provide students with one such site of engagement in NCC, and that students learn in the process how powerfully their writing can serve them.

When NCC was inaugurated, a number of faculty involved in creating the first-year courses had participated in previous curricular revisions and at least some WAC activities. Other faculty had little experience in teaching writing, particularly in interdisciplinary settings, and expressed concern about their ability to do so effectively. Despite these anxieties, teachers of these first-year courses have demonstrated an impressive commitment to teaching writing. As a member of the faculty teams for the Community of Learners and Self as Citizen courses, one of my roles has been to assist faculty by planning WAC workshops, creating WAC materials, and being available for consultation, just as my colleagues from other disciplines share their expertise in teaching and content areas. From my experience in WAC activities at the university prior to the organization of NCC, I had learned to value what I came to call "the other side of WAC." When I was a returning graduate student a decade before NCC began, I initially understood WAC as the means by which writing teachers took the new knowledge in composition studies (chiefly about writing process) to less enlightened but well-intentioned colleagues in other disciplines. Later, I began to appreciate the reciprocal nature of WAC when I taught advanced composition classes focused on writing in the disciplines. Attending WAC discussions and learning more from colleagues in other disciplines about writing in their fields was vital to my growth as a writing teacher. A third stage of my understanding of WAC developed when I began to collaborate with colleagues from across campus in curricular revision and assessment projects. In common with other composition faculty teaching in learning communities at George Mason, I have found this WAC experience key to learning how to do the difficult but rewarding work of collaborating across epistemologies and perspectives.

In her description of linked courses, Terry observes instances of growth in writing instruction by noncomposition faculty. Likewise, faculty in NCC learning communities note changes in the way they teach writing—revisions that can be described as ranging from local to global. From her experience in NCC, a political scientist responds differently to writing, which includes no longer editing her students' journals. A psychologist who teaches both general education and upper-division learning communities reports that she incorporates a significant amount of reflective writing "along with A.P.A. [American Psychological Association] writing." A professor of religious studies describes how he revised the values thread he taught in the fourth first-year learning community, Self as Citizen. This component was designed around writing assignments; the writing, he emphasizes, was more integrated into the course than in courses he had taught in the traditional curriculum. Like Terry, I believe composition teachers have valuable knowledge—about writing processes, language, rhetoric, critical inquiry, and pedagogy—to share with faculty teams. I also believe that experienced writing teachers can be WAC change agents while learning in turn from their colleagues. In addition, I believe significant growth in the teaching of writing can occur whenever faculty are committed to collaborative learning and attentive to student outcomes.

Cross-Unit, Year-Long Writing Assignment

As the introduction to this volume notes, one of the aims of learning communities has been to help students achieve a more coherent and integrated educational experience, in part through making connections between and among various components of the curriculum. In each of New Century's four general education learning communities, students are asked to find connections between and among course readings, themes, ideas, and experiences and to be self-aware constructors of knowledge. One of the ways students integrate their learning and make connections across the entire first-year curriculum is through a year-long research and writing project known as "Transformation." This assignment, created by an interdisciplinary faculty team representing each of the four first-year courses, is described by a math colleague as "a biography with numbers." At the beginning of the year, students identify an individual whose life they would like to learn more about. This subject may be either a famous person or someone personally known to the student. After completing a sequence of assignments culminating in a research proposal in the first course, students continue to research and write about their subjects in the context of the issues and questions of the three subsequent courses. For example, in the second learning community, The Natural World, students identify a population of which their subject was or is a member and perform statistical analyses of that group. At the end of the year, students place all four chapters of their research project in their year-end portfolios, along with self-evaluation and a reflection on their learning throughout the project.

This project gives new meaning to the phrase "writing across the curriculum" because it asks students to write within and across an entire year's course work and to begin to consider how discourse and research conventions vary from one context to the next. In addition, the Transformation assignment creates a sustained "research across the curriculum" opportunity by systematically integrating instruction in information literacy throughout the year. University instructional reference librarian Jim Young has a central role in mentoring this project, for both the faculty team and students. In a year-end assessment of this assignment, students frequently cite Young not only as a valuable source of information about research but also as a guide and facilitator of their learning. Students sometimes ask Young and other instructional reference librarians to read and respond to their drafts. In addition, Young works with faculty, helping us refine the project and design appropriate research exercises. As the information age advances, "literacy" increasingly implies sophisticated acquisition, evaluation, and use of information. The linkage of WAC and information literacy then would seem a natural alliance, one that would benefit teaching and learning on all campuses. In the next section, Terry and I discuss what assessment of both the Linked Courses Program and NCC has shown us about changes in faculty and student practices around writing and writing assignments.

Assessing WAC in Learning Community Programs

While writing and/or writing courses may be the "connective tissue" holding learning communities together, as we noted earlier in this chapter, we have rarely seen listed as criteria for measuring LC programs either growth in students' writing abilities or faculty growth in using writing in their teaching.[4] This is not to say that samples of faculty assignments and students' writing are not collected and measured; they are. Generally, however, these data are being used to measure criteria other than gains in writing and teaching with writing. Typical assessment criteria for student success and satisfaction in learning communities may include, for example, persistence, course completion, cognitive development, appreciation of diversity, involvement in the campus and wider community, ability to work in groups, and intellectual focus. Faculty development tends to be measured by factors such as whether the program stimulates teaching and curriculum improvement both within and beyond the LC program, degree of collaborative effort, willingness to continue teaching in the program, and so on. (See the Washington Center's report on "Elements of Effective Learning Community Programs," for example.) With slight revision, the criteria for faculty could also be applied to WAC programs. Criteria for measuring administrative support for LC programs are also quite similar to WAC programs, e.g., the program has an administrative "home," departments get behind the program, faculty are recognized and rewarded for their efforts, and budget resources are allocated for workshops, curriculum planning, and staff assistance.

By contrast, there is an entire body of literature on students' gains in writing in composition courses. In 1998 Richard Haswell posted a bibliography on "Gain in First-Year College Composition Courses" on the WPA listserv that lists almost one hundred entries divided into three categories: Quantitative Studies Finding Gain, Exit and Alumni Reports, and Theoretical Problems of Measuring Gain in a Writing Course. Nearly half of the citations fall into the last category. Problems of reliability and validity in measurements of growth in writing are intensified when the effectiveness of entire programs is being assessed, as Condon discusses in his contribution to this volume (Chapter 2). Early in the development of the Linked Courses Program, in which FYC has always played an integral part, we attempted to design assessment criteria to measure student gains in writing in the disciplines as well as teachers' attitudes about writing. We asked students to agree or disagree or rank their satisfaction with aspects of their writing in the linked courses. While the categories we included for measuring student attitudes reveal a great deal about the influence of expressivist writing theories on our teaching practices at that time, we found that most of the student responses could just as easily apply to unlinked FYC courses. We also ruled out the idea of comparing students' grades on writing assignments in linked and unlinked courses. Attempts to interpret grades on writing assignments and/or to use those interpretations as data are fraught with problems. (For example, when students in one link wondered why they had received higher grades on a dual-submission assignment from the government teacher than from the writing teacher, even though the evaluative comments were quite similar, they were encouraged to ask the government teacher. He told the students that he gave them a higher grade than they actually deserved on their writing because he wanted to compensate for the low scores they had received on their midterm Scantron exam.)

Not surprisingly, in its 1992 report on the linked program, George Mason University's Office of Institutional Planning and Research concluded that the question of whether students in linked courses perform better in writing remained unanswered. The report did note, however, that students said they liked the idea of being able to write on the same topic for two classes, and that some linked faculty said they were asking students to do more writing and that their students seemed to be more receptive to feedback. For a number of years following this initial foray into assessment, we attempted to get at attitudes toward writing in linked courses by conducting student and faculty focus groups and by asking select faculty to keep logs with observations about students' writing processes and products. These faculty logs provided useful insights into how WAC was working in linked courses. A philosophy teacher wrote, "Students showed remarkable ability to handle some quite complex texts and to summarize philosophies and synthesize material. The papers were lengthy and much more complex than most first-year writing." A government professor reported her discovery that "students seem to appreciate the one-on-one [conferencing on papers,] and it helped me to establish a relationship of sorts with students and point out my way of responding to their work." A history professor said he learned to "make reflection a routine part of the course" by asking students to write about the strengths of a paper, their growth in writing, and what they learned from doing the writing.

Albeit anecdotal, these kinds of self-reflections do provide useful assessment data, as Jean MacGregor argues in her 1998 address to AAHE on "Assessment of Powerful Pedagogies: Classroom, Campus, and Beyond," and they are, in themselves, a "powerful pedagogy" enabling faculty to "deepen their conversations about teaching and learning."[5] Consistent with NCC's commitment to powerful pedagogies, both students and faculty engage in self-reflection and self-evaluation as part of an ongoing assessment process. Students create portfolios of their work, accompanied by self-evaluation, at various points in their academic careers. Some individual learning communities require portfolios, and students also construct portfolios at the end of their first year and again as a graduation prerequisite. In the latter two portfolio assignments, students include samples of work from across an extended period of time, accompanied by self-evaluation and commentary about how these samples demonstrate their work in nine competency areas.[6] Faculty likewise engage in self-assessment by constructing course portfolios, in which they explain and reflect on choices they make in creating learning communities, choosing and using texts, structuring assignments, and so on. Together with findings from classroom assessment exercises, the course portfolio provides teachers with an important means for learning and teaching.

While these practices produce valuable information for program assessment as well as for curriculum and faculty development, as MacGregor noted, accomplishing meaningful analysis of writing outcomes in learning communities presents special challenges, especially when faculty assessors come from different disciplines. In order to design effective assessment, it is crucial to consider how writing may be different—and more complex—in these settings. Genre, in particular, is a source of complication. In a 1996 focus group of NCC first-year students who entered college with advanced-placement credit, students expressed pride in the amount of writing they did (in contrast, they maintained, to friends and roommates in the traditional curriculum), but they also indicated they needed more help with "the different kinds of writing" they were assigned. Likewise, a focus group of a 1998 senior capstone class revealed that students had difficulty keeping straight the different kinds of writing in some learning communities. Students said the confusion stemmed in part from the amount of writing required and from the overlapping nature of some of the genres they were assigned. Because of the innovative nature of collaborative and experiential learning, teachers often create new and different writing assignments, including writing projects for which they do not have models. In some cases, the differing perspectives of faculty partners or team members making the assignment may also contribute to the confusion students experience. As David Russell notes (Chapter 11, this volume), writing tasks are more difficult when students lack clarity about the underlying motivations and epistemological values.

Not only do the forms of writing often differ in learning communities but, as we have said earlier in this chapter, both the social dimensions and the uses of writing often differ as well. In many of the linked-course clusters and in NCC, students write to integrate, reflect, connect, find oppositions, and construct knowledge, and they frequently do so in a collaborative and public way. One of the implications seems to be that we need to attend carefully to understanding what students see as their purposes in writing. For all these reasons, it is crucial that we continue to include the affective domain in our assessment plans, both for the information it provides about how students perceive their learning experiences and for the insights it provides into teaching. In sum, the inventive nature of most learning communities requires new and creative approaches to assessing what and how students learn through writing. We suggest that Stephen Ehrmann's work on the Flashlight Project, a set of evaluation tools for studying the effects of technology on higher education, offers some useful guidelines for thinking about WAC and LC assessment (Ehrmann and Milam).

In his introduction to the Flashlight materials,[7] Ehrmann, who is affiliated with AAHE's Teaching, Learning, and Technology Group, says that the project developed out of a felt sense that new evaluative tools and paradigms were needed to find out what happens when technology is integrated into the curriculum: "[T]he educational consequences of technology investment are notoriously difficult to detect," he writes, likening the difficulty to attempts to assess the results of any education innovation. How does one isolate the effects of technology from the effects resulting from the entire program, he asks. "The process of evaluation is *always* like using a small, dim flashlight to glimpse what sort of animal might be in front of you in a huge dark cave. The cave is the nature of the whole innovation—everything that is happening." Ehrmann's metaphor is applicable to the effort to assess WAC in LC programs, in which, as Ehrmann says about technology use, "each evaluative question is the equivalent of pointing the tiny beam in a particular direction in order to see what walks into the light" (Ehrmann and Milam ix).

The principles and assumptions Ehrmann lays out in a talk on evaluating technology projects seem especially relevant to the issues surrounding measuring the effectiveness of both WAC and LC programs as well as WAC within LC programs, beginning with debates over the definitions of the terms "traditional" and "innovative."[8] Education—"traditional" or otherwise, Ehrmann points out—is never uniform and certainly not always well understood. In fact, he argues, the labels "traditional" and "innovative" are not particularly useful when they are attached to programs without accompanying descriptions of individual program objectives and the learning outcomes expected of students. Similarly, a WAC or LC label does not begin to capture the variety of these programs, as we have shown in our descriptions of the linked program and NCC, and as Thaiss discusses in "Theory in WAC" (Chapter 12, this volume). Part of the difficulty of assessing WAC programs, Thaiss notes, is that definitions of "writing," "learning to write," and "writing to learn" vary "from school to school, teacher to teacher, class to class, assignment to assignment, even from thought to thought within a teacher's response to a group of papers or to a single paper" (p. 303). Far from being a liability, most WAC adherents argue, the variety of definitions ensures the vitality of WAC programs; when WAC is confined to narrow definitions in order to derive a set of assessment criteria, programs run the risk of becoming inflexible and obsolete. Assessment might best be left to individual disciplines and perhaps even individual teachers, as Thaiss suggests.

Whether left to individual teachers or disciplines, good assessment is generally tied to program objectives. In the case of new or innovative programs, however, the objectives might be articulated one way at the beginning of the project and reshaped as the program evolves. Evaluation paradigms, according to Ehrmann, assume that we understand "what the innovation is and what it's for in advance," meaning, in a sense, that we are trying to hit a moving target, given that the innovations themselves change as the project evolves and "underlying ideas emerge" (Ehrmann and Milam 2). Moreover, as Ehrmann argues, most program evaluation occurs well before much of the impact on students' lives has begun (2). Additionally, the paradigm assumes that the learning objectives are the same for every student, that the objectives will affect all students in the same ways, albeit with varying degrees of achievement, and that the impact can be measured apart from all the other variables that may have influenced learning and students' lives (14–15). Ehrmann calls this assumption a "uniform impact" perspective. As difficult as this perspective might be in the academic settings we are accustomed to, the difficulty is multiplied in learning communities, in which students are given many more educational choices, and it cannot be presumed a priori what constitutes "important" things learned. Instead, we suggest, we need to look for "unexpected learning," designing measures that focus on the individual participants in learning communities—students, faculty, and other campus professionals (e.g., librarians, information technology specialists, student services staff).

Ehrmann calls this a "unique uses" perspective, one that asks: What were the most important outcomes for each learner? A "unique uses" perspective is, we believe, most consistent with the goals and values of LC practitioners (although we hesitate to make that claim for WAC practitioners whose funding typically depends on concerns about student writing and a desired outcome of *uniform* "good writing"). Ehrmann's general question can be paraphrased as, What happens to individual writers? What do they say were the most important writing outcomes they experienced—both with writing to learn and written products? NCC's self-reflective, self-evaluative portfolios, which Ashley described earlier, are a step in this direction. Another way to get at student and faculty perceptions of important, individual outcomes is through focus groups. As we have mentioned, both linked-course and NCC students and faculty have participated in focus-group assessment. Their responses, some of which we have already reported, can be used to provide a more detailed picture of important outcomes as experienced by individual learners. But what is to be made of those individual outcomes in terms of our LC programs?

In order to evaluate a program—whether a grant-funded technology project such as those Ehrmann discusses or, in our case, WAC in LC programs—the question of individual outcomes needs to be followed by another question, which is, according to Ehrmann, "How plausible is it that what I'm seeing is an outcome of the program being evaluated?" The program evaluators must then consider what the individual cases imply about the success of the program being studied. While learning is always cumulative, Ehrmann believes that "coherent patterns of instructional events . . . are more likely to have a predictable, perceptible effect on most graduates' lives than are single assignments or courses that are not related to anything else in the college" (Ehrmann and Milam 17). One of the common goals of LC programs is to foster cross-curricular connections and thereby create for students (and faculty) a more coherent academic experience than is typical with stand-alone courses; thus, we can say with some confidence that the changes we see in faculty and student attitudes about and approaches to writing are, at least in part, a result of their LC experiences, just as changes in their attitudes about themselves (both faculty and students) as learners might be attributed in part to their writing experiences.

One type of program assessment, then, might entail looking for patterns in faculty and student responses to questions about important individual outcomes. So far, individual students are telling us—in written assignments, portfolios, and focus groups—that their relationship to writing is shifting in important ways. In both linked courses and NCC, a large number of students seem to have a greater confidence about writing, a sense of themselves as "college writers," compared to students in stand-alone FYC courses. They value the experience of having learned to ask new and different questions in their writing—"hard" questions—and they are proud of what they write in response. In turn, they sense that they have become more fluent writers with more to say than their peers in stand-alone courses. Faculty seem to share the perception that students are writing in more complicated ways about complex topics.

Like the students in our LC programs, writing instructors in LC arrangements tend to experience their professional role and their work quite differently from instructors in traditional courses. At our university, as at most institutions, those of us who teach composition—whether in learning communities or stand-alone courses—tend to be non-tenure-track faculty. While we acknowledge that there are legitimate reasons to be concerned about non-tenure-line faculty (who are typically women) being further subordinated when they teach in linked arrangements, more often these instructors say they feel they have a more visible—and valued—role in learning communities than they do when they teach in isolation. They also list as important outcomes professional growth and the sense of connectedness they experience when they work with colleagues across the campus. One important result of this collaborative work, faculty note, is that their writing assignments tend to become more complex and interesting; along with more challenging assignments, however, come higher expectations for what students can produce. The downside for some faculty is that students don't always meet these expectations. In the case of linked courses, the downside for students is that their grades are sometimes lower than those of their peers in stand-alone FYC courses, as comparisons of grades for linked and nonlinked FYC courses reveal. It is interesting to consider the reasons one experienced writing instructor gave for refusing to sign on for a second year of teaching in a three-course link. The interdisciplinary assignments—developed by all three instructors—were, he felt, too difficult for first-year writers and the expectations for what they would produce too high. An assessment of WAC in LC programs needs to account for all of these competing, and sometimes contradictory, outcomes and expectations.

Is It Still WAC?

If at the end of the 1980s Susan McLeod could speak confidently about the "second stage of some WAC programs" ("Writing"), now, at the beginning of a new century, we find it difficult to know what generation, stage, or phase of WAC might apply to writing in LC arrangements. And, given the variety of LC programs, it seems clear that even if one could confidently apply this terminology, some learning communities would belong to a different generation than others, just as linked courses and New Century College seem to belong to different branches of one very large extended family. While we have used WAC throughout this article as a descriptor of what happens to writing instruction and, more important, writing practice in learning communities, we realize that the acronym does not accurately characterize the reality. Not only have new meanings accrued to "across the curriculum," but also the "cast" at the scene of writing has expanded to include librarians, information technologists, student services staff, and other campus professionals, each representing different discursive cultures. A more apt descriptor, as we suggested in the opening, might be Writing Across Curricular Cultures. Yet no matter how we play with the acronym, we argue that WAC may be most fully realized within the LC movement, which shares its values of inclusiveness, conversation, and collaboration, and the belief that writing should be a central mode of learning in a learning-centered pedagogy.

Notes

1. Gabelnick et al. describe three typical structures for learning communities: student cohorts in larger classes, such as "freshman interest groups" and "federated learning communities"; paired or clustered classes; and team-taught coordinated studies programs. Freshman interest groups—FIGS—generally consist of a trio of courses offered around an area of interest, an interdisciplinary theme, and/or courses related to a major. Most FIGS also include a breakout discussion section led by a graduate student or peer advisor. Federated learning communities register a cohort of students (not just first-year students) in a three-course cluster organized around a common theme and linked by an integrative seminar. These typically occur within the student's major.

Linked or paired courses focus on curricular coherence and on integrating skills and content learning. Faculty coordinate syllabi and assignments and teach the same cohort of students, but they teach their classes separately. Similarly, learning clusters entail coordinated syllabi and separately taught courses with an explicit thematic link rather than a skills link.

A team-taught integrated studies program is the most complex and labor-intensive LC model. The goals of this model include intensive student and faculty involvement in the interrelated topic under study. Faculty are explicitly positioned as learners as well as teachers. In a "full-time" coordinated studies model (New Century College at George Mason University, for example), faculty teams work with students who take their entire course load within the coordinated community, making scheduling for collaborative projects, experiential learning, and so forth quite flexible.

2. We don't want to be overly optimistic, however. As Walvoord notes, although both writing intensive and linked courses can be used to point

out WAC achievements, they have sometimes led to a narrower vision of WAC when faculty and administrators limit WAC support to these initiatives (66).

3. In 2000 the Linked Courses Program was redesigned and renamed the Mason Topics Program.

4. We also acknowledge that we have not looked systematically nor looked at a wide range of LC assessment reports to determine whether growth in writing has been measured. Our sense is that it has not.

5. In the list of "powerful pedagogies," MacGregor included collaborative and cooperative learning, active and interactive learning strategies such as writing and technology, problem-centered learning, service and civic learning, interdisciplinary courses and learning communities, capstone experiences, and assessment as learning.

6. These competency areas are communication, critical thinking, problem solving, valuing, social interaction, global perspective, effective citizenship, aesthetic response, and information technology.

7. This essay, a summary of a talk given to NEH in April 1997, is taken from a packet of materials Ehrmann distributes when he gives workshops on the Flashlight Project. Included in this packet is a section called "Resource Essays and Case Studies," a collection that covers essays and presentations Erhmann has developed in connection with his work for FIPSE and AAHE.

8. We recognize, of course, that instructors drawn to teaching in LC arrangements typically already share many of the same learning-centered values and teaching practices.

Works Cited

Angelo, Thomas A., and K. Patricia Cross. *Classroom Assessment Techniques: A Handbook for College Teachers*. San Francisco: Jossey-Bass, 1993.

Bazerman, Charles. "The Life of Genre, The Life in the Classroom." *Genre and Writing: Issues, Arguments, Alternatives*. Ed. Wendy Bishop and Hans A. Ostrom. Portsmouth, NH: Boynton/Cook-Heinemann, 1997.

Bruffee, Kenneth A. *Collaborative Learning: Higher Education, Interdependence, and the Authority of Knowledge*. Baltimore: Johns Hopkins UP, 1993.

Connors, Robert J. "The Abolition Debate in Composition: A Short History." *Composition in the Twenty-first Century: Crisis and Change*. Ed. Lynn Bloom, Donald A. Daiker, and Edward M. White. Carbondale: Southern Illinois UP, 1996. 47-63.

Crowley, Sharon. *Composition in the University: Historical and Polemical Essays*. Pittsburgh: U of Pittsburgh P, 1998.

Ehrmann, Stephen C., and John H. Milam Jr. *The Flashlight Cost Analysis Handbook: Modeling Resource Use in Teaching and Learning with Technology*. Washington, DC: Teaching, Learning, and Technology Group of the American Association for Higher Education, 1999.

Eyler, Janet, Dwight E. Giles, and Angela Schmeide. *A Practitioner's Guide to Reflection in Service-Learning: Student Voices and Reflections*. Nashville, TN: Vanderbilt University, 1996.

Fischer, Ruth. "Writing Across/Beyond the Curriculum: Connecting Experience with Concept in the Community Service Link." Writing Across the Curriculum Third National Conference. Charleston, SC. Feb. 1997.

Gabelnick, Faith G., et al. *Learning Communities: Creating Connections among Students, Faculty, and Disciplines*. New Directions for Teaching and Learning Series 41. San Francisco: Jossey-Bass, 1990.

Griffin, C. W. "Programs for Writing Across the Curriculum: A Report." *College Composition and Communication* 36 (1985): 398–403.

Haswell, Richard H. "Gain in First-Year College Composition Courses." 30 Sept. 1997 <ftp://ftp.csd.uwm.edu/pub/sands/gain.doc>.

MacGregor, Jean. "Strand Keynote—Assessment of Powerful Pedagogies: Classroom, Campus, and Beyond." American Association for Higher Education Assessment Conference. 14 June 1998.

McCarthy, Lucille Parkinson. "A Stranger in Strange Lands: A College Student Writing Across the Curriculum." *Research in the Teaching of English* 21 (1987): 233–65.

McLaughlin, Tim. "Taking a Look at Learning Communities Nationally." *Washington Center News* 10 (1996): 6–8.

McLeod, Susan H. "Pygmalion or Golem? Teacher Affect and Efficacy." *College Composition and Communication* 46 (1995): 369–86.

———. "Writing Across the Curriculum: The Second Stage, and Beyond." *College Composition and Communication* 40 (1989): 337–43.

Mullin, Joan. "WAC and the Restructuring of First Year Composition." Writing Across the Curriculum Third National Conference. Charleston, SC. Feb. 1995.

O'Connor, John. Personal interview. 24 Sept. 1997.

Office of Institutional Planning and Research. "Paired Courses at George Mason: A Report on the Fall 1992 Experience." Fairfax, VA: George Mason University, 1992.

Thaiss, Christopher. "A 'Linked Courses' Initiative within a Multi-faceted WAC Program: Administrative Problems and Solutions." Writing Across the Curriculum Third National Conference. Charleston, SC. Feb. 1997.

———, ed. *Writing to Learn: Essays and Reflections on Writing Across the Curriculum*. Dubuque, IA: Kendall/Hunt, 1983.

Walvoord, Barbara. "The Future of WAC." *College English* 58 (1996): 58–79.

Washington Center for Improving the Quality of Undergraduate Education. "Elements of Effective Learning Community Programs." Unpublished workshop materials. Olympia, WA: Evergreen State College.

Young, Dennis. "'Doing the Right Thing' from Plato to Spike Lee: Linking Philosophy, Government and Composition." Writing Across the Curriculum Third National Conference. Charleston, SC. Feb. 1997.

CHAPTER SIX

ESL Students and WAC Programs: Varied Populations and Diverse Needs

ANN M. JOHNS

San Diego State University

During the years since the WAC movement was initiated, the student populations in many college and university classrooms have become increasingly linguistically diverse.[1] This ethnic diversity is due to an influx of new immigrants, the result of changes in the immigration laws (as noted by McLeod and Miraglia in the introduction to this volume), and, to a lesser extent, to increased enrollment of international students. In states such as California, Florida, Illinois, New York, and Texas, the growth in the immigrant population has been dramatic. There has also been considerable growth in unlikely states such as Alabama, Arkansas, Nevada, North Carolina, and South Carolina.

These linguistically diverse students present new challenges to faculty in the disciplines, who may have planned their curricula with native speakers of English in mind, who may feel alienated from diverse students (Zamel),[2] and who have what may be unrealistic expectations about the level of proficiency a non-native speaker can attain in written prose. In order to work with these faculty, it is important for those involved in writing across the curriculum to review the literature on second-language acquisition, error, and contrastive rhetoric; examine how the "foundation" ESL writing courses, if any, are taught; and consider how best to help faculty in the disciplines (perhaps including composition and rhetoric faculty) work with ESL writers. Before we examine these issues, however, let us first look at who these writers are.

Who Are the Linguistically Diverse Students?

Perhaps the most important point to be made about our ESL students is that they are diverse in many ways: they vary in their proficiency levels in their first languages and in English, in their professional aims and literacy theories, and in their academic expectations. In order to sort out some of these differences, educational experts have somewhat artificially separated diverse students into categories. The largest and most dispersed of these groups consists of naturalized citizens and documented or undocumented aliens—students who were born in another country, have come to the United States, generally with their families, and intend to remain. Many of these students are identified in primary and secondary schools as limited English proficient (LEP)—that is, as not having achieved the academic language proficiencies necessary to compete with monolingual English-speakers.[3] The LEP student population increased more than 100 percent in U.S. public schools (K–12) between academic years 1985–86 and 1994–95, jumping from 1,487,549 to 3,132,201 students (Olsen 6). In some states, such as California, Texas, and New York, this population represents the majority in many urban schools. When these students enter colleges and universities, they may be required to enroll in ESL or basic writing classes in addition to a full complement of university-level courses.

Of course, some immigrant students are no longer limited English proficient when they enter universities. Nonetheless, they may have cultural backgrounds or values that are considerably different from those of North American academic cultures (Johns, "Interpreting" 380; Welaratna). Immigrant students tend to select from a limited set of majors, dictated by their cultural values or the need for immediate family income, as well as by their English proficiencies. Many of the Asian immigrant students, for example, select technical and engineering majors because they are concerned about competing with monolingual English-language speakers in professions requiring extensive written and spoken communication (Takaki 26). Additionally, the parents of many of these students immigrated or got their green cards because of their technical skills, so there is family pressure to follow a career path that has proven successful. Often, immigrant students must work long hours to put themselves through school while helping their families adjust to a new cultural and linguistic context. Thus, they may view courses in the humanities and social sciences, and writing assignments in these courses, as extraneous to their goals.

A second, related group of linguistically diverse students consists of emergent English-dominant learners, "children of immigrants who have oral competency in English and the cultural references of native English speakers" (*California Pathways* 19). These students may lack expertise in academic writing in both their first, or "heritage," language[4] and in English, particularly in the use of vocabulary and standard grammar. In many cases, emergent English-dominant learners continue to make errors that have become so much a part of their language that they do not recognize them as nonstandard and therefore cannot correct them. Teaching about these errors is difficult for the students' instructors for a variety of reasons: because the rules for use are extremely complex; because the standard English usage is illogical grammatically; because grammatical usage in the first language continues to be dominant in the student's mind; or because of fossilization.[5] Errors such as the misuse or omission of the definite article "the" occur in the discourse of many Asian-origin and some Arabic-speaking students and fall into the "extremely complex rules" category. Errors related to using the third-person singular -s form ("I know, you know, she/he know") fall into the illogical category and are found in the discourse of students from many language groups. In Romance languages such as Spanish and French, speakers inflect adjectives; thus, students from these backgrounds sometimes transfer this feature into English ("the beautifuls girls") because in the case of this grammatical feature, the heritage language remains dominant. Fossilization, resulting in permanent "interlanguage"[6] or between-language errors, occurs among many of these students for a variety of reasons. This error type may have developed over time because of large classes, insufficient teacher input, or other factors affecting a student's primary and secondary education in North America. Many overworked public school teachers fail to give students sufficient feedback on their written work, and unfortunately, if second-language

(L2) learners function for a long time in a language without being corrected, they may not develop full control of English grammar, syntax, and semantics. In fact, their English-language development may stop, or fossilize, before they have acquired all of its central features (*California Pathways* 19; for a useful list of fossilized errors, see Leki, *Understanding*).

This emergent English-dominant group of students, made up of the children of immigrants, is the one about which ESL and developmental composition instructors in postsecondary institutions are often most concerned. Their difficulties with English tend to be intractable, and like their monolingual English-speaking counterparts but unlike their international student peers, they may not have acquired a metalanguage—language about language (Johns, *Text* 133)—that enables them to talk about the features of their written, or spoken, discourses.

A third, considerably smaller, linguistically diverse student group consists of international students. Since 1954 this population has increased in U.S. postsecondary education by 1,200 percent, from 34,232 to 453,787. Currently, international students represent 3.1 percent of the total college and university enrollment. This figure is misleading, however, because of concentrations in certain levels of education, in certain regions, and in a few majors. Students from this group generally hold F-1 or other student visas and represent 2.5 percent of the four-year university enrollments, 10.1 percent of graduate enrollments, and 33.0 percent of doctoral degree enrollments. The majority of these students are enrolled in large public, and a few large private, universities concentrated in the Northeast, Midwest, and Pacific West Coast. The most popular majors for international students are business and management (20.2 percent) and engineering (16.1 percent). Twelve of the top fifteen countries of origin are in Asia: Japan, Korea, Thailand, Indonesia, Taiwan, Hong Kong, India, Pakistan, Sri Lanka, Singapore, Malaysia, and the Philippines (Davids 12–15). International students, in contrast to many immigrant and English-emergent students, tend to be academically proficient in their first languages and to use a metalanguage when discussing English grammar because of their English as a Foreign Language (EFL) educations in their home countries.

Reviewing the Research on Second-Language Acquisition, Error, and Contrastive Rhetoric

All three groups of students may fall under the ESL rubric at our universities, though they may respond differently to our classes and face very different obstacles to attaining their degrees. For these reasons, it is important that WAC administrators, and the faculty with whom they work, be aware not only of the variety among the "ESL" groups but also know something about the literature on second-language acquisition, error, and contrastive rhetoric. This literature demonstrates that language learning processes are complicated and idiosyncratic, sometimes resulting in fossilization into nonstandard grammatical and lexical forms. Some of the best and most accessible discussions of second-language acquisition (SLA) as it relates to ESL writing include Sridhar's article "A Reality Check for SLA Theories"; Silva, Leki, and Carson's "Broadening the Perspective of Mainstream Composition Studies" (which discusses second-language acquisition research and writing instruction, noting the importance of each to the understanding of diverse student populations); and Leki's *Understanding ESL Writers: A Guide for Teachers*. Leki is especially helpful because the volume includes a discussion of the types and possible sources of student mistakes. She makes this comment on current theories about sources of error: "It does seem clear that students' first languages have an influence on the kinds of problems they will have with English . . . . But although a small number of errors can be associated with particular language backgrounds, the vast majority . . . resemble each other and, therefore, seem to be a result of the structure of English itself" (110). Thus, according to current theory, particular features of the English language itself contribute most to the fossilization of errors in student discourses.

Leki also makes these important comments about second-language acquisition processes and error variation:

A learner's progress [in learning a second language] is not stable but is characterized by movements backwards and forwards along the path toward the second language, as new input, previously too complex to take in, is analyzed and processed. . . . This analyzing and processing causes previously in-place interlanguage features to shift.

Sometimes, under certain conditions, a seemingly acquired correct second language form is dropped in favor of an error. . . . This phenomenon occurs in a variety of situations: if the learner must suddenly deal with new or difficult subject matter in the second language, experiences anxiety, lacks practice in the second language, or slackens attention. (*Understanding* 111–12)

These comments should be useful for faculty, for they explain why L2 learners make errors on timed written examinations that they would not make if provided with sufficient time to revise; why complex assignments sometimes result in error-ridden papers; and why drafts written under relaxed or ungraded conditions might also result in unusual errors. The best conditions for L2 student writing are those in which students understand the content[7] and the expected format of the required paper, have practiced the task assigned, have time to conscientiously correct their errors, and know that their instructors consider error correction sufficiently important to make it part of the grade.[8]

Another topic that is central to understanding the ESL student populations is contrastive rhetoric, a research area that has become increasingly sophisticated over the years in its analyses of relationships between discourse and culture. Sources particularly accessible to faculty are Leki's *Understanding ESL Writers* and two excellent collections: Connor and Kaplan's *Writing Across Languages* and Purves's *Writing Across Languages and Cultures*. Two important contributions to contrastive rhetoric are a chapter by Hinds (in Connor and Kaplan), in which he argues that American English texts are "writer-responsible" and thus rhetorically quite different from "reader-responsible" texts in more homogeneous cultures, and an article by Matalene ("Contrastive Rhetoric: An American Writing Teacher in China"), one of the most culturally sensitive essays in the literature. Hinds argues that in "writer-responsible" cultures, such as those in North America, readers are more heterogeneous and thus writers must lead them through the texts in ways not necessary in more homogenous cultures such as China and Japan. This "writer responsibility" involves many tactics, including the use of metadiscourse, which tells readers where they have been and where they are going ("In the last section, we discussed XXX; now we turn to YYY"), and conjunctions of various types (e.g., "however," "in conclusion") that signal readers about changes or continuations in argumentation or discourse function (see Williams 28 for a thorough discussion of metadiscourse features). Western academics require such metalanguage and sometimes penalize writers for not including it. Matalene suggests that various historical influences on Chinese writing persist in modern prose, despite the vicissitudes of the Cultural Revolution and other major upheavals affecting education. She discusses the influences of Confucian thought, the features of the "8-legged essay" that was characteristic of civil service examinations for centuries, and other cultural influences that leave their traces on the discourse of modern writers from China.

Examining the "Foundation" Writing Courses

Once WAC administrators acquaint themselves with the literature, they should take a careful look at how ESL, and other writing classes in which ESL students are enrolled, is taught in their universities. When preparing this manuscript, I sent out this query on the WAC list: "How do you integrate the teaching of ESL students into your WAC programs?" One response was from the irate director of a writing program with many enrolled ESL students who are taught, for the most part, by graduate students in a Teachers of English to Speakers of Other Languages (TESOL) M.A. program. He complained that because his university's TESOL M.A. students do not take classes in the teaching of writing, they believe that writing is "nothing more than a string of sentences in no way distinct from language skills." He argued, quite convincingly, that many TESOL graduate programs around the country still do not devote sufficient time to the teaching of academic reading and writing.[9]

This perceived difference between some TESOL graduate programs and programs in composition and rhetoric is an important one for our understanding of students' theories of writing and writing tasks derived from their writing classes. In a study at one comprehensive university, Atkinson and Ramanathan found considerable disparity between writing programs for monolingual English-speakers (MES) and those courses for ESL (particularly international) students. ESL teachers assumed that students did not have native competence in "American culture," whereas the MES programs assumed considerable knowledge of the "Western" way of life. The MES programs valued originality, creativity, Western logic, and rationality as commonsense notions in composition, whereas the ESL writing courses valued academic writing that followed certain discourse conventions, particularly the "modes" (e.g., comparison/contrast, cause/effect). The ESL writing courses emphasized form at both the discourse and sentence levels; the MES courses focused on writing development. Atkinson and Ramanathan concluded that "some of the very approaches to writing that are rewarded in [one] program appear to be stigmatized in [the other]" (563).

These findings are useful to WAC administrators because research indicates that linguistically diverse students bring to all of their academic classrooms theories of writing and how writing tasks should be approached that have been developed in their first cultures and in their writing classrooms in their home countries and in North America. These theories undoubtedly influence the ways students conceptualize, plan, and execute their writing assignments in all of their classes. Wise WAC administrators will begin thinking about ESL writing issues by talking to the teachers of ESL or basic writing in their own institutions about pedagogies employed.

Helping Faculty in the Disciplines Understand ESL Students

After educating ourselves, there are a number of steps we can take to assist other faculty in understanding the issues and in improving the academic achievement and motivation of ESL students. In particular, WAC administrators can help faculty recognize the variety of needs, language proficiencies, and cultural contributions among linguistically diverse students, and to understand that linguistically diverse students' notions about academic writing and writing in the disciplines may differ from those of the dominant university culture.

Faculty have no doubt already been advised to administer early needs-assessment surveys to determine who their students are, what they are studying, and what they expect from their classes. An early survey is particularly important in classes in which linguistically diverse students are enrolled. These assessments can help faculty identify the various student populations represented and what these students might be able to contribute to a particular classroom. Assessment questionnaires can also assist faculty in identifying those who might have difficulty with speaking, reading, or writing assignments. Questions such as the following might be posed in a survey: "What is your first language?"; "Do you read and write in this language?"; "How long have you lived in the United States?"; "What English language writing difficulties do you have, if any?"; "What university-level writing classes have you completed?"; "What is your major?"; "Why did you select it?" (Johns, "Language"). On my own campus, we have found that faculty who are aware of the diverse students in their classes tend to model and scaffold their assignments more conscientiously and to recommend a writing center or tutor when the need arises.

Faculty can use the information about diverse students gathered from needs assessments to enhance class discussion and presentations and to bring a more international or multicultural approach to a course. In an article from an excellent collection on cultural diversity and cultural literacy, Walters has this to say about the contributions of diverse students to our classes: "Research demonstrates the strengths that students from various cultural and linguistic groups might possess, strengths that could be used as a starting point for our pedagogy and shared with classmates so that they can learn from each other" (15). The literature suggests many ways for faculty to draw from ESL students' strengths. In linguistics, language, literacy, and education classes, students can provide examples from their spoken or written first languages to exemplify certain teaching points. In anthropology, students can discuss the kinship terms used in their families; in sociology, the various cultural norms of student groups can be a topic for discussion or writing. Postmodern historians can draw from students' own views of U.S. history or of the history of their own countries or families, demonstrating that historical retelling is socially constructed. Even in the sciences, students' first-culture theories about evolution or other topics can be discussed as ways of viewing natural phenomena.

As noted earlier, ESL students bring to academic classrooms their own ideas about what good writing is and what roles they should play as writers as they both produce and process texts. Though this statement may be true of all students to some degree, the gap between what is expected in our academic classrooms and the students' own literacy expectations and experiences may be even greater when those enrolled are linguistically or culturally diverse.[10] In a useful discussion of this issue, Basham, Ray, and Walley make the following comment:

> When . . . teachers ask students to read a text and then to respond in writing, whether to summarize, criticize or comment, they do so with certain underlying assumptions about the nature of texts, of literate practices in general, and more specifically, about what constitutes "academic discourse." The fact that these underlying assumptions are often left *implicit* can cause problems for students, particularly those second language learners who come to university with very different expectations about discourse in general and academic discourse in particular. For example, Asian students may incorporate whole phrases from known texts in their writing (Matalene 1985, Scollon and Scollon 1991). . . . Problems can also occur when students' culturally determined rules for spoken discourse affect their writing. Within the cultural experience of most Alaskan Native groups, for example, there are limits to the authority a speaker may claim on a topic. . . . The resulting circumspection of assertion is in direct variance with demands of academic writing. (299)

Central to this argument is the fact that many students do not "naturally" share with faculty an understanding about the values that underlie the discourse of a particular academic subject. Thus, they would benefit from instructor explanations or classroom discussions about how a successful paper for that particular context is organized, what content should be included, and how the argumentation is made (see Belcher). If students are given some clues about the values and "ways of being" (Geertz) that are realized in texts in particular academic disciplines, they may begin to develop an appreciation for or a critical stance toward those values and an understanding of why they may need to acquire discourse repertoires for certain academic contexts.

Other issues relating to "good" writing and thinking may be at odds with the cultural and discourse experiences of ESL students. Muchuri, Mulamba, Myers, and Ndoloi (175–98) note that an insistence on the use of personal voice, common to some composition and humanities classes, is anathema to students who come from cultures in which drawing attention to oneself is discouraged. In some parts of Africa and Asia, for example, writers are encouraged to take on not personal but community voices: of local leaders, of mythical characters, or of famous heroes of the past. In a related article, Ramanathan and Kaplan (1996) argue that "voice and audience are largely culturally constrained notions, relatively inaccessible to students who are not full participants in a culture within which they are asked to write" (22).

Most U.S. faculty value "critical thinking," a variously defined concept that has become an increasingly controversial topic in the ESL literature. Fox, for example, speaks of this concept as deeply rooted in U.S. culture and in the particular academic stances that academics reward (125). Atkinson, after discussing the variety of approaches to critical thinking in North American pedagogy, concludes that

> critical thinking is cultural thinking. Thus, I have suggested that critical thinking may well be in the nature of social practice— discoverable if not clearly self-evident only to those brought up in a cultural milieu in which it operates, however tacitly, as a socially valued norm. . . . [The literature points to] vastly different understandings across cultures of three notions directly implicated in critical thought: individualism, self-expression, and using language as a tool for learning. (89)

These comments reveal why many ESL students major in the sciences or engineering. According to L2 speakers in science and technology disciplines (Johns, "Written Argumentation," "Interpreting"; Swales), the specific directions for how critical thought can be achieved, the exploitation of visuals, repeated standard text structure, the use of the passive to subdue or omit the personal agent, and multiple authorship of scientific and technical writing appeal to many students for whom the personal nature of other writing and vague suggestions for critical thinking pose difficult problems. Instructors in the humanities and social sciences might consider a variety of ways for students to complete an assigned task, thereby encouraging involvement of students' own cultural "ways of being" as they think and write (see, e.g., Leki, "Coping Strategies").

The initiatory practices of faculty in the disciplines have also been interrogated in the ESL literature. In an important discussion of this issue, Casanave presents the story of a young Hispanic woman who eventually dropped out of a Ph.D. program in sociology because she could not conform to the pseudoscientific values of her professors or to the register in which they required her to write, and because the faculty steadfastly refused to acknowledge her values or approaches to texts. Casanave notes that "[this study] leads us to ask . . . whether disciplines should socialize all students into a preordained set of values and practices, or whether they should accommodate the cultural diversity of the populations they serve and thus open themselves to change" (148–49). Villanueva elaborates on this issue in "The Politics of Literacy Across the Curriculum" (Chapter 7, this volume).

The Casanave essay is part of an expanding literature on the challenges and difficulties that ESL students face as undergraduates (see, e.g., Johns, "Toward," "Text"; Leki, "Coping," *Understanding*) and as graduate students (see Schneider and Fujishima; Connor and Kaplan) in North American universities. In this literature, instructors are advised to listen for and respect student difference by encouraging students to draw from their own experiences and interests to complete academic tasks, or to contribute to classroom discussion or group work in ways with which they are comfortable. Also important to faculty understanding are examinations of their own assumptions about what it means to be academically literate or to think critically in their classrooms. The more explicit faculty can be about their assumptions, goals, and expectations, the more their diverse students will understand the language registers and academic cultures in which they are attempting to succeed. And, like all students, those who speak English as a second language need to have opportunities to talk to knowledgeable students and faculty about drafts of their assigned texts, thus encouraging critique and discussion of their progress before a grade is awarded (Belcher).

Confronting Errors

Many faculty members complain vociferously about the sentence-level errors in ESL students' written texts, though, as Belcher points out, others ignore errors in student writing, grading only for content. The first group tends to stigmatize students. They associate errors with inadequate thinking, "thus conflating 'bad language' and 'insufficient cognitive development'" (Zamel 507). They complain that students "can't write" or that they "can't think," when they actually mean that students have difficulty correcting minor errors in their assigned writing. Fully as problematic are those faculty who completely ignore error, for by ignoring mistakes they do not help their students learn the discourse features of their disciplines.

What can we do about and for these two groups of faculty? This is a complex question that has been discussed exhaustively in the ESL literature, and the research findings are contradictory. Some research has dealt with faculty tolerance for error. Vann, Myer, and Lorenz found that faculty were tolerant of ESL mistakes that monolingual English-speakers make such as misspellings, comma splices, and subject-verb disagreement. They were forgiving of article ("the/a/an") and preposition errors because these are considered minor and "tricky." Faculty could not forgive other types of ESL errors, however, such as those in which verb affixes were incorrectly used or one verb tense was substituted for another. Santos, on the other hand, found that faculty were most annoyed by errors that both ESL and native-speaking students make, such as those involving subject-verb and pronoun agreement. They were most forgiving of "foreign" grammatical and mechanical errors, but they would not tolerate misuse of disciplinary vocabulary or weak argumentation by any of their students. Interestingly, Santos found that professors in the humanities and social sciences were more lenient toward ESL errors than those in the physical sciences, older professors were more lenient than younger ones, and (perhaps most interesting) non-native-speaking professors were *less* lenient than monolingual English-speakers.

No doubt we all have stories from our own campuses that support the findings cited here. One of my experiences involves a very intelligent Chinese-speaking student whose history instructor, like some whom Zamel mentions, confused error with poor thinking and could not extricate the content from the grammar. He noted all of the missing definite articles ("the") in her well-constructed paper and wrote in red ink across the top of it, "You shouldn't be in college!" For the most part, however, faculty are well-meaning but bewildered by the problems in ESL student writing that neither they nor, in some cases, the students can identify or correct.

When should errors become a major issue? WAC administrators might recommend that faculty have different standards for in-class examination essays and out-of-class assignments, requiring careful editing only in out-of-class papers. Linguistically diverse students tend to write more slowly and take more time to plan; often they can correct their work if they are permitted to draft their papers and edit them over time. Faculty should also be aware of the growing number of English-emergent students who have acquired fossilized errors. After producing these errors in their spoken and written English for years, these students cannot hear or see their mistakes, nor can they identify them in their own written work. Thus, under some circumstances, students should be permitted to work with a competent monolingual English-speaker in correcting their sentence-level errors. In addition, faculty might recommend a general handbook written by an ESL expert. At my own institution and many others, Raimes's *Keys for Writers* has been adopted because the author has been an ESL teacher for most of her professional life and her ESL section is intelligently written. (I have included at the end of this essay a brief description of this and other useful resources for WAC directors to consult as they work with faculty on ESL issues.)

Heading Off Plagiarism

As we all know, plagiarism is considered a major academic crime in North American universities (see Mallon). Nearly every college catalog includes warnings against plagiarism and lists the penalties that infractions of the rules can bring. Many faculty mention plagiarism in their syllabi, and some spend hours in the library attempting to determine which sections of a student paper have been plagiarized. Pennycook suggests some reasons for faculty wrath: "Plagiarism . . . undermines the authority of both teacher and text; . . . the ferocity of this hunting down of borrowed words may be seen as part of a desperate rearguard action against changing textualities" (215).

This is a useful argument, but one that will not be readily accepted among faculty who have been chasing down and punishing plagiarists over the years. What may be more acceptable are Pennycook's suggestions for teaching students who have learned in their home cultures that memorizing and copying the "greats" without citation are essential elements in the written work of a learned person:

> Part of any discussion of citation, paraphrase, textual borrowing, and so forth needs . . . to include a discussion of how and why these notions have been constructed, how authorship, authenticity, and authority are linked, and how these practices may be in a process of flux. . . . Also needed is an attempt to understand the other side of the coin—our students' textual and language learning worlds as well as the constraints upon their lives and their perceptions of how academic norms operate and may be flouted. (227)

In addition to understanding some of the motivations behind the issues of authorship and authority, diverse students need to practice summary and paraphrase. A volume that many students have found useful for this purpose is Braine and May's *Writing from Sources: A Guide for ESL Students,* particularly the long chapter "Using and Acknowledging Sources" (119–138).

In some academic classrooms, however, "plagiarism" means more than copying text and not acknowledging sources. In one classroom on my campus, for example, if a student models a paper on the organization of another student's paper, she or he will receive an F. Thus, as Pennycook and others have noted, plagiarism can refer to copying ideas, to using language without appropriate citation, or, in rare cases, to mimicking the organization of another text. Clearly, each faculty member must determine what he or she believes plagiarism is and make the definition, and penalties, clear to the students in the class. It would also be useful to diverse students to see examples of plagiarism and adequate paraphrasing in student papers so that they can avoid the standard pitfalls.

Final Thoughts

Like many of the topics discussed in this volume, the issues of ESL writing and the nature of writers are complex and the research findings are contradictory. If there were a single L2 literacy instead of many literacies (McKay), if there were easy methods to eradicate errors or explain our academic cultures and discourses, then teaching diverse students would be much easier. But the very complexity of the issues is what makes them interesting. As a teacher of academic literacies, I learn a great deal from students who are linguistically and culturally different from me, and, like many of my faculty colleagues, I enjoy the polyphony (as Laurence terms it) of my classes. Certainly, discoveries about the diversity within our classrooms and our worlds, and an appreciation for difference, must be two of the most important achievements of a North American liberal education.

Notes

1. "Linguistically diverse," though awkward, appears to be the most appropriate term for the variety of bilingual and ESL students in our classes. I also use "ESL," but readers should note that this term is considered derogatory by many students and teachers, particularly in Latino communities.

2. A faculty member Zamel interviewed said he had so many diverse

students in his classes that he thought he was in a foreign country. Recently, an instructor on my campus came to me during the first week of class to complain that "none of [his] students speak English," because so many appeared to be of Asian parentage.

3. Most experts agree that it requires at least six years of concentrated instruction in academic English for most students to attain proficiency. Some students, however, do not attain this goal even after twelve years (Scarcella).

4. A large number of these students are not literate in their family's first language.

5. This first-language dominance was called "interference" by second-language acquisition theorists in the 1960s; now it is referred to as "negative transfer."

6. In second-language acquisition, we refer to the language students use as they attempt to become proficient as "interlanguage." Many of the emergent English language speakers are fossilized into a particular interlanguage period. As a result, they continue to make errors that they themselves cannot identify. Here are a few examples from Leki (*Understanding*), Chapter 9:

> Cut down more trees creates hotter conditions.
>
> This compromise succeeded to bring about a ceasefire.
>
> A real revolution was occurred with her election.
>
> The man he is very interesting in being there.

7. See Berkenkotter and Huckin and Giltrow and Valiquette for interesting discussions of uses of content in the disciplines.

8. A remarkable number of ESL students with good grades in their disciplinary courses are enrolled in basic writing classes in North American colleges and universities. Many claim that their instructors in the disciplines are interested only in their understanding of content, not in their errors. In some cases, especially in engineering, most of the faculty are former ESL students themselves, and a "foreign accent" in written work has become acceptable (Johns, "Written Argumentation").

9. The opposite problem arises in some rhetoric and composition studies programs in which *no* discussion of grammar and its rhetorical purposes takes place.

10. It is important to note here that reading may be fully as challenging as writing for some ESL students, as well for other students in our classes. In California we have found that many more students have difficulty with the reading section of the English Placement Test (a diagnostic examination, administered when students enroll) than with the writing section.

Works Cited

Atkinson, Dwight. "A Critical Approach to Critical Thinking in TESOL." *TESOL Quarterly* 31 (1997): 71–94.

Atkinson, Dwight, and Vai Ramanathan. "Cultures of Writing: An Ethnographic Comparison of L1 and L2 University Writing/Language Programs" *TESOL Quarterly* 29 (1995): 539–68.

Basham, Charlotte, Ruth Ray, and Elizabeth Walley. "Cross-Cultural Perspectives on Task Representation in Reading to Write." *Reading in the Composition Classroom: Second Language Perspectives.* Ed. Joan Carson and Ilona Leki. Boston: Heinle and Heinle, 1993. 299–314.

Belcher, Diane. "How Professors Initiate Nonnative Speakers into their Disciplinary Discourse Communities." *Texas Papers in Foreign Language Education* 1 (1989): 207–25.

Berkenkotter, Carol, and Thomas Huckin. *Genre Knowledge in Disciplinary Communication: Cognition/Culture/Power.* Hillsdale, NJ: Erlbaum, 1995.

Braine, George, and Claire May. *Writing from Sources: A Guide for ESL Students.* Mountain View, CA: Mayfield, 1996.

California Pathways: The Second Language Student in Public High Schools, Colleges, and Universities. Glendale, CA: CATESOL, 1997.

Casanave, Christine P. "Cultural Diversity and Socialization: A Case Study of a Hispanic Woman in a Doctoral Program in Sociology." *Diversity as a Resource: Redefining Cultural Literacy.* Ed. D. E. Murray. Alexandria, VA: TESOL, 1992. 148–82.

Connor, Ulla, and Robert B. Kaplan, eds. *Writing Across Languages: Analysis of L2 Text.* Reading, MA: Addison-Wesley, 1987.

Davids, Todd M., ed. *Open Doors, 1995/96* (Report on International Educational Exchange). Institute of International Education, 809 United Nations Plaza, New York NY 10017-3580.

Fox, Helen. *Listening to the World: Cultural Issues in Academic Writing*. Urbana, IL: NCTE, 1994.

Geertz, Clifford. *Local Knowledge: Further Essays in Interpretive Anthropology*. New York: Basic, 1983.

Giltrow, Janet, and Michele Valiquette. "Genres and Knowledge: Students Writing in the Disciplines." *Learning and Teaching Genre*. Ed. Aviva Freedman and Peter Medway. Portsmouth, NH: Heinemann-Boynton/Cook, 1994. 47–62.

Hinds, John. "Reader versus Writer Responsibility: A New Typology." *Writing Across Languages: Analysis of L2 Text*. Ed. Ulla Connor and Robert B. Kaplan. Reading, MA: Addison-Wesley, 1987. 141–53.

Johns, Ann M. "Interpreting an English Competency Examination: The Frustrations of an ESL Science Student." *Written Communication* 8 (1991): 379–401.

———. "Language and Culture in the Classroom." *Multicultural Diversity and College Teaching*. Ed. Helen Roberts. Newbury Park, CA: Sage, 1994. 60–76.

———. *Text, Role, and Context: Developing Academic Literacies*. New York: Cambridge University Press, 1997.

———. "Toward Developing a Cultural Repertoire: A Case Study of a Lao College Freshman." *Diversity as Resource: Redefining Cultural Literacy*. Ed. Denise E. Murray. Alexandria, VA: TESOL, 1992. 202–32.

———. "Written Argumentation for Real Audiences: Suggestions for Teacher Research and Classroom Practice." *TESOL Quarterly* 27 (1993): 75–90.

Laurence, Patricia. "The Vanishing Site of Mina Shaughnessy's *Errors and Expectations*." *Journal of Basic Writing* 12 (1993): 18–28.

Leki, Ilona. "Coping Strategies of ESL Students in Writing Tasks across the Curriculum." *TESOL Quarterly* 29 (1995): 235–60.

———. *Understanding ESL Writers: A Guide for Teachers*. Portsmouth, NH: Boynton/Cook, 1992.

Mallon, Thomas. *Stolen Words: Forays into the Origins and Ravages of Plagiarism*. New York: Ticknor, 1989.

Matalene, Carolyn. "Contrastive Rhetoric: An American Writing Teacher in China." *College English* 47 (1985): 789–808.

McKay, Sandra. *Agendas for Second Language Literacy.* New York: Cambridge UP, 1993.

Muchuri, Mary N., Nshindi G. Mulamba, Greg Myers, and Deoscorous B. Ndoloi. "Importing Composition: Teaching and Researching Academic Writing beyond North America." *College Composition and Communication* 46 (1995): 175–98.

Olsen, Roger E. Winn-Bell. "Enrollment, Identification, and Placement. *TESOL Matters* (Aug./Sept. 1996): 6.

Pennycook, Alastair. "Borrowing Others' Words: Text, Ownership, Memory, and Plagiarism." *TESOL Quarterly* 30 (1996): 201–230.

Purves, Alan, ed. *Writing Across Languages and Cultures: Issues in Contrastive Rhetoric.* Newbury Park, CA: Sage, 1988.

Ramanathan, Vai, and Robert B. Kaplan. "Audience and Voice in Current L1 Composition Texts: Some Implications for ESL Writers." *Journal of Second Language Writing* 5 (1996): 21–34.

Santos, Terry. "Professors' Reactions to the Academic Writing of Nonnative-speaking Students." *TESOL Quarterly* 22 (1988): 69–90.

Scarcella, Robin. "Secondary Education in California and Second Language Research: Instructing ESL Students in the 1990s." *CATESOL Journal* 9 (1996): 129–52.

Schneider, Melanie, and Naomi K. Fujishima. "When Practice Doesn't Make Perfect: The Case of a Graduate ESL Student." *Academic Writing in a Second Language: Essays on Research and Pedagogy.* Ed. Diane Belcher and George Braine. Norwood, NJ: Ablex, 1995. 3–22.

Silva, Tony, Ilona Leki, and Joan Carson. "Broadening the Perspective of Mainstream Composition Studies." *Written Communication* 14 (1997): 398–428.

Sridhar, S. N. "A Reality Check for SLA Theories." *TESOL Quarterly* 28 (1994): 795–805.

Swales, John M. "Discourse Communities, Genres, and English as an International Language." *World Englishes* 7 (1988): 211–220.

Takaki, Ronald. *From Different Shores: Perspectives on Race and Ethnicity in America.* New York: Oxford UP, 1994.

Vann, Roberta J., D. E. Myer, and F. O. Lorenz. "Error Gravity: A Study of Faculty Opinion of ESL Errors." *TESOL Quarterly* 18 (1984): 427–40.

Walters, Keith. "Whose Culture? Whose Literacy?" *Diversity as Resource: Redefining Cultural Literacy.* Ed. Denise E. Murray. Alexandria, VA: TESOL, 1992. 3–29.

Welaratna, Usha. "A Khmer Perspective: Connections between Khmer Students' Behaviors, History, and Culture." *Diversity as Resources: Redefining Cultural Literacy.* Ed. Denise E. Murray. Alexandria, VA: TESOL, 1992. 135–47.

Williams, Joseph. *Style: Ten Lessons in Clarity and Grace.* 3rd ed. Glenview, IL: Scott, Foresman, 1989.

Zamel, Vivian. "Strangers in Academia: The Experiences of Faculty and ESL Students Across the Curriculum." *College Composition and Communication* 46 (1995): 506–21.

Other Resources

Overviews of the Major Issues

Belcher, Diane, and George Braine, eds. *Academic Writing in a Second Language: Essays on Research and Pedagogy.* Norwood, NJ: Ablex, 1995. This sixteen-chapter collection is particularly useful for WAC practitioners working with upper-division and graduate classes. Among other sections of the volume, the introduction and a chapter by Joel Bock and Lan Chi on use of citations in Chinese and English are particularly helpful. This volume and Swales and Feak, listed in the works cited, should greatly benefit faculty teaching more advanced ESL students.

California Pathways: Second Language Students in Public High Schools, Colleges, and Universities. Glendale, CA: CATESOL, 1997. (Address: California Teachers of English to Speakers of Other Languages, 1146 N. Central Avenue, #195, Glendale, CA 91202. (818) 502-4ESL or Browning@cccd.edu.) Compiled by ESL educators at all levels of instruction, this report discusses the different categories of ESL learners, challenges to acquisition of academic English, cultural factors affecting student achievement, and writing proficiency assessment. Though the volume was written for a California audience, the information, approaches, and list of resources are valuable in most ESL contexts.

Connor, Ulla. *Contrastive Rhetoric: Cross-Cultural Aspects of Second-Language Writing.* New York: Cambridge UP, 1996. This is the latest of three modern volumes on contrastive rhetoric (see also Connor and Kaplan and Purves in the works cited). Here, Connor traces the evolution of contrastive rhetoric (CR), beginning with the famous Kaplan 1966 "doodles" study; she then discusses the CR interface with various theoretical and disciplinary camps: rhetoric and composition, textual linguistics, cultural studies, translation, and genre studies. To understand CR issues, WAC administrators might consult all three of the volumes mentioned here for specific chapters of interest.

Huckin, Thomas, Margot Haynes, and James Coady, eds. *Second Language Reading and Vocabulary Learning.* Norwood, NJ: Ablex, 1993. If we were to ask the ESL students in our classes to name the one major problem they face in acquiring academic literacies, they would undoubtedly say "learning vocabulary." This rich collection discusses ways in which L2 students in academic environments confront issues of vocabulary acquisition, sometimes with negative consequences. Chapters such as "False Friends and Reckless Guessers: Observing Cognate Recognition Strategies" (Holmes and Ramos) and "Too Many Words: Learning the Vocabulary of an Academic Subject" (Parry) should be particularly useful to WAC practitioners.

Leki, Ilona. *Understanding ESL Writers: A Guide for Teachers.* Portsmouth, NH: Boynton/Cook, 1992. If there were only one volume on ESL purchased for a WAC library, this book would be the choice of many ESL specialists. Of particular interest to WAC practitioners is Leki's short and accessible discussions of second-language acquisition, the differences among ESL and basic writers, characteristics of ESL students, major findings from second-language composition research, modern issues in contrastive rhetoric, and common sentence-level errors. Using this volume, WAC administrators could provide a complete and focused ESL workshop for faculty.

Murray, Denise M. *Diversity as a Resource: Redefining Cultural Literacy.* Alexandria, VA: Teachers of English to Speakers of Other Languages (TESOL), 1992. With a foreword by Shirley Brice Heath and some excellent chapters, this volume approaches literacy issues from a cultural perspective, arguing that much of what faculty object to in the writing of linguistically diverse students can be traced to cultural mismatches rather than to contrastive rhetoric or student error. Chapters are written from a number of cultural perspectives, and issues of cultural literacy are raised and critiqued.

Roberts, Helen, et al. *Teaching from a Multicultural Perspective.* Thousand Oaks, CA: Sage, 1994. This volume is devoted exclusively to providing practical suggestions for understanding, teaching, and assessing the nontraditional student and encouraging university administrations to recognize and embrace changes in student populations. WAC administrators can consult this volume for discussions of collaborative learning and ESL, designing initial needs assessments, involving students in class discussion, and other practical topics.

Silva, Tony, Ilona Leki, and Joan Carson. "Broadening the Perspective of Mainstream Composition Studies." *Written Communication* 14 (1997): 398–428. In this article, three of the most prominent ESL literacy specialists argue that ESL composition research and theory have been neglected by mainstream professionals. The authors discuss two topics that are central to the ESL literature: second-language acquisition research and second-language writing instruction, noting the importance of each to understanding diverse student populations.

Handbooks

Azar, Betty S. *Understanding and Using English Grammar.* Englewood Cliffs, NJ: Prentice-Hall, 1981. For those WAC practitioners and other faculty who need to develop a metalanguage about grammar or who want to refresh their memory about "traditional grammar," this textbook for ESL students will provide an accessible reference. In addition to fifteen chapters on topics in English grammar, it includes an appendix that defines basic grammar terms. This is in fact a series of volumes for students at different English-language proficiency levels.

Raimes, Ann. *Keys for Writers: A Brief Handbook.* 2nd ed. Boston: Houghton Mifflin, 1999. If faculty want to recommend a handbook written by an ESL expert, *Keys for Writers* is probably their best choice. In addition to being a useful handbook for all students, this volume devotes twenty-one pages to ESL issues, concentrating on some of the major student errors and common editing questions that ESL students ask. The handbook has another attractive feature: boxes throughout the text that highlight "Language Across Cultures" issues. On page 258, for example, the author discusses the implications of the fact that only English capitalizes the first-person singular pronoun "I." The volume also has a good section on citing sources and avoiding plagiarism.

Swan, Michael, and Bernard Smith, eds. *Learner English: A Teacher's Guide to Interference and Other Problems.* Cambridge: Cambridge UP, 1988. For those who would like to know more about the features of the languages their students speak, this volume is invaluable. It provides a brief discussion of verb tense and aspect and other characteristics of written languages, such as punctuation.

WEB Sites

◆ At California State University, Los Angeles, where an estimated 80 percent of the students are linguistically diverse, M. Anne Snow and others have been conducting workshops with faculty on ESL issues for a number of years. They have developed Web sites such as http://web.calstatela.edu/centers/write_cn/esltyp.htm that deal specifically with ESL issues. CSULA sites are also devoted to ESL literacy in specific disciplines, such as this one on philosophy: http://web.calstatela.edu/centers/write_cn/. With its large ESL population and its commitment to writing in the disciplines, CAL State L.A. is a good source for WAC faculty.

◆ At Washington State University, ESL experts have set up an ESL "Help Desk" which lists books and resources for students, advice for faculty, and ESL classes in the English department; Lynn Gordon, the faculty member who set it up, answers questions from non-native speakers of English from all over the world: http://www.wsu.edu/ gordon/ESL/.

◆ Purdue University's online Writing Lab provides tutoring by e-mail and dozens of helpful documents. For information, send a blank e-mail message to owl@sage.cc.purdue.edu (with the subject "owl-request").

CHAPTER SEVEN

The Politics of Literacy
Across the Curriculum

VICTOR VILLANUEVA
Washington State University

Is There a Politic in the House?

*I return to school after all the years in the Army, my
GED in hand, and walk into my first-year composition
course, taught by a South Asian woman, Ratna Roy, who
speaks of her maids back in India, tells of her literacy
test that awarded her a scholarship in English at Oxford: the Rhodes scholar wearing a sari at Tacoma Community College. There is a politic here—in the life she
once knew and discussed, in the surplus value gained in
having a Rhodes scholar teaching first-year comp at a
community college (which is not to denigrate first-year
comp or the community college, only the combination of
money and power and national origin or race or racism).
I know there is a politic. But I can't make sense of it.*

*Her assignments are open. I write of race, of my "ex-
istential situation." Get accused of plagiarism, though
I'm vindicated through a timed writing in her office.*

*At the university, my first assignment concerns
Spenser: a 36 out of a possible 100—for my imagina-
tion, the professor writes on my paper. Success depends
on researching the publications of my professors. Mimicry. My politic suppressed—suppressed until the first time
I write of the political exigencies of my existence as an
academic, as an academic of color, of poverty, as I write
in narrative. As I write within the conventions of the acad-*

emy, my suppressed politic festers, a dream deferred while
another pursued, but not deferred indefinitely.

I'm a skeptic when it comes to writing across the curriculum. I
have no problems with the WAC idea of literacy across the
disciplines or even of sharing the responsibility of literacy instruction (as outlined by McLeod and others), and I long ago
accepted writing as epistemological, as a way of knowing. But
for just as long, I've accepted writing and the teaching of writing
as inherently political. And WAC, it seems to me, has tended to
be assimilationist, *assimilation* being a political state of mind more
repressive than mere accommodation:[1] we begin by having students invent the university, perhaps, then move on to having students invent the disciplines.[2] This isn't the politic I'd prefer. We
in composition studies might assume a closer connection between
language and epistemology, but "writing to learn" doesn't go far
enough, doesn't historicize our conceptions of language and knowing, keeps us tied to a Platonic mind-set.

That Platonic mind-set is embedded even in our discussions
of politics. Our conversations are quick to blur distinctions between culture, ideology, and politics. The political involves more
than culture. Culture can be kinship and community (as one category) and aesthetics (as another). And there is culture as the
material (particularly the economic).[3] But this last is often absent
from our discussions. We stay aloft, away from the material. And
that has something to do with WAC. So I want to argue for a
reconsideration of what happens in WAC, maybe suggest a way
to a culturally sensitive and politically conscious edge in how we
approach literacy, even as students of color and others venture
into the conventions of academic discourse—now—during the
time it takes for us all to reconceptualize the discourse of the
academy.

The Platonic Mind-set

Not all at once, not just in that first class on rhetoric, I
discover some things about writing, my own, and about

the teaching of writing. I find some of modern composition's insights are modern hindsights. I don't mind the repetition. Some things bear repeating. The repetitions take on new significance and are elaborated upon in a new context, a new time. Besides, not everyone who teaches writing knows of rhetoric, though I believe everyone should.

VICTOR VILLANUEVA, Bootstraps

The curriculum we write across prides itself on being a "higher learning," something above the day-to-day. We are still "the academy," tied to Plato and to his epistemology in one sense or another. We know that in his *Republic* and in the two dialogues dealing directly with rhetoric he draws a distinction between true arts and forms of flattery, "flattery" as a pleasing deception. Rhetoric falls under the heading of a form of flattery for Plato, insofar as its concerns are decidedly tied to the temporal and to the material. This is even more true for literacy, since there is no talking back to the text (a matter Volosinov will take issue with centuries later). For Plato, rhetoric can be salvageable, can be a true art, if it works in the service of dialectic, potentially liberating the mind from the temporal and sensorial to the plane of the infinite, the Idea of the Good. The academy might have grown to be a huge megaversity, but it remains rooted in the Platonic liberal arts, so much so that our discussions of rhetoric or literacy and surely composition studies remain to a great extent apart from the material. Even our opening discussions on class tend to remain tied to class as culture but not to class as political economy, an uncomplicated notion of class as socioeconomic status rather than as a relationship between economic systems (material) and political processes (temporal).[4]

It's little wonder that literacy, after so long a legacy, could so easily be set aside as an academic responsibility even while being touted as essential to the historical base of the academy. We are steeped in Plato.

From the fifth century B.C.E. to the nineteenth century, rhetoric and its literacy have been central to education, particularly within the liberal arts, those kinds of knowledge that will elevate

— 167 —

and in some sense free the mind. Though the English literary arts tend to be concerned with the politics which surround their authors and poets, these politics are necessarily abstractions, calls for contemplation more than calls for action, the contemplation having value, certainly, but in that sense proffered by Quintilian: as a means of forming better folks down the line.

By the nineteenth century rhetoric had lost its centrality. The center of the academy belonged to the new sciences. In some schools, the social sciences became aligned with the liberal arts, rhetoric and literacy becoming defined as an introductory course or two on writing for college, until a convergence of circumstances (Woods Hole, Dartmouth, Janet Emig's study of writing as a mode of learning) returned rhetoric and literacy to a reconsideration of language and psychology, language and epistemology, if not literacy as political—a move more difficult to make, given the Platonic in our midst.

This realization of literacy as epistemological, as ways of learning about the self, the context in which the self is oriented, and the context as defined by an academic discipline, captures WAC through the "second stage"—literacy as accepted across the disciplines as a way of learning. The third stage, to some extent the call of this volume and invoked by Donna LeCourt ("WAC as Critical Pedagogy: The Third Stage?"), would have us look more closely at the need to reform pedagogy, taking into account the rise of new technology; the question of WAC and writers whose primary literacy is in languages other than English; and politics, particularly (for me) as reflected in racism.

Multicultures—and One Dominates

Excerpt from a note to an editor concerning a reviewer's comments, maybe 1993: "The reviewer wants me 'to avoid the charge of bias, of raising the British-French-Americans to a level of behavior unparalleled in history.' I really do think American imperialism has attained 'a level of behavior unparalleled in history.' I'm with Fernand Braudel, Noam Chomsky, Karl Polanyi,

Immanuel Wallerstein, and the rest of a long list (of which I have not mentioned one Marxist) who think so too. So I skipped the fairness task." Why pretend to the scientistic notion of objectivity in discourse when such a thing is unattainable, even within the conventions that precede us, since language and dialect are always steeped in convention?

For all the sympathy inherent in multiculturalism, it tends to fail because by and large it tends not to be antiracist. As I argue elsewhere ("Rhetoric," "Reading"), the problem with multiculturalism is that it relies on a conception of cultural pluralism, an ideal (a Platonic "Good"), but given the political economy of the day (no matter what the school of "political economy"), the idea of all cultures living together in mutual understanding is not yet practical. So we do an injustice in our acting as if a mutuality already exists. Further, there is a political economy in the conception of cultural plurality historically, as when Glazer and Moynihan argue that the United States is the melting pot, assimilation is the norm, and failure is a cultural fault, not a matter of racism (Omi and Winant 17–21). Cultural pluralism will not be achieved by pretending it already exists or can exist by simple avowal.

Rhetoric, composition studies, the third stage in WAC—all of us concerned with language and discourse and the desire for a more equitable society—will need to move beyond the cultural to the relations among discourse, the cultural, the political (not only as ideology but also as political power more broadly conceived), and the economic. Gayatri Spivak begins to approach this as she writes not only of epistemology in poststructural terms that give credence to the power of discourse as ideological, but also as she writes of the epistemology of other politically economic forces, what she calls an episteme of violence.

In terms of racism, we can stand to learn from those other disciplines while we inform them of the ways of writing pedagogy. That is, the third stage, as I see it, will be the stage of a true dialectic between the disciplines we work with. We can learn from folks in business who have economists among them, from historians, from political scientists, from sociologists, as well as from the literary figures and critical theorists we have grown accustomed to learning from. We give something to the disciplines—matters of literacy and rhetoric grounded in the sociopolitical; and they give us something—their considerations of the political and the economic. It's time. And it's bound to succeed, since the old resentments of the "missionary" would simply pass, given reciprocity.

If we are to proffer our understanding of the value of cross- and interdisciplinary literacy, we have an obligation to proffer the social dimensions of our research, theory, and discussion as well. And we have the obligation to learn from those to whom we pass on our knowledge of the teaching of writing. If WAC is no longer (or perhaps never was) missionary in its method, then we should be engaging the other minds across the disciplines who also face the students we face. We should enter into a dialogue across the disciplines so as better to understand the social processes that could relegate such a large number to the trouble-heap: the poor and the racial or ethnic majority. All of us can use the tools at our disposal to circumvent reproducing a school system that has traditionally failed to educate the woman, the poor, or the person of color at the same rate of efficiency as others. Time for the third stage.

WAC Critical!

The Calling

The calling came to me
while I languished
in my room; while I
whittled away my youth
in jail cells
and damp *barrio* fields.

It brought me to life,
out of captivity,
in a street-scarred

and tattooed place
I called body.

Until then I waited silently,
a deafening clamor in my head,
but voiceless to all around me;
hidden from America's eyes,
A brown boy without a name,

I would sing into a solitary
     tape recorder,
music never to be heard.
I would write my thoughts
in scrambled English;
I would take photos in my mind—
     plan out new parks;
     bushy green, concrete free,
     New places to play
     and think.

Waiting.
Then it came.
The calling.
It brought me out of my room.
It forced me to escape
night captors
in street prisons.

It called me to war;
to be writer,
to be scientist
and march with the soldiers
     of change.

It called me from the shadows,
out of the wreckage,
of my *barrio*—from among those
who did not exist.

I waited all of 16 years
for this time.

Somehow, unexpected,
I was called.

Luis J. Rodríguez

While *process* and *consensus* become the catchwords of writing across the curriculum pedagogy, rhetorical theory and composition theory look to how language is not just the conveyor of knowledge but is also the way knowledge becomes known. The question becomes how to convey writing in a way that doesn't alienate. One suggestion, well articulated by Donna LeCourt, is to add the pedagogy of Paulo Freire to the imperatives of meaningful college literacy. Freire offers a particular brand of social theory for education that we in composition studies have tended to adopt for the work we do within our own programs but have only half-heartedly conveyed across the curriculum. In other words, we should say that writing is not only a way of learning but also a way of fostering critical consciousness, more than a means of problem solving but also a means of problem posing.

Patricia Bizzell notes that Freire, in *Education for Critical Consciousness*, argues a case that sounds decidedly like our pronouncements on college literacy, our justification for writing across the curriculum:

> Knowledge [Freire writes] necessitates the curious presence of subjects confronted with the world. It requires their transforming action on reality. It demands a constant searching. It implies invention and reinvention. It claims from each person a critical reflection on the very act of knowing. It must be a reflection which recognizes the knowing process, and in this recognition becomes aware of the *"raison d'être"* behind the knowing and the conditioning to which that process is subject. (qtd. in Bizzell 100–101)

This is the very knowledge we ought to be fostering: the self as situated within a discipline and within the world, confronting racism head on as well as other situations that distance women, the poor, and others from the dominant discourse and its racialized and gendered assumptions. For LeCourt the means is through a politicized personal narrative with which to interrogate students' relations to the disciplines for which they are writing. This is the means whereby the critical has been introduced to first-year composition, as LeCourt acknowledges, and it should work well, particularly in introductory courses throughout the disciplines.

But at a certain point, students need to break free from the personal as the sole genre of engagement. How then to maintain the critical and one's sense of identity and agency when called on to break from personal narrative?

Many writers of color have written about a conscious mimicry of the discourse of power. In *Puerto Rican Jam*, for instance, sociologists Grosfoguel, Negrón-Muntaner, and Georas describe the strategy employed by many Puerto Ricans given a particular political economy. Puerto Rico's situation is one in which political power makes colonialism (at least five hundred years of colonialism) no longer tenable, yet given its economic situation, nationalism is not feasible. The trick then is maintaining a cultural identity while complying with dominance. That's achieved through *jaibería*, a "subversive complicity," analogous to shining someone on. The authors describe the concept this way:

> According to Diana Fuss in her essay on Frantz Fanon,[5] there is a tendency within postcolonial and psychoanalytic discourse to distinguish between the practices of mimicry and masquerade. While in psychoanalysis, masquerade is understood as the unconscious assumption of a role, mimicry, according to Homi K. Bhabha, is understood as a colonial strategy of subjugation. Fuss, however, stresses that there can be a mimicry of subversion where the deliberate performance of a role does not entail identification. The performance's contexts thus become crucial in determining its subversive potential. . . . [In] both Fanon's and Fuss's texts, the most powerful example of subversive mimicry is that of the Algerian Nationalist woman militant who "passes" as a Europeanized subject in order to advance the cause of National liberation. (Grosfoguel, Negrón-Muntaner, and Georas 26–28)

Two of the essays in Keith Gilyard's collection *Race, Rhetoric, and Composition*, one by Malea Powell and one by Gail Okawa, explore strategies similar to *jaibería*, one calling on the

American Indian icon of the trickster, the other calling on Mitsuye Yamada's masks (though not masquerade), masks that intentionally conceal. In rhetorical terms, there is *imitatio*, best described by Quintilian, a Spanish subject of the Roman Empire. Here, however, I'm calling for *imitatio* with an antiracist critical pedagogy, *imitatio* taking on a particular mental state—a *jaibería*, a masking, a discursive trickery—while students and everyone involved in WAC work on discourse, work critically and consciously on conventions, and work on swapping what other disciplines are discovering about economics and political power.

Although the expression *jaibería* is new to us in composition studies, the practical workings of how one moves from the discourse of the individual and the individual's culture to the discourse of the academy are not. I have described, perhaps best in *Bootstraps*, a drafting process which begins with the personal as political and moves through conscious translations to the conventions of academic discourse. It entails a conscious understanding of Aristotle's logic (the teaching of which has been laid out as a practical pedagogy best by Ed Corbett in *Classical Rhetoric for the Modern Student*). And it involves a conscious process through which the discoveries made in the narrative process are revised or translated to fit within the conventions of academic discourse. I have used the process successfully for many years with students from other cultures (even white students residing in what Walter Ong, following Marshall McLuhan, calls a "secondary orality": an awareness of the sound of literacy but literacy devised to be orally delivered only). Others under my direction have used the method as well.

Within faculty workshops, our co-workers can be shown that the organizational patterns and other discourse markers (matters other than simple mechanics) that are manifest in students' early draft writing are not necessarily signs of disorganization but of other-cultural organization (see Ann Johns in Chapter 6 of this volume on issues of contrastive rhetoric). While we all explore ways of helping students translate their ways with words into the conventions of particular disciplines, we can also listen and learn from other disciplines about the political economies that give rise to difference, opening a door whereby we might agree to changes in conventions that will better situate cultural differences. In being conscious of the conventions as conventions, in remaining conscious of our own predispositions in early drafts to give free rein to cultural discourse, we stand a chance of doing our job of assuring students' access to the places they wish to go by way of the academy without erasing where they've been. It can be done. It has been done. WAC should pass it on.

Notes

1. I mention accommodation because Donna LeCourt, who argues persuasively for a critical pedagogy in WAC, tends to see the basic problem in writing in the disciplines as its tendency toward an accommodationist mind-set. But I would argue that we all accommodate—either in the conventions we adopt (or even mimic) or in the body of knowledge we lean on within particular disciplines. Although I believe her intent is to point to assimilation, her reliance on the language of Henry Giroux's version of resistance theory provides her with the term(s) (*accommodation, opposition,* and *resistance*). Rather than Giroux (who, like LeCourt, I am surely indebted to in pursuing the lines of argument presented here), I am calling on others, who I will at the very least allude to in this essay.

2. LeCourt wonders at how the politics that are played out in first-year comp courses might be carried over to WAC. Although it is true that composition studies has entered into the political in its discussions, as have many other disciplines (as LeCourt acknowledges), composition studies has hardly solved the problems of the political, has not as a discipline, for example, ventured into the political as containing more than the superstructural—the cultural. In some sense, then, the politic of the classroom remains safe, a necessity, as far as I can see, since the first-year course does remain a gateway course into the university's discourses. Although others have argued that Bartholomae's pedagogy is no less assimilationist than other pedagogies (a defanged Freire, I'd say), it does confront the dilemma—that of meeting what we see as a political dimension to our work and the need to provide the gateway function. What results from this near paradox is critical thinking, a problem solving, in which the problems are disciplinarily conscribed, rather than a critical consciousness, a problem posing, in which the problems are themselves to be uncovered by the student writer. LeCourt does try to address this, finally arguing for Freire as writing the personal within the disciplines (which is as far as any of us in composition studies has gone).

3. These three factors comprise social historian Fernand Braudel's "set of sets" or economist Andre Gunder Frank's "three legged stool" on which world systems sit, or Karl Polanyi's anatomy of political economics.

4. I think here of *Coming to Class: Pedagogy and the Social Class of Teachers* edited by Shepard, McMillan, and Tate, an interesting collection, but one that tends not to complicate the notion of class.

5. "Interior Colonies: Frantz Fanon and the Politics of Identification." *Diacritics* 24 (1994): 20–42.

Works Cited

Bartholomae, David. "Inventing the University." *When a Writer Can't Write: Studies in Writer's Block and Other Composing Process Problems.* Ed. Mike Rose. New York: Guilford, 1985. 134–65.

Bizzell, Patricia. *Academic Discourse and Critical Consciousness.* Pittsburgh: U of Pittsburgh P, 1992.

Braudel, Fernand. *The Wheels of Commerce.* Vol. 2 of *Civilization and Capitalism: 15th–18th Century.* Trans. Siân Reynolds. London: Collins, 1982.

Corbett, Edward P. J. *Classical Rhetoric for the Modern Student.* New York: Oxford UP, 1965.

Emig, Janet. "Writing as a Mode of Learning." *College Composition and Communication* 28 (1977): 122–28.

Frank, Andre Gunder. *ReOrient: Global Economy in the Asian Age.* Berkeley: U of California P, 1998.

Freire, Paulo. *Pedagogy of the Oppressed.* Trans. Myra Bergman Ramos. New York: Herder, 1970.

Glazer, Nathan, and Daniel Patrick Moynihan. *Beyond the Melting Pot: The Negroes, Puerto Ricans, Jews, Italians, and Irish of New York City.* Cambridge: MIT P, 1963.

Grosfoguel, Ramón, Frances Negrón-Muntaner, and Chloé S. Georas, "Beyond Nationalist and Colonialist Discourses: The *Jaiba* Politics of the Puerto-Rican Ethno-Nation." *Puerto Rican Jam: Rethinking Colonialism and Nationalism.* Ed. Frances Negrón-Muntaner and Ramón Grosfoguel. Minneapolis: U of Minnesota P, 1997. 1–36.

LeCourt, Donna. "WAC as Critical Pedagogy: The Third Stage?" *JAC: A Journal of Composition Theory* 16 (1996): 389–405.

McLeod, Susan H. "Writing Across the Curriculum: An Introduction." *Writing Across the Curriculum: A Guide to Developing.* Ed. Susan H. McLeod and Margot Soven. Academic.Writing Landmark Publications in Writing Studies: http://aw.colostate.edu/books/mcleod_soven/ 2000. Originally published in print by Sage (Newbury Park, CA), 1992. 1–11.

Okawa, Gail. "Removing Masks: Confronting Graceful Evasion and Bad Habits in a Graduate English Class." *Race, Rhetoric, and Composition.* Ed. Keith Gilyard. Portsmouth, NH: Heinemann, 1999. 124–43.

Omi, Michael, and Howard Winant. *Racial Formation in the United States: From the 1960s to the 1990s.* New York: Routledge, 1994.

Ong, Walter J. *Orality and Literacy: The Technologizing of the Word.* New York: Methuen, 1982.

Plato. *Gorgias.* Trans. Robin Waterfield. New York: Oxford UP, 1994.

———. *Phaedrus.* Trans. R. Hackforth. Cambridge: Cambridge UP, 1952.

Polanyi, Karl. *The Great Transformation.* New York: Farrar & Rinehart, 1944.

Powell, Malea. "Blood and Scholarship: One Mixed-Blood's Story." *Race, Rhetoric, and Composition.* Ed. Keith Gilyard. Portsmouth, NH: Heinemann, 1999. 1–16.

Quintilian. *Quintilian on the Teaching of Speaking and Writing: Translations from Books One, Two, and Ten of the* Institutio Oratoria. Ed. James J. Murphy. Carbondale: Southern Illinois UP, 1987.

Rodríguez, Luis. "The Calling/*El llamado.*" *Puerto Rican Writers at Home in the USA: An Anthology.* Ed. Faythe Turner. Seattle: Open Hand, 1991. 123–25.

Shepard, Alan, John McMillan, and Gary Tate. *Coming to Class: Pedagogy and the Social Class of Teachers.* Portsmouth, NH: Boynton/Cook, 1998.

Spivak, Gayatri Chakravorty. *A Critique of Postcolonial Reason: Toward a History of the Vanishing Present.* Cambridge: Harvard UP, 1999.

Villanueva, Victor. *Bootstraps: From an American Academic of Color.* Urbana, IL: NCTE, 1993.

———. "On the Rhetoric and Precedents of Racism." *College Composition and Communication* 50 (1999): 645–61.

———. "Reading Rhetoric outside and in: Theory, Pedagogy, and Politics in Race, Rhetoric, and Composition." *JAC: A Journal of Composition Theory* (2000): 195–204.

CHAPTER EIGHT

Writing Centers and WAC

JOAN A. MULLIN
University of Toledo

While writing across the curriculum and writing centers both have histories with roots in the nineteenth century, the current connections between them date back to the early 1970s. Researchers claim that this recent linkage began as a response to open admissions, a population explosion, and increased pressures for job-related skills instruction and educational accountability (Carino, "Early" 103; Russell 271). It is worth noting that these same forces exerted themselves at the turn of the century, and in both eras educators were confronted with student populations that challenged their previously held ideas about language instruction. The response in the late nineteenth century included the beginnings of a composition course that, in some cases, included collaborative peer work and the vestiges of writing across the curriculum. It is interesting that the response to a student population whose language skills didn't match faculty expectations in the 1970s was similar to the response of nearly a century before: a growth in the *discipline* of composition, writing centers, and writing across the curriculum.

Today we find our educational assumptions challenged yet again by new but familiar forces. Society and technology herald a millennium in which alternative educational communities and the languages of hypertext, Internet, and cyberspeak compete with previous understandings of communication and disciplinarity. Added to these forces, increased access to education and the population's need for retooling in a quickly changing job market create cross-generational classrooms. As Lester Faigley points out, "More than 80 percent of students enrolled in postsecondary education do not live in dormitories. Close to half are older than

25. . . . A different college population with different needs and expectations is bringing different models of learning," which in turn require different models of teaching (14–15). The recent growth and collaboration of WAC and writing centers owe much to practices that allow a quick response to such changing conditions within institutions.

Current social forces and the added collaborations of community and college, industry and university, create an increasingly multi- and interdisciplinary system that demands services tailored to specific needs. Electronic classroom delivery, both face-to-face and screen-to-screen instruction, changes the traditional teacher-learner dynamic and threatens traditional notions of education. It remains to be seen whether, in an era of challenge similar to those mentioned earlier, the academy will turn again to a historically powerful philosophy that promotes writing and learning as skills to be learned discretely. At the moment, practices of writing across the curriculum programs and writing centers seem to have successfully met many of the educational and social needs of the last decade and are poised to respond to those of the new millennium.

Intersecting Histories

David Russell notes that often, from the end of the nineteenth century on:

> When [administration and faculty] did require writing as part of regular courses in the disciplines, that writing was less likely to be integrated into the activity of the course or program and more likely to be seen merely as a favor to the English department or the institution, as a way of enforcing standards of correctness or reinforcing general-composition courses, or as a means of evaluation. (8–9)

Articles on early writing labs likewise establish a connection between enforcement of standards, remediation, and required classroom "lab" attendance (Carino, "Early" 104). Russell and Carino note that contending perspectives of language learning in educational and public forums influenced writing centers and fledgling writing programs (Carino, "Open" 39). In both cases, the pedagogy used was created in response to these competing perspectives, but it was also shaped in response to each successive student population.

For example, while the dominant theories at the beginning of the last century spurred the growth of composition programs, these theories did not support any attempts to spread active responsibility for the teaching of writing to disciplinary faculty other than English. Historians of writing agree that at that time, students "whose writing did not conform to a particular community's standards were thought to exhibit some deficit, which had to be remedied *before* they could be admitted to the [academic, disciplinary] community" (Russell 15). Not particularly enthusiastic about assuming this task, departments of English questioned the assignment of writing instruction to their literature faculty or were overwhelmed by the inability of their practices and theories to "remedy" student writing. So writing instructors and labs were elected to take care of those deficiencies. Nonetheless, with each new cultural challenge, with each incoming first-year group of students, the problem of writing continued to grow across the curriculum. Writing centers and writing classroom instructors with their smaller class sizes and concentrated work environments began to experiment, testing new theories and developing responsive pedagogies.

Despite decades of practices that sought to remedy writing discretely, writing centers attempted early on to connect language learning with a discipline or tutoring lab methods with classrooms. The latter gained strength in the military training of the 1940s that recognized the importance of individualized instruction in the form of lab-connected classrooms (see Redford; Weigle; Wykoff). Some of these practices were adopted by university writing programs throughout that decade, with an important addition in communications programs, which focused on the affective domain (Carino, "Early" 107). Likewise, some writing center practitioners at the time also recognized the need to go beyond surface correction, or skill-and-drill, and sought to identify and work with an individual context—holistically.

Exerting another force on writing practices were the "progressive methods . . . founded or reorganized along the Deweyan lines between the world wars" (Russell 224). Emphasizing interdisciplinarity and what we might today call service learning, private colleges tied writing instruction to disciplines and to the connections between them and learning (see Clark; Jones). Such efforts in writing centers and early WAC initiatives, however, were overwhelmed by the educational theories which separated learning "skills" (such as writing) from content (e.g., Russell 10–12, 108), or separated the affective from the intellectual (Carino, "Early" 107–8). Writing centers and writing teachers were caught between an acquired cultural image of themselves as remedial centers focusing on skill-and-drill and their successful experiences with real writers.

In the 1970s, language learning again came under fire from within and outside the academy. The response was twofold: evaluate composition teaching and establish more writing centers. Writing centers along with other "cross-curricular writing programs were almost always a response to a perceived need for greater access, greater equity. They set out to assimilate, integrate, or . . . initiate previously excluded students by means of language acquisition" (Russell 271). This time, however, the work of writers such as Elbow, Graves, Macrorie, and Moffett gave writing center practitioners a student-centered pedagogy that corroborated affective practices already woven into the traditional skills-centered response to writers. Many histories of individual centers maintain that during this period, they "rejected their imposed roles as course supplement responsible for remedial grammar and developed an innovative student-centered writing pedagogy that competed with classroom work" (Carino, "Open" 31). Influenced by "mass education" in the 1960s and the concomitant increase of diverse student backgrounds in the classroom (Russell 274), writing center practitioners in their one-on-one interactions learned that teaching students an all-purpose academicspeak, one that would serve in all classrooms across the curriculum, was not effective. Center practitioners began interacting across the disciplines to find out what faculty expectations were, how they constructed language in their disciplines, and to what questions their students must respond.

The same forces "gave to the WAC movement its focus on the classroom as community; its student-centered pedagogy, often with a subversive tinge; and its neoromantic, expressivist assumptions" that focused on the individual (Russell 273), as well as on the individual disciplinary classroom. Perhaps unconsciously, faculty began to believe that English teachers couldn't teach everything about writing in one composition class. They began attending writing workshops in an effort to discover "what to do," and research on the nature of writing in the disciplines grew. While there never was a single evolutionary line that both writing centers and WAC programs followed, their mutual philosophies began to develop mutual theories and practices. These created a context for current programs that traverse disciplinary lines and challenge traditional ways of thinking about writing and learning content in a world in which writing and learning contexts constantly change.

Who Begets What in WAC/Writing Center Connections?

One of the tenets oft repeated in writing center circles is that any center must shape itself according to its local context. That is, writing centers will exist with their audience in mind, will build on the purpose of their assignment, and will respond to the tacit conventions of the institution within which they operate. The same is true of WAC programs: models are useful for stimulating ideas but should be seen as menus from which ideas can be chosen—or generated. So while numerous variations exist, two basic models drive WAC-writing center connections: writing centers beget WAC programs or WAC programs beget writing centers.

Our program at the University of Toledo followed the first model: while the College of Arts and Sciences wanted to establish a WAC program, faculty decided that they first needed a writing center as a resource; the writing center in turn established the WAC program. As is typical in some universities, such as Purdue, WAC may not be a formal program, but the writing center performs WAC activities as part of its pedagogy and because of the perceived need for faculty interaction across the curriculum (see Harris). In the second model, a WAC program may be established and then administrators find it necessary to establish or change the mission of a writing center as faculty assign more writing across the curriculum. At the University of North Dakota, for example, Joan Hawthorne reports, "The connection with WAC happened during about the fourth year of our WAC program, when we [the WAC program] first began hiring undergrads from disciplines outside of English in a conscious effort to build liaisons with departments where lots of writing was happening." All of these universities responded to their contexts in different ways, yet all of their WAC programs—official or unofficial—are vital and thriving.

WAC and WC Partnerships

Partnerships between WAC and writing centers seem obvious because they both draw from some of the same theories, engage in shared practices, and are similarly placed within the academic community (often not reporting to departments or working across traditional curricular lines). Even the debates between WAC and writing center practitioners parallel each other: in disciplinary writing, the issue is summarized in the philosophical and semantic contest between the WAC proponents (characterized as forwarding writing to learn) and WID (Writing in the Disciplines) proponents (characterized as favoring writing as disciplinary genres). In writing centers, the same debate takes shape between those who claim that generalist tutors, with their "outsider" status, provide the most effective feedback to writers in any discipline and those who claim tutors must have disciplinary knowledge in order to maintain maximum effectiveness with writers (see Soven, Chapter 9, this volume). In each case, though, and in the WAC and writing center movement toward workplace literacy, there are several common agreements:

◆ Each discipline has genres, ways of performing, or conventions specific to its manner of constructing, supporting, and questioning knowledge.

- ◆ No discipline can effectively act alone: this fact implies a call for workplace alliances, interdisciplinary planning, and multidisciplinary exchanges of theory and practice.

- ◆ The most effective pedagogy is one-on-one or small-group instruction.

- ◆ Assessment of teaching and learning effectiveness is a complex, continual, reflective activity.

Because these commonalities are in line with what we know about teaching and learning, it is no surprise that these two programs serve as model educational initiatives. *Returning to Our Roots*, a report of the Kellogg Commission on the Future of State and Land-Grant Universities, outlined three primary changes institutions must initiate in the new century: they must become *"genuine learning communities"*; they must be *"student centered"*; they must "emphasize the importance of a *healthy learning environment* that provides students, faculty and staff with the facilities, support and resources to make this vision a reality" (v–vi). WAC and writing centers are natural partners when it comes to shared theory and practice, but they also form strong partnerships for changing curriculum and administrative practices, and for examining the ways faculty and students think about writing, learning, and evaluation. In so doing, they create a faculty-student connection—a loop of feedback and response—that promotes student-centered learning communities and provides a healthy environment that supports risk taking and innovation.

Recent educational movements—the federally supported School-to-Work Initiative, the current growth of service learning in universities (see Jolliffe, Chapter 4, this volume), the growth of corporate-school-university relationships, and the new corporate universities—all point to the need to closely align instruction with workplace or vocational competencies. The importance of genre studies in WAC research (see Russell, Chapter 11, this volume) parallels this emphasis in professional contexts. Both WAC programs and writing centers continue to develop ways to read rhetorical situations, deconstruct them, respond to them, and mirror or challenge their practices. There are several areas in which effective partnerships can be built on this common ground.

I discuss four: faculty development, tutor- and technology-linked courses, assessment, and community connections.

Faculty Development

If a director of WAC or of a writing center learns one thing, it is this: faculty members do not want to be told how to teach their classes, how to write assignments, or how to evaluate assignments. While they may well solicit help for any of these—and many of them do—they do not want to be *told* they have to shift their way of thinking about writing, teaching, or learning. The advantage of being a writing center director, therefore, is that the focus of discussion with faculty members can be the student, even while the object of the discussion may be to change teacher pedagogy or philosophy. WAC directors maintain the same focus and objective in faculty conversations since WAC proponents likewise want to have an effect on teaching practices. On the forefront of effecting pedagogical change by promoting reflective practice among faculty, WAC and writing centers can use their discussions with faculty and their work in partnerships to stimulate curricular change.

The blurring of disciplinary boundaries, now a common topic of discussion in academe, has some roots in WAC and writing centers even as such centers acknowledge disciplinary contexts. This dual perspective again puts writing centers both at the edge of educational reform and in paradoxical conflict with the tradition of "disciplinarity." Conflict 1: The most difficult concept for faculty and students to understand is that writing is not a matter of correct surface features, but a product of a disciplinary culture; nonetheless, at many points disciplines need to speak to each other and to the larger community through accepted conventions that demand interdisciplinary surface correctness. Conflict 2: If WAC and writing centers recognize discipline-specific proficiency, they risk alienating the very discipline from which they evolved (English); yet if they align themselves too closely with English departments, they risk being seen as an arm of composition programs—a remedial lab for those who need emergency treatment. Conflict 3: If a WAC program or writing center is connected to a "home" English department, it risks aligning it-self with the position that writing should be taught discretely, that it is only the purview of those who overtly teach language, and that other areas or disciplines have no obligation to do so. If it is not connected to any department, a WAC program or writing center may be perceived as lacking disciplinary scholarship— the currency of the academy. Working together despite these conflicts, WAC programs and writing centers can serve as models for ways in which education might structure itself as a *knowledge-building community*, responding to blurred concepts of disciplinarity and conflicting political and social agendas in a fluid culture.

In efforts to establish learning communities, WAC program and writing center directors use many forms of engagement, but workshops have been their primary venue. In the late 1980s, writing centers reported a variety of ways in which they were called on or sought to interact with faculty: books such as Fulwiler and Young's *Programs That Work*, Kinkead and Harris's *Writing Centers in Context*, Fulwiler's *Teaching with Writing*, a handbook of faculty development workshops, or Web sites like that of the Citadel (http://www.citadel.edu/citadel/otherserv/wctr/index.html), serve as examples of faculty outreach through such means.

In addition to workshops, some directors facilitate monthly talks during which a faculty member discusses the writing done in class. In tandem, WAC programs and writing centers may host writing groups made up of faculty across the disciplines who are working on their own articles, grant proposals, or textbooks. These collaborations can prove rich sources for modeling how to respond to writing, for learning that writing is a complex activity, and for discovering that faculty do write differently in other disciplines—and that maybe students need that explained to them. Such public activities build a culture of writing and a community of writers while providing supportive resources.

Community building also occurs through daily conversations between WAC or writing center directors and their colleagues. The Department of Electrical and Computer Engineering in the College of Engineering at the University of South Carolina began understanding writing in that discipline when center staff engaged in corridor conversations, and when Kristin Walker interviewed faculty about their writing and cultural practices as engineers. Conversations in offices, during lunch, and in corridors are as effective as formal workshops because faculty feel less threatened about asking questions and less reluctant to seek advice in this private forum. WAC seminars and writing centers, with their lively atmospheres, serve as spaces where faculty feel comfortable enough to discuss the one activity that previously had no forum: their teaching.

The practice of working with faculty in these ways arises from conversation pedagogy essential to writing centers (see Farrell-Childers). When students from a class have a particularly rough time figuring out or responding to an assignment, writing center staff typically contact the faculty member, explain that many of his or her students are running into difficulty, and ask how best they can work to support the faculty member's goals. These conversations are rich teachable moments for both sides; writing centers learn more about the discipline and that individual faculty member's style of teaching and assumptions about learning, while faculty members learn more about the writing center, disciplinary writing, and their own discipline's way of communicating (something many of them have not considered before). Phone or e-mail conversations also lead to collecting faculty syllabi, writing guidelines, and assignments for files or Web pages; they lead to invitations to faculty to speak to tutors at monthly inservices about their expectations, assumptions, assignments, and disciplines. In *The Writing Center Resource Manual*, Joe Law outlines these and other general faculty development initiatives common to both WAC and writing centers, and Barnett and Blumner's *Writing Centers and Writing Across the Curriculum Programs* offers a menu of initiatives that help draw together student and faculty constructions of each other and of education.

Tutor reports provide another means by which writing centers can educate faculty about WAC and from which WAC directors can learn of faculty needs. The University of Toledo has developed a double-column, process-oriented tutor report, for our own record keeping but also to be sent to instructors if students choose to have us do so (see Figure 8.1). On the left side is a checklist describing where the student was in the writing process (revision, draft, brainstorming, etc.) and what the primary areas of concentration were in the tutorial (organization, conventions of American culture, surface features, etc). On the right side is a blank column where tutors—along with tutees, if they choose—summarize what was worked on during the tutorial. Faculty responses to these reports have been positive: "I never thought about the difficulty Kim might be having with culture, not just language," or "Thanks for the feedback on the students. I see I needed to explain more thoroughly what 'describe' means in music theory!" Using resources like the tutor reports, WAC and writing centers can work together to develop a language by which writing and disciplinarity can be discussed across the disciplines.

Tutor and Technology-Linked Courses

An effective outgrowth of both WAC and writing centers has been the tutor-linked classroom. Margot Soven discusses such linkages in Chapter 9, and many writing center Web sites point out the availability of tutors for writing intensive classes. It is worth noting that this activity provides another link between teaching and learning by creating a collaborative group rooted in the classroom (see Mullin, Reid, Enders, and Baldridge, "Constructing"). Faculty working with a viable writing center have confidence that tutors placed in their classes will enhance not only their students' abilities, but also provide a "teaching mirror" through which they can determine the effectiveness of their instruction, assignment, and feedback. Such an association with faculty provides not only an opportunity for the director to talk about disciplinary writing, but also a nonthreatening co-instructor in the form of a tutor.

For more than a decade, tutor-linked associations have demonstrated that they contribute some of the richest instruction to both faculty and students; they also provide the director of the writing center and WAC with disciplinary insights never gleaned without being in a classroom—something I also do by linking

---

Writing Center Tutor Report

Name of Student: <u>Larry Wolzniak</u>　　　# *Visits this semester:* <u>2</u>

Tutor: <u>Mullin</u>　　　　　Date: <u>Sept.9</u>　　Time: <u>60 min</u>

Instructor and Department: <u>M. Perri, Educational Foundations</u>

Type of Writing Assignment: <u>Report</u>

Intended Audience:＿＿＿＿＿＿＿＿＿＿＿＿ Unspecified: <u>x</u>

Did the student have an assignment sheet? <u>Yes</u>

Writer is at what stage of the writing process?

＿＿ Prewriting
＿＿ ▶Reading/thinking/talking about topic
＿＿ ▶Researching
＿＿ ▶Exploratory writing
＿＿ ▶Outlining
_x_ Rough draft
＿＿ Revising
＿＿ Editing
＿＿ Final draft
＿＿ Rewriting previously turned-in paper

Writer needed assistance with *content*:
＿＿ Understanding the subject matter
＿＿ Determining a main idea (thesis) for the paper
＿＿ Using logic
＿＿ Developing ideas through explanations and examples
＿＿ Adopting appropriate tone and diction for the situation, purpose, audience

Writer needed assistance with *organization* or *format*:
＿＿ Organizing information in a way that is easy to follow and makes sense
＿＿ Arranging information into introduction, body and conclusion
_x_ Following the specific format required

Writer needed assistance with *grammar* or *mechanics*:
＿＿ Using correct punctuation
＿＿ Understanding subject-verb agreement
＿＿ Eliminating fragments, run-on sentences
＿＿ Using correct spelling

This <u>international student</u> needed assistance:
＿＿ Finding adequate vocabulary to express ideas
＿＿ Using appropriate articles, prepositions, verb endings
＿＿ Understanding American cultural conventions

Comments:
Larry had written a draft for his education course, but found he wasn't sure what went into an abstract that was required. We looked at some models in the writing center, and he began constructing his own.

　As we read through his paper to find major concepts for his abstract, I noticed some awkward syntax. It turned out that English is Larry's second language—that Polish is still spoken at home. We talked a bit about second language/first language translation, and how Polish differs from English, centering on verb constructions that he used. We both constructed a way for him to think about editing those areas where he "forgets his English."

　Larry continued through his paper, rewriting phrases, choosing main ideas for his abstract, and smoothing out transitions which changed as a result of his revision. He made an appointment to return with his final draft in two days.

UT Writing Center - White Hall, Lower Level - Ext. #4939

FIGURE **8.1.** *Sample tutor report.*

myself to classes. As a colleague engaged in teaching with another, I have the opportunity of suggesting not only teaching practices, but also research practices which lead to discipline-specific, classroom-based inquiries that join my writing center expertise and perspectives on language with a faculty member's knowledge of content and convention (see Mullin, Holiday-Goodman, Lively, and Nemire, "Development"; Mullin and Hill; Putney; Stoecker, Mullin, Schmidbauer, and Young). In such associations, faculty members gain insights on the hidden agendas or tacit assumptions lodged in their discipline and therefore their teaching practices—as do I. These insights, passed along to writing center tutors, benefit the students they work with across the curriculum.

With the advent of technology in the classroom, faculty struggle to add a new expertise to their disciplinary repertoire, one based on technological knowledge making (see Reiss and Young, Chapter 3, this volume). The addition of a WAC/writing center perspective can help faculty focus on how this new writing tool, the computer, changes the way information may be presented, processed, and communicated. Online activities (ranging from tutor-linked electronic classrooms, to presentations about network researching, to the e-mailing of tutor reports and working with student papers online) affect the ways students use language and how they measure its validity. Partnering of WAC and writing centers helps faculty discover how the technological classroom has immense repercussions on discipline-specific knowledge making.

OWLs (Online Writing Labs) offer the academy and outside community many forms of support. One of the best known OWLs is Purdue University's at http://owl.english.purdue.edu; however, the National Writing Centers Association homepage (http://nwca.syr.edu) lists nearly three hundred sites that offer many uses of this new medium. In every case, the connection between instructor, student, and WAC and writing centers provides generative feedback through continual reflective assessment about the learning process; in every case, language is being renegotiated, and faculty, students, and center are responding to immediate contextual needs.

Assessment

One of the most difficult problems any WAC director faces is "proving" to faculty that the pedagogies promoted do indeed improve learning and communicating (see Condon, Chapter 2, this volume). While more evidence has accumulated over the last few years (e.g., Walvoord and McCarthy; Mullin, Holiday-Goodman, Lively, and Nemire, "Development"; Russell), there is still more to be learned. Writing centers can be of help with WAC assessment efforts. Directors of WAC programs may not get to see the range of writing processes and products demanded within the disciplines or within a particular discipline the way a writing center director often does. Even in the inexperience of our first year, tutors at my institution immediately saw the discrepancies between what faculty thought they were doing in the classroom and through their assignments and how students interpreted those activities. Writing centers often target this gap between theory and theory in practice.

While writing centers can serve as the locus for gathering student portfolios for formative and summative assessment projects, they also can stimulate more effective assessment practices within the classroom. Students often perform for their teachers; they answer assignments as they think they should be answered (see Bartholomae), fail to ask questions for fear of appearing "stupid," or don't realize they don't understand an assignment or course content until they have to write about it—often the day before the assignment is due. Close alignment of writing center observations with classroom practices can provide ongoing assessment that forestalls the continuation of lore about student abilities (e.g., "The material is difficult, that's why only a few students understand it"; "Students just don't know how to write").

Tutor-linked classes, calls to faculty about the difficulty students are having with an assignment, the ability to "arm" students with questions they are not afraid to take back to instructors: these are all writing center strategies that can fold into assessment. They are uniquely available in tutorial situations where the absence of performance evaluation allows the student the freedom to make errors—to learn in a way that is not always possible in the classroom. Unless this information is communicated to faculty members (through tutorial reports, phone, or e-mail), however, teachers may have no way of knowing whether their writing assignments are clearly stated, whether their students are engaging in critical thinking or in outguessing the instructor, or whether their WAC objectives are being met. Web sites, such as the University of Missouri's, demonstrate the kind of assessment through feedback necessary to maintain the writing center-WAC loop (see http://cwp.missouri.edu).

Of course, the advantage to the writing center of working with faculty across the disciplines is that directors can draw on the measurement expertise of these disciplines. A sociologist might choose to help construct a case study of a WAC classroom participant; a political scientist might construct a quantitative study of her WAC practices and those students who use the writing center; a pharmacist might measure, by means of pre- and post-tests, the power of WAC strategies to help students learn scientific content as well as to convey scientific information to patients and customers. Because a WAC or writing center director might not necessarily construct an assessment that is disciplinarily precise, and because the writing center is a rich source of teacher-researchers, there exists in the association of WAC and writing centers new and extensive possibilities for assessment and research, both short term (classroom) and long term (curricular).

Local and national cross-curricular work (e.g., Berkenkotter and Huckin; Connolly and Vilardi; Young and Fulwiler) has been used to inform writing center pedagogies and their follow-up assessments for the disciplines. All of these help complete the teaching-learning circle necessary to viable, active, and ever-changing pedagogies. The research and practice also provide a means of extending WAC beyond the university walls.

Community Connections

Writing centers might have more opportunities to interact with the community in various ways than WAC programs (though many high school WAC programs have evolved on their own).

Farrell-Childers, Gere, and Young's *Programs and Practices* describes how high school writing centers have been instrumental in starting WAC programs (some by linking to university programs). College, university, and secondary writing centers also may serve as community literacy centers, help not-for-profit organizations with grants, run workshops for businesses, or start writing centers in high schools or grade schools. This last project stems from a belief that promotion of WAC at early levels of education ensures less "remedial" work at the university level. In addition, by educating parents through work in the schools, writing centers also touch the business, industrial, and service communities in which parents work—and vote.

The educational community has realized rather belatedly that self-promotion has been needed for the last fifty years. Now it is difficult to gain the ear of the community and legislature with our theories and practices—unless we have sound assessment data and a cadre of people within those areas who can speak for and with us. Often schooled in an environment of skill-and-drill, with competition instead of collaboration as the motivator, many of those who make laws and fund schools can and must be drawn into the learning communities established by WAC and writing centers. This proves especially true as the programs become more actively involved in the service learning initiatives being promoted around the country.

Perhaps one of the best examples of successful service learning that grows out of a WAC-writing center is the Write for Your Life initiative of Project CONNECTS at Michigan State University. In this program, undergraduate and graduate students, faculty, and teaching consultants from across the curriculum work with schoolchildren. Based on the research of Deborah Protherow-Sith, dean of the Harvard University School of Public Health, the project rests on the "observation that students learn more easily and better when they undertake new study in terms of the images and experiences they bring to it from their home communities" (Stock and Swenson 154). Responding to students' personal narratives, the university consultants work to develop with the writers a topic "of inquiry, subtopics, if you will, of the broader course of study in which they are engaged, a course that might itself be named 'American Adolescents: Challenges to Their Health and Well-Being'" (154). Such service learning projects demonstrate vital ways writing centers can collaborate with the community to promote WAC objectives.

The Bottom Line

Finally, there comes the bottom line, the administrative and budgetary reason for linking WAC and writing centers: public relations. While this subject is closely tied to issues of assessment and to the need to explain ourselves to the larger community (as well as to our own), it also closely affects the changing landscape of education and the places where our combined knowledge about writing and thinking can be enacted. Through joint efforts in assessment, for example, writing centers and WAC programs can provide recruitment offices with the promotional tools they need to demonstrate that the university does care about the real-world abilities with which students should graduate. Admission efforts that involve highlighting both WAC and writing centers can also help to change assumptions about the inability of academe to prepare students for the world, which in turn have negatively affected our ability to construct curricula and programs which create reflective, critical thinkers and writers.

Likewise, combined efforts to provide assessment demonstrate that our practices—and the theories which back them—retain students in the institution by engaging, motivating, and stimulating learning. We know that the one-on-one interaction of writing centers and the student-focused classroom provided by WAC programs change the teaching and learning culture. (We also need to be sensitive to the language with which our institutions recognize the value of what we do—*retention* is one, but only one, buzzword that brings automatic, positive support.)

Twenty-five current and former presidents of state and land-grant institutions summarized best how we need to prepare our students for the new millennium; they called for "seven action commitments that"

- ◆ revitalize partnerships with (K–12) schools

- ◆ reinforce commitment to undergraduate instruction

- ◆ address the academic and personal development of students

- ◆ strengthen the link between education and career

- ◆ strive for the highest quality educational experience for students while keeping college affordable and accessible

- ◆ clearly define educational objectives to the public

- ◆ provide experiential learning environments for students (Kellogg 22–23)

If this is an accurate description of the future, then WAC and writing centers have laid the ground for all these initiatives (see Stock). We

- ◆ already reach out to schools

- ◆ have revitalized the undergraduate curriculum

- ◆ address student and faculty development holistically

- ◆ create links outside academe with real-world writing practices and service learning

- ◆ help make college educationally accessible by improving teaching and learning

- ◆ stress clear assessment strategies through clearly stated objectives in assignments

- ◆ participate in discovery learning practices—part of many WAC and writing center initiatives linked to real-world writing

The same opportunity that WAC and writing centers offers students and faculty is offered to the surrounding communities: education in how we have come to understand the linked processes of writing and thinking within contexts. In working to further these linked processes, WAC and writing centers can partner to respond to shifting contexts and serve as a source for effecting needed changes in the new millennium.

Works Cited

Barnett, Robert, and Jacob Blumner, eds. *Writing Centers and Writing Across the Curriculum Programs: Building Interdisciplinary Partnerships*. Westport, CT: Greenwood, 1999.

Bartholomae, David. "Inventing the University." *When a Writer Can't Write: Studies in Writer's Block and Other Composing Process Problems*. Ed. Mike Rose. New York: Guilford, 1985. 134–65.

Berkenkotter, Carol, and Thomas N. Huckin. *Genre Knowledge in Disciplinary Communication: Cognition/Culture /Power*. Hillsdale, NJ: Erlbaum, 1995.

Carino, Peter. "Early Writing Centers: Toward a History." *The Writing Center Journal* 15.2 (Spring 1995): 103–15.

——. "Open Admissions and the Construction of Writing Center History." *Writing Center Journal* 17.1 (Fall 1996): 30–48.

Clark, Burton R. *The Distinctive College: Antioch, Reed & Swarthmore*. Chicago: Aldine, 1970.

Connolly, Paul, and Teresa Vilardi, eds. *Writing to Learn in Mathematics and Science*. New York: Teachers College P, 1989.

Faigley, Lester. "Writing Centers in Times of Whitewater." *Writing Center Journal* 19.1 (1998): 7–18.

Farrell-Childers, Pamela. "A Unique Learning Environment." *Intersections: Theory–Practice in the Writing Center.* Ed. Joan Mullin and Ray Wallace. Urbana, IL: NCTE, 1994. 111–19

Farrell-Childers, Pamela, Ann Ruggles Gere, and Art Young, eds. *Programs and Practices: Writing Across the Secondary School Curriculum*. Portsmouth, NH: Boynton/Cook, 1994.

Fulwiler, Toby. *Teaching with Writing: An Interdisciplinary Workshop Approach*. Portsmouth, NH: Boynton/Cook, 1987.

Fulwiler, Toby, and Art Young, eds. *Programs That Work: Models and Methods for Writing Across the Curriculum*. Portsmouth, NH: Boynton/Cook, 1990.

Harris, Muriel. "A Writing Center without a WAC Program: The De Facto WAC Center/Writing Center." *Writing Centers and Writing Aross the Curriculum Programs*. Ed. Robert Barnett and Jacob Blummer. Westport, CT: Greenwood, 1999.

Hawthorne, Joan. E-mail to the author. 27 June 1999.

Jones, Barbara. *Bennington College: The Development of an Educational Idea*. New York: Harper, 1946.

Kellogg Commission on the Future of State and Land-Grant Universities. *Returning to Our Roots: The Student Experience*. Washington DC: National Association of State Universities and Land-Grant Colleges, 1997.

Kinkead, Joyce, and Jeanette Harris, eds. *Writing Centers in Context: Twelve Case Studies*. Urbana, IL: NCTE, 1993.

Law, Joe. "Serving Faculty and Writing Across the Curriculum." *The Writing Center Resource Manual*. Ed. Bobbie Silk. Emmitsburg, MD: NWCA, 1998. IV.4.

Mullin, Joan, and Bill Hill. "The Role of Continual Assessment in the Process of Learning: Formative Evaluation in a History Class." *Clearing House* 71.2 (1997): 88–92.

Mullin, Joan A., Monica Holiday-Goodman, Buford T. Lively, and Ruth Nemire. "Development of a Teaching Module on Written and Verbal Communication Skills." *American Journal of Pharmaceutical Education* 58 (1994): 257–62.

Mullin, Joan A., Neil Reid, Doug Enders, and Jason Baldridge. "Constructing Each Other: Collaborating Across Disciplines and Roles." *Weaving Knowledge Together: Writing Centers and Collaboration*. Ed. Carol Peterson Haviland, Maria Notarangelo, Lene Whitley-Putz, and Thia Wolf. Emmitsburg, MD: NWCA, 1998.

Putney, Richard H. "The Civil War and Its Monuments: Visualizing the Past." *Articulating: Teaching Writing in a Visual Culture*. Ed. Joan Mullin, Eric Hobson, and Pamela Childers. Portsmouth, NH: Boynton/Cook-Heinemann, 1998.

Redford, Grant H. "The Army Air Force English Program and the Schools of Tomorrow." *College English* 5 (1944): 276–80.

Russell, David. *Writing in the Academic Disciplines, 1870–1990: A Curricular History*. Carbondale: Southern Illinois UP, 1991.

Stock, Patricia Lambert. "Reforming Education in the Land-Grant University: Contributions from a Writing Center." *Writing Center Journal* 18.1 (1997): 7–29

Stock, Patricia Lambert, and Janet Swenson. "The Write for Your Life Project: Learning to Serve by Serving to Learn." *Writing the Com-*

munity: Concepts and Models for Service-Learning in Composition. Ed. Linda Adler-Kassner, Robert Crooks, and Ann Watters. Washington DC/Urbana, IL: AAHE/NCTE, 1997. 153–66.

Stoecker, Randy, Joan Mullin, Mary Schmidbauer, and Michelle Young. "Integrating Writing and the Teaching Assistant to Enhance Critical Pedagogy." *Teaching Sociology* 21 (1993): 332–40.

Walker, Kristin "The Debate over Generalist and Specialist Tutors: Genre Theory's Contribution." *Writing Center Journal* 18.2 (1998): 27–46.

Walvoord, Barbara F., and Lucille P. McCarthy. *Thinking and Writing in College: A Naturalistic Study of Students in Four Disciplines*. Urbana, IL: NCTE, 1990.

Weigle, Frederick H. "Teaching English in an Army Air Force College Training Program." *College English* 5 (1944): 271–75.

Wykoff, George S. "Army English Experiences Applicable to Civilian Postwar English." *College English* 6 (1945): 338–42.

Young, Art, and Toby Fulwiler, eds. *Writing Across the Disciplines: Research into Practice*. Portsmouth, NH: Boynton/Cook, 1986.

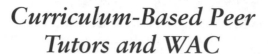

Curriculum-Based Peer Tutors and WAC

MARGOT SOVEN
La Salle University

At the dawn of the new millennium, writing across the curriculum (WAC) is undergoing a transformation. The faculty workshop that used to be the mainstay of WAC no longer exists at many institutions with established programs or even at schools about to start WAC programs. In the first group of schools, faculty have already attended at least one workshop and perhaps also participated in follow-up meetings. These instructors are familiar with the basic principles of WAC, such as using writing as a teaching tool and encouraging students to engage in all phases of the writing process, but they often need additional support to implement these ideas. And schools with new WAC programs that are trying to introduce WAC concepts and strategies often lack the funding for faculty workshops.

Enter peer tutoring as the new mainstay of many WAC programs. In the early days of WAC, peer tutoring was often regarded as a support service and was confined to the writing center. As a consultant evaluator for the Council of Writing Program Administrators, when invited by a school to evaluate its WAC program I would routinely ask, "Do you have a writing center?" I wanted to be sure that students who could not get sufficient help from their instructors—because their instructors lacked either the expertise to deal with common writing problems, especially at the sentence level, or the time to meet with students after class—had a place to go. In those days, it was the peer tutor's job to supplement classroom instruction in writing and to meet with weak writers who required a great deal of assistance.

But times have changed, as Joan Mullin points out in Chapter 8, "Writing Centers and WAC." The writing center plays an increasingly important role in the WAC program. The peer tutors who often staff writing centers not only help students with generic writing problems, but they also help them learn the rhetorical and stylistic features of writing in different disciplines. Increasingly, faculty come to the writing center for workshops and informal conversations about writing.

But the most dramatic change in the role of the peer tutor vis-à-vis WAC is the emergence of curriculum-based peer tutoring programs. Joan Mullin describes the courses in these programs as "tutor-linked courses." In this chapter, I demonstrate how the development of these programs coincided with the evolution of the WAC movement. I point out how the role of the course-linked peer tutor differs from the role of the writing center peer tutor, and how ongoing controversies related to peer tutoring also affect curriculum-based peer tutoring programs, from here on referred to as CBPT programs. The chapter concludes with some practical information about choosing, training, rewarding, and supervising peer tutors in CBPT programs and a brief discussion about evaluating such programs.

Many CBPT programs are the descendants of the Brown University Writing Fellows Program, although Brown was not the first school to assign undergraduate writing tutors to courses. Harriet Sheridan pioneered the idea of linking peer tutoring to WAC programs at Carleton College and then helped to establish a similar program at Brown. The credit, however, goes to Tori Haring-Smith of the English department at Brown University for popularizing curriculum-based peer tutoring. Once Haring-Smith got the Brown program started in the early 1980s, with Sheridan's assistance, she invited faculty and tutors from other schools to peer tutoring workshops and conferences at Brown. Those of us who participated marveled at the enthusiasm of both Brown faculty and students for this new program. Although Haring-Smith had initiated CBPT to develop a WAC program at a research university where faculty did not relish the idea of attending WAC workshops, other schools (such as La Salle University) that already had WAC programs saw the potential of CBPT as an invigorating agent in existing WAC programs.

The eight objectives of the Writing Fellows Program at Brown University are similar to the principles and practices endorsed by most WAC programs:

To demonstrate that all faculty and students share responsibility for writing.

To explore ways in which writing and learning are connected.

To change both student and faculty attitudes towards writing.

To make writing an integral part of the curriculum, not a feature of isolated courses.

To encourage students to practice good writing habits, including revision.

To involve all students, not just weak writers.

To reward faculty for their attention to student writing.

To provide students with feedback for revision before their writing is judged and graded. (Haring-Smith 177).

It was clear to those of us who directed WAC programs that by placing peer tutors in the classroom we could give faculty members a "WAC buddy." Tutors would become our emissaries, our intermediaries, with the special strengths that only peer tutors can bring to the table. Those of us who started CBPT programs have not been disappointed. Karen Vaught-Alexander at the University of Portland, in her response to an e-mail survey I conducted in 1997, calls her course-linked tutors "'gentle subversives' who have created more change in the departments than any faculty workshop on clear writing assignments." Barbara Sylvester at Western Washington University says, "My Dean of General Education/Honors mentioned the other day that when he visits other departments they are often holding discussions about writing. He said that ten years ago writing was not a topic of conversation on campus." Deidre Paulsen describes writing fellows as "unintimidating catalysts for discussion about writing at all levels because they are a safe sounding board for professors; they clarify writing for students entering majors through their workshops; they help students clarify their thinking through their mentoring, and in the process of translating for everyone else, their own writing improves." She goes on to say,

> They have caused whole departments (from engineering to religion) to sit down to ponder appropriate assignments and sometimes ask help drafting them. Whereas once we brought in WAC consultants (and I wish we still could), today we recognize that over the long haul, Writing Fellows are there for the entire semester or longer to support a faculty member as she experiments with various kinds of write to learn as well as transactional assignments. (Soven, "Writing")

It is interesting to note that as early as 1904 there are accounts of the success of one-on-one classroom writing instruction, at that time called the "laboratory approach." Teachers, not peer tutors, were working one on one with students, but from the beginning they were advised to behave like peers. In an essay by an instructor on the subject of the lab approach, he reports with obvious satisfaction that one of his students said, "You aren't the dignified teacher I used to think you were. You seemed like one of the boys, and I have learned to like English in laboratory work." The value of an approach to CBPT in which the teacher was less authoritarian was beginning to be recognized (Carino 104)

One-on-one classroom instruction had more in common with CBPT than with writing center tutoring programs. Most important, its goal was not remedial. All students had the opportunity for lab instruction when teachers reviewed their papers at different stages during the writing process. Writing centers began with a similar agenda, but rapidly became places for remediation in order to accommodate the needs of underprepared students, especially during the influx of college students after World War II and during open enrollment in the 1960s (see Mullin, Chapter 8, this volume).

In "The Politics of Peer Tutoring," one of the first essays to appear on CBPT, Kail and Trimbur point out that originally CBPT programs were attached to the first-year composition program, the curriculum-based model providing a required lab component in writing courses. Students worked one on one with a peer tutor as part of their course work. Some schools still reserve classroom tutors for courses in the writing program. At the City College of New York, for example, tutors from the campus writing center are each attached to a section of composition (Soliday). In the last fifteen years, however, CBPT programs not only expanded to other disciplines as WAC programs grew, but some also incorporated activities beyond reading drafts and conferencing. For example, peer tutors often coordinate with the course instructor to provide in-class tutoring. At La Salle University, course-linked tutors, called writing fellows, are occasionally asked to conduct discussions about or give classroom presentations on common errors. In any case, in the curriculum-based model, peer tutors are written into the plan of instruction. They are part of the course, which gives them a distinctly different role than that of the writing center tutor.

The Brown University workshops led to the establishment of CBPT at a diverse group of schools. Large state institutions (e.g., Western Washington State University, Illinois State University), Ivy League institutions (e.g., the University of Pennsylvania, Barnard University), and liberal arts colleges (e.g., Swarthmore College, Lafayette College) began to recruit faculty and students for their own CBPT programs.

In a survey I conducted in 1993, I found that the largest number of responding curriculum-based peer tutoring programs conform to the Brown model (Soven, "Curriculum-Based"). At these schools, tutors are selected from all fields. They receive training and are assigned to courses in a variety of disciplines where they read the drafts of all the students in the course, the theory being that all students, not just the weak writers, can benefit from draft review. This is also a major tenet of WAC programs, strongly endorsed by modern composition theory and research. In many programs, tutors give both written and oral feedback, usually meeting with their students after having read the drafts. The tutee is free to accept or reject the tutor's comments. Some schools assign peer tutors to special projects rather than to courses. At Seattle University, for example, course-linked tutors work with students in the School of Engineering on special projects. At La Salle University, the Biology department assigns tutors to the senior writing project. In all cases, whether they are assigned to courses or department projects, course-linked tutors reinforce the idea that revision is an integral part of writing in all courses.

CBPT and the Peer Tutoring Controversy

As CBPT becomes more popular, old controversies about peer tutoring have resurfaced, along with new questions specific to CBPT programs and the role of the peer tutor in the context of WAC. Perhaps because in CBPT programs the tutor is built into the plan of instruction, these questions have assumed even greater importance than in the past, when most peer tutors were assigned to writing centers. Both instructors and students can ignore the peer tutor in the writing center, an impossibility with the course-linked tutor. Typically she has been assigned to a course for the semester at the request of the instructor. It is understood that the tutor will work with *all of the students* in the course that semester. Karen Vaught-Alexander at the University of Portland tells her course-linked tutors to think of themselves as part of a team involving the client, the tutor, and the faculty. The coordinator of the CBPT program is also a part of that team. At the beginning of the academic year, I tell the writing fellows at La Salle University and their sponsoring instructors, "We are all in this together. Therefore, only by working together can we make this program a success."

The close working relationship between the teacher, the student, and the peer tutor forces us to revisit the questions underlying all controversies about peer tutoring: What is the appropriate role of the peer tutor in relation to the teacher and the students? How does the tutor's role differ from the instructor's role? What kind of help and how much help should tutors provide for students? Mary Soliday, in her essay "Shifting Roles in Classroom Tutoring," notes that in the early stages of an experimental program involving course-linked tutors, "students, teachers, and tutors alike had trouble 'placing' the tutor within a classroom's hierarchy and defining the tutor's role" (59). Theorists and researchers who study peer tutoring, and instructors who work closely with peer tutors, continue to grapple with this issue. Many peer tutoring theorists (e.g., Bruffee; Goodlad and Hirst) believe that the tutor's strength resides in his special peer relationship with the students. In their view, to maintain that relationship the peer tutor must disassociate himself from the instructor and be "non-judgmental and non-directive" as opposed to the teacher who is "directive and evaluative" (see Raines). Raines argues, however, that this is a false dichotomy and recommends that conversation about this issue be conducted as a dialectical exchange between the two positions. Raines says that during the last fifteen years we have learned that both the tutor and the instructor learn from one another. Sometimes the tutor may need to be more directive and judgmental, depending on the student, and frequently the instructor may need to assimilate into her teaching style the less directive and less judgmental strategies of the peer tutor.

Some teachers, however, cannot see the role identification issue in any but dualistic terms. They are apprehensive about sharing their authority with peer tutors and experience difficulty working with a tutor who is more directive. In the CUNY program described by Soliday, in which tutors were present in the classroom, teachers found it difficult to share their authority with another person and were concerned about the tutor's criticism of their performance. At La Salle University, instructors who find it impossible to relinquish authority to peer tutors usually withdraw from the program after a semester. This happens rarely because most of the instructors who request a writing fellow have been participants in our Writing-Across-the-Curriculum workshop and they have, or have "converted" to, theories about teaching revision that emphasize the value of peer review.

Some instructors would like the peer tutor to behave as a faculty clone, an understudy who fills in for the absentee teacher when writing comments on student drafts and conducting conferences. For these instructors, the most effective tutor is the tutor who is a good reporter—that is, he reports the instructor's messages to the students. In this case, the tutor's authority to respond to the student's paper as a peer is seriously undermined.

These issues of authority are symptomatic of how many instructors think about learning. Teachers who believe that learning is based on instructional delivery have a hard time relinquishing authority. But those teachers who have been exposed to social constructivist theories of learning, which emphasize the importance of collaborative learning and conversation, are more apt to view the tutor as a valuable link in the learning process. These teachers often use some form of collaborative learning, such as small-group discussion, in their classrooms.

The main question when evaluating the success of any peer tutoring program is, Which tutoring approach "better delivers the knowledge it takes to learn to write well?" (Kail and Trimbur 7). When we ask that question in the context of the goals of writing across the curriculum, we use as criteria for the program's success more than the quality of the completed paper. We are also interested in knowing whether the students being tutored have increased their competency in several areas: their understanding of the writing process, the ability to use writing as a learning tool, knowledge of the rhetorical conventions of academic discourse in a variety of disciplines, and the acquisition of a vocabulary for talking about writing. We continue to debate which role is most effective for the tutor to adopt to help students acquire these competencies and how to help tutors develop this role.

When WAC and CBPT are related, the issue that receives the most attention is the effectiveness of the generalist versus the specialist peer tutor. In "Look Back and Say 'So What': The Limitations of the Generalist Tutor," Kiedaisch and Dinitz argue for the benefits of tutors who know the subject matter of the discipline in which they are tutoring writing. After videotaping twelve tutoring sessions, they concluded that only those tutors familiar with the discipline in which the student was writing could ask questions that would improve the quality of the analysis in a paper, though knowledge of the discipline did not always guarantee that the tutor could help a student achieve this goal. The tutors' general knowledge about academic writing did not help students writing literature papers move beyond plot summary. The students who were being tutored never arrived at a "controlling insight" for their papers, and their ideas seemed randomly ordered, although each idea was well developed. Furthermore, some tutors had difficulty applying the general tutoring strategies they had learned when working with unfamiliar discipline-specific assignments. Despite these drawbacks, however, students who worked with generalist tutors still rated their sessions with the tutor very positively. Kiedaisch and Dinitz say,

> We know we can't reach conclusions based on this small number of cases, but in the sessions we looked at, the tutor's knowledge of how to think and write in a discipline did seem important. Good tutoring strategies were not enough. All these tutors were trained to address global before local concerns, to use questioning to draw out students' ideas, and to refrain from appropriating the student's paper. All of them had had numerous tutoring sessions with students in introductory writing courses in which they had successfully demonstrated these strategies. But David, Michelle, and Jill [peer tutors in the study] seemed unable to apply [these strategies] when working with students on assignments other than [those in] their own [major]. (72)

Not at all discouraged by their findings, Kiedaisch and Dinitz draw three conclusions, which directors of CBPT programs should take to heart:

1. We feel if students are satisfied and motivated they have benefited. A session that is less than it can be is not a bad session

2. In many cases assignments do not require a knowledgeable tutor, especially assignments in introductory courses.

3. Even when tutors cannot help students master the thinking patterns or rhetorical patterns of writing in a discipline, they can help instructors teach them these skills by explaining to the faculty what they have learned about student difficulties (73).

Kiedaisch and Dinitz discovered that tutors who are not familiar with disciplinary conventions might still help students learn about the writing process; although these tutors do not always ask all the right questions, they demonstrate that asking questions helps the tutees build audience awareness. Kiedaisch and Dinitz's third finding suggests that in addition to being accepted as peers by their tutees, tutors were also accepted as "authorities" by their sponsoring instructors, especially on matters related to understanding the problems students faced when writing.

The discussion about the effectiveness of the generalist versus the expert peer tutor is further complicated by another consideration—namely, does competency in one area of knowledge hinder the tutor's performance in another area? For example, in Susan Hubbuch's essay "A Tutor Needs to Know the Subject Matter to Help a Student with a Paper: ____Agree ____Disagree ____Not Sure," she argues that a tutor who is knowledgeable about the subject matter being written about is apt to treat writing as a product rather than a process and therefore proceed to try to "fix" the paper. The peer tutor may ask the right questions to help the student improve the content, but in doing so may give the student too much direction, thereby encouraging the kind of passivity which will draw attention away from the process of writing. Hubbuch goes on to say that these expert tutors may persuade students that all rhetorical decisions are either right or wrong rather than explaining to them that some rhetorical decisions are simply better than others in any given communication situation.

While Hubbuch acknowledges some of the benefits associated with tutoring in the major, she believes that the negative effects far outweigh them. Because she believes that passivity is the greatest obstacle to effective writing, Hubbuch argues that the tutor's ability to motivate the tutee to take charge of her own writing is more apt to be compromised by the knowledgeable tutor.

Haring-Smith is one of the strongest supporters of the generalist tutor model. She argues that "only with courses relying heavily on technical vocabulary or foreign language courses must the writing fellows have a particular expertise; the writing fellow in most courses acts as an educated lay reader, who can honestly report when she is confused by what a student is trying unsuccessfully to say" (179). For Haring-Smith, the expert tutor can subvert the goals of peer tutoring. Assigning peer tutors to courses outside their majors became an important part of the Brown credo. Haring-Smith's discussions about peer tutoring emphasize the mission of the peer tutor to promote one of the major objectives of WAC—to use writing as a tool for clarifying what students want to say about the course content, thereby reinforcing the idea that writing is a tool for learning the course content.

Kenneth Bruffee, one of the earliest proponents of collaborative learning in writing instruction, places more emphasis than Haring-Smith on the ability of the peer tutor to teach the conventions of thinking and writing in the disciplines. For Bruffee, however, disciplinary knowledge does not detract from the peer tutor's role as a peer, nor does it interfere with imparting knowledge about writing. The two issues are not connected for Bruffee; he defines a tutor's knowledge of the content and the rhetoric of a discipline in process-oriented terms. When speaking to a group of peer tutors at Brown University in 1993, Bruffee said,

> What you do as a tutor, as I understand it, is to help a tutee cross the boundary between one knowledge community and another. You do that by helping the tutee learn the language of the new community. Knowledge communities, or if you prefer, discourse communities, are groups of people who talk the same way. The boundaries between knowledge communities are defined by the words, turns of phrases, and styles of speaking and writing that communities agree on as they construct the knowledge that is their common property. (3)

Bruffee considers this to be a constructive process. The tutor does not *tell* or *show* the tutee this language but, through conversation, helps the tutee understand these new languages and use them. He says, "My premise here, then, is that the most important expertise you gain in learning to be a peer tutor is the linguistic flexibility required for helping students translate from one language to another—from the languages you and your tutees speak to languages that the faculty speak" (3). In Bruffee's view, conversation is an integral part of the process of learning how to write, and therefore discipline-specific knowledge facilitates learning how to write by increasing the effectiveness of the conversation between tutors and their tutees.

Bruffee's theories about peer tutoring mesh well with WAC theory, which emphasizes the connections between form and content in writing. Many WAC theorists believe language is not separate from content, but *is* content. This is where there is a "disconnect" between WAC theory and the guidelines adopted by many peer tutoring programs, based on the Brown program and WAC theory. In the program at La Salle (described in a later section), I no longer worry about peer tutors commenting on content, but I stress the fine line between enabling students to revise their work and revising their work for them.

Curriculum-Based Programs: Progress and Change

In the early years of curriculum-based peer tutoring programs, most programs followed Brown's approach of assigning tutors to courses outside their major. My 1997 e-mail follow-up survey of some of these programs indicates, however, that these programs have either become more flexible or they have completely abandoned this practice. The program directors I surveyed agree that knowledge in the discipline is an important factor when assigning tutors, but they take into account other variables as well. Western Washington University, Brigham Young University, and La Salle University's approaches are representative of the departure from the Brown model.

Western Washington University

At Western Washington University, writing fellows work with the required 300-level writing proficiency courses. Knowledgeable tutors are assigned to their majors only in science courses. First-year tutors are assigned to courses that best match their particular strengths, which might include knowledge in a discipline but can also mean their writing ability or their interpersonal skills. Experienced writing fellows choose courses that interest them. Barbara Sylvester, the director of this program, reports that "these Fellows have demonstrated for some ten years now effective but different ways to comment on student papers, certainly one factor in the present groundswell to create more systematic and comprehensive approaches to writing for students approaching their major" (Soven, "Writing"). She believes that knowledgeable peer tutors do not necessarily sacrifice the traditional role of the peer tutor. Once they understand their role, the temptation to be overly directive is not as strong.

Brigham Young University

Brigham Young University assigns students to courses in their major. Deidre Paulsen, the director of that program, says,

> I started out following Brown University's dictum—something written well should be clear to any educated lay audience. I'm sure that guide can work at a liberal arts college (except perhaps in philosophy) but we have too many professional programs at BYU for it to work well. After having my WF's become quite intimidated by fellowing in a philosophy 400 course, and in an engineering course, I now ask specialized departments to recommend students in their fields for me to train, so they can be trained to work in that field.

Paulsen, while recognizing the pitfalls in assigning knowledgeable peer tutors to advanced courses, believes that the benefits outweigh the limitations. Although she agrees with Haring-Smith's concern about commenting on course content, she uses Bruffee's terminology to discuss the role of her tutors. According to Paulsen, "my Writing Fellows serve as visiting archeologists to translate various cultures to the students who are confounded by the cultural differences in disciplines" (Soven, "Writing"). Like many coordinators of peer tutoring programs, Paulsen finds some theoretical statements more useful than others for describing her program.

La Salle University

La Salle University assigns tutors to advanced courses in their own field of study, but we often do the same for introductory courses. After thirteen years directing a curriculum-based peer tutoring program, during which time I have trained and supervised more than 250 tutors, I have come to believe that the knowledgeable tutor—that is, the tutor who is familiar with the subject matter of the course—more effectively communicates the various understandings about writing promoted by WAC than the generalist tutor, the tutor who is unacquainted with the course content. In all these years, we have had only one tutor whose knowledge of the subject matter clearly jeopardized his role as a peer tutor. This writing fellow was viewed by the students he tutored as impatient and arrogant. Instead of falling into the typical trap of knowledgeable peer tutors—i.e., giving his students too much help because he saw them as "hopeless"—he tended to be abrupt and condescending. Fortunately, his was an isolated case.

More studies similar to the one by Kiedaisch and Dinitz are needed. Until more systematic research on the effectiveness of the knowledgeable tutor is conducted, however, we must rely on surveys and reports of instructors, students, and the peer tutors themselves. Thirteen years of these internal evaluations at La Salle University indicate that most teachers, tutors, and students believe that the program is more successful with knowledgeable tutors, though they praise the efforts of generalist tutors as well.

The knowledgeable tutor is more necessary in advanced courses than introductory courses, in which the papers assigned are sometimes (but not always) of a more general nature. At La Salle, I usually assign new tutors to introductory courses because assignments are often not discipline specific and the expectations of instructors in different disciplines are similar. For example, the book review is a common assignment in history, philosophy, and religion classes. Most instructors want a brief summary of the text, followed by a critique based on general criteria, such as personal interest and clarity of presentation. Even in these introductory courses, however, the tutor who is tutoring in her major usually outperforms her generalist counterpart.

Sometimes I purposely assign new tutors to introductory courses in their major because they seem apprehensive about their first tutoring assignment. Tutors, like all students learning a new field, go through developmental stages. They often start out with "high hopes and nagging doubts" (Kail and Trimbur 21). Kail and Trimbur note that new tutors are often "insecure about their mastery of rhetoric, style, grammar and usage" (11). To add to these insecurities by assigning some of these tutors to a course in an unfamiliar discipline is not wise, as the following remarks by April White, one of the La Salle University tutors, suggest. In her Semester Review Report, she wrote,

> During the fall semester I worked with Brother Fagan's introductory English course. As an English major, I found myself chal-

lenged by my new responsibilities as a Writing Fellow, not the subject I was tutoring. This semester, now more comfortable with the role of Writing Fellow, I was confronted with a new discipline, education. Although the writing process is similar in both fields, the assignments and therefore my tutoring approach in conferences was very different. Bro. Butler, in his Education 101: The Role of the Teacher course, gave three assignments. In the first, an educational biography, I concentrated mainly on focus and structure issues, because many students wrote a straightforward unanalytical story about their lives from nursery school until now. I also stressed specific grammatical problems that Bro. Butler highlighted for me.

The second assignment was a review of selected journal entries. These journals, often handwritten, detailed students' experiences while observing in classrooms around the city. This assignment, while easier for the students than the first, was a challenge for me. Its style did not lend itself to the Writing Fellows forms I have become accustomed to using. Instead in conferences I focused on grammar errors and discussed observation skills. By asking students about their observations in the classroom, I attempted to improve their ability to translate their experiences into writing.

April's comments indicate that she appreciated being assigned to a course in her major during her first semester as a peer tutor, although she found her placement in a course in education during the second semester more challenging. In both cases, she felt she was helping students improve their writing. She cites what she believes to be an advantage of tutoring in an unfamiliar discipline when she says, "my unfamiliarity with the discipline led to a closer interaction with the professor and a better understanding of the criteria he uses to evaluate papers."

Interestingly, April's comment weakens one of the major arguments of those who favor generalist tutors. They assume that the generalist tutor will be better able to assume the role of an "intelligent peer" than the knowledgeable tutor, who may start playing teacher. But if what April says is true for other tutors—that tutors will seek more guidance from the teacher when they are tutoring outside their discipline—it is possible that generalist tutors will behave more like miniteachers than peer tutors. Her comment also reminds us that for tutoring situations to be positive learning experiences, the tutor as well as the tutee must find the experience satisfying.

After having said I favor assigning tutors to courses in their discipline, however, my experience also demonstrates that tutors with no previous expertise in a field often do convey many of the understandings about writing advocated by WAC without relinquishing their role as a peer. Perhaps we have exaggerated the influence of knowledge in the major as the factor most responsible for shaping the role of the peer tutor and determining his success. Most CBPT programs provide rigorous training that introduces peer tutors to strategies for commenting on students' papers, conducting conferences, and following the conventions of academic discourse in a variety of disciplines. CBPT peer tutors are encouraged to learn "peer tutor talk": to ask questions, to be nonjudgmental, and to be nondirective. They are taught to be sensitive to students' special needs and to give advice about disciplinary conventions only when they are familiar with them. The La Salle University training program also includes a segment on the development of writing ability in college-age students. Training programs remind students of their role as peer tutors and may prevent them from losing sight of this role when they are tutoring students in their discipline or working with faculty who would prefer them to behave as mini-instructors.

Implementing Curriculum-Based Peer Tutoring Programs

Training peer tutors is only one component of implementing a CBPT program. Implementation begins with recruiting both faculty and students for the program. At La Salle, we start both processes simultaneously. Faculty in all disciplines receive an invitation to apply for a writing fellow for the coming semester. In the same letter, I ask them to send me the names of students who have demonstrated good writing skills in their classes. I then write to all of the students who have received a faculty recommendation, urging them to apply to the program. This procedure is effective in motivating students to consider submitting an application. Many students, especially those who are not English majors, assume they do not write sufficiently well to become writing fellows. Knowing that their writing has impressed Prof. X often helps them overcome worries about their qualifications. (See the appendix to this chapter for the faculty and student letters and application form.)

Students who nominate themselves for the program must include the name of a faculty member who will serve as a reference. All applicants then submit to a selection committee two academic papers they have written at La Salle. They also agree to attend an interview during which the selection committee learns the nominee's purpose in wanting to become a writing fellow and attempts to evaluate his interpersonal skills. Brown University involves the current writing fellows in the interview process, and Swarthmore requires the nominee to evaluate a student paper. Other schools with writing fellows programs (e.g., Seattle University, Wesleyan College, and Beaver College) employ some version of this selection process. At La Salle we require that students achieve sophomore standing before they apply to become writing fellows. At some schools, however, such as the University of Pennsylvania, all students are eligible to become writing fellows.

At virtually all schools with CBPT programs, once selected, tutors must participate in some form of training, usually in the form of an academic course, although some schools such as Williams College limit the training to a weeklong workshop. Perhaps because many of these courses are modeled on the course developed at Brown University, they include similar topics such as

> how to write effective comments on student papers and conduct successful conferences, the specific demands of academic writing, and the reasons students have difficulty in meeting these requirements. On the theoretical side, courses emphasize the literature on process approaches to writing, collaborative learning, and the development of writing ability on the college level. (Soven, "Curriculum-Based" 65)

Increasingly, training programs for tutors include a unit of study on diverse student populations such as students with learning disabilities, ESL students, and "thirty something" reentry students.

All training programs give students the opportunity to role-play conferences and evaluate sample papers. At La Salle University, the Writing Fellows course is conducted as a seminar, where, in addition to readings and assignments, students discuss their peer tutoring experiences and faculty give presentations on academic writing in their disciplines. Tutors receive their first tutoring assignment while taking the course, as they do at Brown University and other schools. At some schools such as Swarthmore College, the tutors practice tutoring strategies with one or two students before being assigned to a specific course, which occurs the semester after they have completed their training. Although the amount varies, in most programs the peer tutors receive a stipend for their work as peer tutors in addition to receiving course credit. At La Salle, students are paid $300 a semester for working approximately sixty hours.

During the semester students are taking the course, supervision is relatively easy. At La Salle, our tutoring staff is limited to twenty-five tutors each semester. The new tutors who are taking the course in the fall semester are required to meet with me during each round of tutoring. Together we look at their written comments on several papers and often discuss appropriate tutoring strategies for the writers of these drafts. Those writing fellows who elect to tutor during the year after they complete their training course continue to meet with me each time they receive a new set of papers. In addition, the tutors meet regularly with their sponsoring instructors. At the end of the semester, I encourage the tutors to set up an "exit interview" with their sponsors to review the semester and discuss possible ways to collaborate more effectively in the future. Many tutors work with the same instructor for several semesters. At schools with a large number of tutors, such as Brown and Swarthmore, professional and student assistants help to supervise the tutors.

CBPT programs are communication intensive. Especially since the advent of e-mail, CBPT program coordinators are in constant touch with sponsoring instructors, peer tutors, and the students in writing fellows–assisted courses. (See Reiss and Young,

Chapter 3 in this volume, for more information on WAC and the use of computer technology.) Peer tutors know they can reach me at any time, regardless of the nature of the problem. They may be in a quandary about how to respond to a student paper and need some help. Over the years, I have received several frantic weekend calls from tutors with difficult drafts. Sometimes I am visited by students who cannot find their writing fellows because they forget where to meet them. Often, a faculty sponsor calls because he has lost the peer tutor's e-mail address and phone number! The problems can range from simple to more serious issues, such as the instructor who has postponed deadlines for papers until final exam week, when the peer tutor should not be reading papers.

In addition to on-the-spot supervision, most programs require evaluations from all of the principals in the program—the peer tutors, the faculty sponsors, and the students in peer-assisted courses. I also require the writing fellows to submit a brief report after each round of tutoring, and at midsemester ask faculty to drop me a short note about how things are going. (See the last section of this chapter for more information on evaluation.)

Pitfalls

All programs are subject to pitfalls and CBPT programs are no exception. Tori Haring-Smith lists several problems that may emerge in CBPT programs:

> *Elitism:* Haring-Smith says, "although you want your program to carry a certain amount of prestige, it is important not to let the Writing Fellows become campus celebrities and lose the ability to relate to peers" (184). Tutors need to be constantly reminded of the possible ways their role as peer tutors can be undermined.

> *Tutor Burnout:* Tutors may receive more work than anticipated. At La Salle, faculty send me descriptions of their writing assignments as part of their application for a writing fellow. However, sometimes they change their assignments

or deadlines. The coordinator's first responsibility is tutor protection. I intervene either before or after the fact, but because the tutors know that I am on their side, they rarely become discouraged, even when things do not go as planned.

Program Stagnation: I agree with Haring-Smith that the training program must change to accommodate other changes taking place on campus and in response to new ideas for training. A prerequisite for supervising a CBPT program is flexibility and an adventurous spirit. I rarely say no when asked if the program can be used in a new context, although I never commit the program to a new context on a long-term basis until we have done a pilot. When the faculty in La Salle's graduate program in psychology approached me about assigning tutors to their courses, I responded, "We'll give it a try." The idea of undergraduates tutoring graduate students was a new one for me, but we assigned experienced tutors who were psychology majors to the instructors in the graduate program who had requested the help. Most of the graduate students in their courses, especially the reentry students, were grateful for the assistance.

Our training program has changed in response to recommendations from the peer tutors, what has worked well in the past, my contact with coordinators of other CBPT programs, and new initiatives at the university. When the course was first offered, for example, it included more theoretical readings than it does at present. But students said they wanted more practice and more opportunities to discuss their tutoring experiences in class. They also wanted more discussion on the nature of academic writing. In its newest version, the course requires that students examine academic writing in their major through library research and interviews, in addition to reading articles about academic writing.

Other pitfalls, such as poorly written student drafts or poorly designed assignments by the faculty, come with the territory. Enthusiastic faculty sponsors who understand and support the program can help keep these problems in check. However, the coordinator of a CBPT program must be tolerant of the "less than perfect." Despite the coordinator's best efforts to guide faculty and tutors, many components of these programs are difficult to control. Informal conversations with faculty and peer tutors, rather than drastic action, can go a long way to setting matters straight (Soven, "Curriculum-Based").

Evaluating Curriculum-Based Peer Tutoring Programs

Many CBPT programs rely on written surveys from the student in the classes participating in the program, their instructors, and the peer tutors. At La Salle, I use surveys for the students and faculty but rely on open-ended reports from the tutors. I meet individually with the writing fellows and review the instructors' and tutee's evaluations as well as the writing fellows' own reports. Most coordinators of CBPT programs also compile statistics regarding the number of students served by the program and the number of tutoring sessions, and then write an annual report for the administration. These reports are often crucial for continued funding. At Brigham Young University, good evaluations were responsible for continuing the program. Deidre Paulsen says,

> Although I was certain of my mission (largely defined by Brown University) now others at the university share that vision and that's nice. Whew! It was a lot of proving myself, the program, my kids . . . a pioneering effort . . . but hard work and strong evaluations triumphed, and we are now considered a part of the General Education/Honors program at BYU. (Soven, "Writing")

Many programs also conduct midsemester evaluations. The writing fellows at La Salle submit a midterm report. At the University of Portland, the peer tutor and the tutee write a brief collaborative report about what was covered at the first conference and include plans for future conferences; they then send a copy to the instructor. Portland's approach to evaluation reflects the collaborative approach emphasized in CBPT programs.

Evaluations of CBPT programs tend to rely on self-report rather than an assessment of the writing competencies of students in tutored classes, most likely because of the difficulties involved in attributing improvement in writing performance to a single variable. Furthermore, few coordinators of peer tutoring

programs receive compensation for conducting lengthy evaluations of their programs. At most schools with CBPT programs,
both students and instructors are asked through written surveys
if they believe the program has improved students' understanding of the writing process and has had some effect on the quality
of papers. (See the appendix to this chapter for the La Salle University survey forms). At La Salle, most instructors and students
report that the program has been effective in both areas. Many
instructors at La Salle also report that the writing fellows program has influenced the nature of their assignments.

There are few studies comparing the relative effectiveness of
CBPT programs versus writing center peer tutoring programs and
few studies comparing the writing of students in tutored versus
nontutored classes. Song and Richter, however, compared the
writing competency of students in a remedial program who received both writing center and in-class tutoring to a group of
students who received only writing center assistance. They found
that the students in the first group had a higher pass rate on the
CUNY writing assessment test than the students who received
assistance only from the writing center tutors. In another study
comparing the writing in tutored and nontutored classes, the instructor found that the greatest effect of tutoring came in the
area of "on time performance," though she also observed that
the papers in the tutored class were better written than the papers in the class that did not receive classroom-based tutoring
(Levine 58).

Conclusion

Writing across the curriculum has had incredible staying power
despite the many curriculum revisions and technological innovations that preoccupy institutions of higher education today. Curriculum-based peer tutoring is one of the reasons we can be
optimistic about the future of WAC. Besides the educational benefits, CBPT may be a "must" in today's political climate. As Song
and Richter point out, "Considering the size of today's classes, it
would be very difficult, if not impossible, to achieve the instructional goals of WAC without the help of course linked tutors"

(55). Although most evaluations of these programs are qualitative, the results are promising. Those of us who believe in these programs must continue to experiment with various approaches to curriculum-based peer tutoring and continue to deliberate on the issues that affect them.

Works Cited

Bruffee, Kenneth. "Lost in Translation: Peer Tutors, Faculty Members, and the Art of Boundary Conversation." Tenth Anniversary Peer Tutoring Conference. Brown University. April 1993.

Carino, Peter. "Early Writing Centers: Toward a History." *Writing Center Journal* 15.2 (1995): 103–15.

Goodlad, Sinclair, and Beverly Hirst. *Peer Tutoring: A Guide to Learning by Teaching.* New York: Nichols, 1989.

Haring-Smith, Tori. "Changing Students' Attitudes: Writing Fellows Programs." *Writing Across the Curriculum: A Guide to Developing Programs.* Ed. Susan H. McLeod and Margot Soven. Academic. Writing Landmark Publications in Writing Studies: http://aw. colostate.edu/books/mcleod_soven/ 2000. Originally published in print by Sage (Newbury Park, CA), 1992.

Hubbuch, Susan M. "A Tutor Needs to Know the Subject Matter to Help a Student with a Paper: ____Agree____Disagree____Not Sure." *Writing Center Journal* 8.2 (1988): 23–30.

Kail, Harvey, and John Trimbur. "The Politics of Peer Tutoring." *WPA: Writing Program Administration* 11.1-2 (1987): 5–12.

Kiedaisch, Jean, and Sue Dinitz. "Look Back and Say 'So What': The Limitations of the Generalist Tutor." *Writing Center Journal* 14.1 (1993): 63–74.

Levine, Judith R. "Using a Peer Tutor to Improve Writing in a Psychology Class: One Instructor's Experience." *Teaching of Psychology* 17.1 (1990): 57–58.

Raines, Helon Howell. "Tutoring and Teaching: Continuum, Dichotomy, or Dialectic?" *Writing Center Journal* 14.2 (1994): 150–62.

Soliday, Mary. "Shifting Roles in Classroom Tutoring: Cultivating the Art of Boundary Crossing." *Writing Center Journal* 16.1 (1995): 59–73.

Song, Bailin, and Eva Richter. "Tutoring in the Classroom: A Quantitative Study." *Writing Center Journal* 18.1 (1997): 50–60.

Soven, Margot. "Curriculum-Based Peer Tutoring Programs: A Survey." *WPA: Writing Program Administration* 17.1-2 (1993): 58–74.

———. "Writing Fellows Survey." Unpublished survey materials. November 1997.

White, April. Final Report. Writing Fellows Program. Philadelphia, PA: La Salle University, 1998.

Chapter 9 Appendix

Program Documents

◆ WRITING FELLOWS PROGRAM FACT SHEET

◆ WRITING FELLOWS PROGRAM FACULTY NOMINATIONS

◆ THE WRITING FELLOWS PROGRAM, FALL SEMESTER

◆ LETTER TO POTENTIAL WRITING FELLOW

◆ EVALUATION OF THE LA SALLE UNIVERSITY WRITING FELLOWS PROGRAM

◆ WRITING FELLOWS PROGRAM FACULTY REPORT ON AFFILIATED COURSES

Writing Fellows Program Fact Sheet

What is a Writing Fellow?
A Writing Fellow is a good student writer who is assigned to a
specific course to help students in the course revise drafts of their
assigned papers. Fellows do not grade papers, but through written
comments on the drafts and direct interaction in conferences, help
students during the revision process.

Fellows will work approximately 60 hours per semester and receive a
$300 stipend.

Who is eligible?
Undergraduate day students who have achieved at least sophomore
standing in the Fall semester, in the School of Arts and Sciences,
School of Business Administration and the School of Nursing.

Application procedure
Students must submit two papers (two copies of each), preferably 4 to
15 pages, though we will consider longer papers if they represent your
best writing (no fiction). A brief interview will also be required and
an expressed willingness to enroll in English 360, Writing Instruction:
Theory and Practice (cross-listed as Honors 360) in Fall.

What are the benefits of being a Writing Fellow?
Fellows will have a chance to improve their own writing as a result of
taking the course and tutoring other students. Most professions and
graduate schools often seek out good writers, and the title "undergraduate Writing Fellow" should help convince future employers and
educators of the Fellow's special strength in writing.

WRITING FELLOWS PROGRAM FACULTY NOMINATIONS

You may nominate more than one student.

Your name   Ext.

Student

Major

Course:

Phone # & Address

Student

Major

Course:

Phone # & Address

Would you be interested in the assistance of a Writing Fellow for one of your courses in the Fall?

Please return to Margot Soven, English Department

The Writing Fellows Program, Fall Semester

Are you interested in the assistance of a Writing Fellow for the fall semester?

- Writing Fellows will read the drafts of the papers you assign in one of your courses and give students one-on-one assistance with their writing.

- To obtain the assistance of a Writing Fellow, your course must include at least <u>two papers written for a grade.</u>

- Faculty in <u>all schools and departments</u> may request Writing Fellows. Undergraduate courses <u>at all levels</u> are eligible for the program. Senior Writing Fellows are assigned to advanced courses.

- See the reverse side of the page for a list of the Writing Fellows. You may indicate on the tear-off if you prefer one of these students to be assigned to your course.

- Please contact me for more information about the program.

Name   Phone (campus)   Email
Department   Home Address:
                Phone (home)

Title and Number of Course

Approximate Enrollment

Number of Papers

Writing Fellow Request

Letter to Potential Writing Fellow

Dear Student:

You have been identified as a good writer by one of your instructors. I urge you to apply to the Writing Fellows Program. Many excellent Writing Fellows have been Honors Program students.

You do not have to be an English major to be a Writing Fellow. Some of our best Writing Fellows have been majors in *Chemistry*, *Biology*, *Psychology*, *Foreign Languages, etc.* The program has special benefits whether you are planning to attend graduate school, law school, or you are interested in pursuing a career in teaching or the business world.

Writing Fellows are assigned to one section of a course to help students in that class improve their writing. Students often ask, "How much time will it take?" While the workload varies, most Writing Fellows are busy for about four weeks out of the semester when they are reading drafts of the two papers assigned.

Fellows receive a $300.00 stipend each semester they are in the program, including the first semester when they take the course.

To apply submit two previously written papers. They do not need to be retyped. (See attached sheet for additional information.)

Please feel free to call me at school (x1148) or at home (610-664-0491) if you have any questions, or stop in during office hours (Olney 140), or e-mail me (soven@lasalle.edu).

Sincerely,

EVALUATION OF THE LA SALLE UNIVERSITY WRITING FELLOWS PROGRAM

Dear Student:

    To help us shape the future of the Fellows Program, we need to know your views of the program and how it worked for you in this course. Please complete this evaluation form. Thanks very much.

****

Number and name of course:
Instructor   Your class (FR,SO,JR,SR)
Writing Fellow

****

1.   Generally what did you think about the Fellow's comments?

a) mostly encouraging   mostly discouraging   mostly neutral
b) just right in number   too few   too many
c) mostly helpful   mostly unhelpful

In what ways could written comments have been more useful to you?

2.   Did you follow the Fellow's suggestions?

        always   frequently   sometimes   never

3.   How many conferences did you have with your Fellow?

    (Circle the number)

    0   1   2   3   more than 3

    a) If you had no conferences, why?

    b) How many conferences would you like to have had?

    c) Which was more helpful:

    conferences   comments on papers
    comments and conferences equally valuable

d) The Fellow's comments in conference were:

mostly clear   mostly unclear

In what ways could conferences have been more useful to you?

4. How did the Writing Fellows Program affect your papers in this course?

improved   stayed the same

If you checked "improved":

a) In what ways do you feel working with a Writing Fellow helped you to improve?

b) Are there other areas of writing in which you would like to have had more assistance?

5. How much effort did you give to your draft (check one)?

wrote the draft carefully
wrote the draft with some effort
wrote the draft quickly, with little effort

6. Please circle your overall rating of the program.

very effective   somewhat useful   unsatisfactory

1   2   3   4

7. Please add any further comments or suggestions you would like to make. Thank you for your help.

Writing Fellows Program
Faculty Report on Affiliated Courses

Name: Dept.   Date

Course Title and Number:

Writing Fellow:

Please take a few minutes to fill out this questionnaire. Your responses will help us to evaluate the success of the program and make decisions about future policies.

1. How did the program affect student writing?

2. How did the program affect the structure of your assignments, assignment deadlines, etc.?

3. Were conferences with the Writing Fellow required? If so, did most of your students comply with the requirement?

4. Did most of your students submit drafts on time? If not, how did you respond?

5. Did you require students to submit their drafts along with their final papers?

6. How often did you meet with the Writing Fellow? Were you able to contact the Writing Fellow without difficulty?

7. How can we improve the program? What can we do to make the program more useful to you?

8. Are you interested in being assigned a Writing Fellow during the next academic year?

9. Are you aware of colleagues who might be interested in learning about the program? If so, please let me know and I will contact them.

Dear Writing Fellows:

Please tell me about the semester. I need to know the following information. Please give me as close an estimate as possible for questions which require responses in numbers. This information influences how I assign Writing Fellows in the fall and in no way affects your stipend. Pick up your last check when you bring in the survey. Thanks again for your conscientiousness and expertise.

Please type your responses to these questions and attach them to this sheet.

Name:
Sponsor:
Course to which you were assigned:
Number of assigned papers:

Answer these questions on the pages attached:

1. How many papers did you respond to in writing?
2. How long were most of the papers?
3. How many students did you see in conference? Where did you hold conferences?
4. How many times did you meet with the instructor?
5. What did you learn from this tutoring experience?
6. Were there any problems? If so, how did you handle them?
7. Are you interested in tutoring next year (if you are not graduating!)?
8. Other comments:

Chapter Ten

Writing Intensive Courses and WAC

Martha A. Townsend
University of Missouri

In its nearly thirty-year presence on the U.S. higher education scene, one shape that writing across the curriculum has assumed is the writing intensive (WI) course requirement. In some settings, this curricular-driven form of WAC has proved itself, in the words of Ed White, an "unimagined fiasco" (*Teaching* 161). In other settings, it has worked as an enlightened, if challenging, solution to moving writing instruction beyond the English department. Many institutions have adopted WI, or writing enhanced (WE), or writing in the major (M) designations for courses in which faculty in a variety of disciplines use writing in a variety of ways.

This chapter identifies typical characteristics of WI courses, examines the pros and cons of using the WI or similar designation, describes selected aspects of programs employing WI designations, and highlights factors that appear to make such programs successful. The chapter then examines in more depth how one institution—the University of Missouri, a Research I, land-grant university—has successfully employed writing intensive courses since 1984 by tying the requirement to four campus missions: undergraduate education, graduate education, faculty development, and research. Cautionary comments for those programs considering adopting the WI designation as their campuses move into the twenty-first century are stressed throughout. The chapter concludes with an exploration of new directions that WI courses could take as institutions continue to meet U.S. higher education needs.

Defining Writing Intensive Course Requirements

Experienced WAC practitioners know that for WAC programs to be successful they must be institutionally specific. That is to say, WAC programs must be locally designed to fit within a given institution's particular context. Similarly, WI course requirements should be defined within the local context to ensure the best possible chance for success. The language that defines course requirements at a comprehensive research university may not work at a small liberal arts college or in a large, multicampus, two-year college system. Despite variations in language, however, the guidelines for WI courses at most institutions are surprisingly similar. Farris and Smith provide an excellent overview of features that typify WI courses, paraphrased and summarized here: _

1. Class size or instructor-to-student ratio: Most guidelines call for a maximum enrollment of fifteen to twenty-five students; in larger-enrollment classes, teaching assistants may be provided to reduce the instructor's workload.

2. Who teaches: Many guidelines require that WI courses be taught by faculty rather than teaching assistants.

3. Required number of papers or words: Some guidelines specify a page or word count, which may include a combination of formal and informal writing, in-class and out-of-class writing, and a variety of genres; some guidelines specify the number of formal papers that must be written.

4. Revision: Some guidelines specify how many papers must undergo a complete revision process; some indicate who will read drafts (instructor, peers, teaching assistants); some specify that feedback and revision go beyond correcting surface errors to include substantive rethinking.

5. How writing will affect final grade: Some guidelines stipulate or recommend that grades from writing make up a certain percentage of the course grade; not always easily negotiated, these percentages can vary widely from, say, 20 percent to 70 percent or more.

6. Types of assignments: Guidelines may require or recommend that writing be distributed throughout the course rather than

concentrated in a term paper; some specify particular tasks, e.g., summary, analysis, source integration; some call for assignments typical to the discipline of the course or for controversies in the discipline to be addressed.

7. Assignment-related instruction and evaluation of papers: Some guidelines may suggest, require, or provide teaching techniques such as collaborative work, directed lessons on research techniques, checklists for feedback, and minimal marking.

8. Support services: Some guidelines suggest or require that WI instructors attend workshops or consult with WAC staff, or that their students use a particular writing center for tutoring (Farris and Smith 73–74)

The characteristic that is probably most variable among programs is the amount of writing required. Actually, many WAC directors find page- or word-count stipulations one of the least intrinsically relevant aspects of their programs, but they acknowledge the need to provide them so that faculty and students have some common sense of scope. More meaningful to WI course quality are the frequency of writing, the usefulness of instructor feedback, the opportunity for revision, and, most important, the design of the writing assignments and their "fit" with the pedagogical aims of the course. Usually, WI courses will include some combination of both writing-to-learn and writing-to-communicate assignments, although the balance of these will vary based on instructor preference, course goals, and the course's place in the curriculum, e.g., lower division, upper division, for majors only, for general education purposes. Typically, traditional term papers are discouraged unless they are assigned in sequenced segments with teacher feedback and revision incorporated.

The more astute programmatic guidelines are couched in diplomatic language, allow for flexibility among disciplines, and account for individual instructors' teaching preferences. In most universities, oversight committees responsible for vetting WI courses have little finite authority; moreover, they recognize the perils of constituting themselves as the campus "WI police." Instead, most programs are interested in overall pedagogical change. Susan McLeod, in sharing an anecdote on how WAC had changed one teacher's life, concluded by noting that:

his enthusiasm, many years after his first encounter with WAC, shows what I think is the most important thing about WAC—it is really not about writing, but about teaching and learning. Once faculty change their pedagogies and see the effect that change has on their classes, they can't go back to the lecture mode. . . . That's what introduces a culture of writing on campus—faculty change.

One example of the incorporation of diplomatic language and room for flexibility appears in the definition of WI courses at the University of Rhode Island. URI's guidelines call for a number of the features Farris and Smith mention. But URI further suggests that "if possible," WI courses should include (for example) peer review and collaborative writing, and that "if possible," upper-division WI courses should include a variety of professional writing assignments, such as patient charts, client reports, case studies, lab reports, research reviews, and so on. The WI guidelines at Missouri Western State College blend prescriptiveness with flexibility. In MWSC's ten itemized points, directive statements (as in "major assignments *will* be broken down into stages") are balanced with an almost identical number of optional statements ("peer involvement *could* be used") (my emphasis).[1]

The WI guidelines at George Mason University were derived from a survey of fifty-three WI programs in existence at the time George Mason started its program. A report of that research by John Latona appears in the *Composition Chronicle*. George Mason's WI guidelines can be found at http://www.gmu.edu/departments/wac/wacrec.htm. This site also provides links to numerous other WAC programs with additional WI guideline variations. Several other Web sites are worth noting for their access to WI definitions. The University of Hawaii at Manoa lists its WI criteria at http://mwp01.mwp.hawaii.edu. A fine resource is the extensive WAC Clearinghouse Web site maintained at Colorado State: http://aw.colostate.edu/resource_list.htm. Finally, the WPA-L archives are a rich resource for virtually all issues having to do with writing programs, including WI descriptions. The archive address is http://lists.asu.edu/archives/wpa-l.html. Each subdirectory in the archive is searchable by subject; simply type "writing intensive courses" at the prompt. (To subscribe to the list itself, send a message to listserv@lists.asu.edu; in the message, type <subscribe WPA-L your name>.)

The Case against WI Labels and Curricular Requirements

There are sound arguments against adopting WI designations and solid reasons for institutions to avoid moving to a WAC program that is driven by a curricular requirement. The overarching rationale is that writing—instruction, assignments, assessment—should be embedded in all course work, not isolated or marginalized in a reduced number of "marked" classes. WAC theory, in other words, not to mention the ideals undergirding liberal education, militate against this kind of system. Veteran WAC advocate and practitioner John Bean noted some years ago that faculty at his institution, Seattle University, made a conscious decision to forego a WI requirement by committing to the integration of some writing into all courses. Other institutions, too, successfully practice WAC by means of the "infusion" model without a WI requirement; St. Lawrence University comes to mind, along with many smaller liberal arts colleges.

WAC literature and lore are replete with stories of WI disasters. Lively debates ensue on WPA-L whenever a new correspondent innocently poses the question, "My school is considering adopting a WI requirement. Please describe your institution's WI criteria." Usually such queries focus on the characteristics that define a WI course rather than on the factors necessary to ensure the success of such a requirement. Veteran writing program reviewer and founder of the National Council of Writing Program Administrators' Consultant/Evaluator Service, Ed White is one of the most vocal opponents of WI courses: "I've said it before and I'll repeat it briefly again: I don't like writing intensive courses . . . . [T]hey usually (though not always) wind up as a fraud after a few years. . . . Beware of easy and faddish solutions to basic problems" ("Re: Descriptions"). His short article "The Damage of Innovations Set Adrift" has served as a caution to faculty and administrators for more than ten years. He presents a fuller, more balanced view in *Teaching and Assessing Writing*, concluding that "universities that take writing seriously . . . can make a writing-intensive program work successfully. But no one should minimize either the difficulty or the expense involved over the long term" (164).

Among the arguments against WI designations are these: Budget-wary administrators often view them as a cheap, easy fix to students' writing "problems." Promised support doesn't materialize, or, as budget cuts become necessary, WI courses are easy targets. One recent horror story reported on the Writing Program Administrators' listserv involved administratively mandated WI classes with no resources, no WAC director, no budget, no programmatic support, no criteria for designating WI classes, and no faculty workshops. After unsuccessfully attempting to educate administrators about the basic needs for imbuing the WI courses with minimal rigor and integrity, writing faculty (all tenured) resigned as a group from the general education reform committee. In some scenarios, students progress through the curriculum, taking the requisite number of WI courses, without even understanding what "WI" refers to. In others, the requirement is regularly waived so as not to prevent students from graduating, thereby turning the "requirement" into a campus joke. In the worst scenarios, non-WI faculty quit using writing in their courses because "the WI classes are doing this now and we don't have to." Students complain when writing is assigned in non-WI courses. The net effect can be less writing in the curriculum than before the WI requirement took effect.

Not least, it is hard to make WI programs work. In some institutions, WI teaching assignments are often given to the worst, or youngest, teachers. The least attractive or inappropriate courses are made to carry the WI designation. Enrollment management is difficult. Curricula are not well thought out. Assessment is difficult or not done at all. Faculty in the disciplines are not sufficiently prepared to offer WI courses and are not supported, either during the teaching process or at tenure and promotion time. Faculty find that certain criteria, especially eliciting meaningful revision and providing feedback on student papers, are daunting. Larger institutions, particularly those with research missions and/or uncooperative registration offices, find the logistics a hassle. Committees overseeing the requirement find it difficult to strike a balance between enforcement and support—if they are too tentative about course integrity, faculty are not invested in the process and the program lacks substance; if they are too strident, faculty resist what they perceive to be interference in their academic freedom. As David Russell puts it, "On an *institutional* basis, WAC exists [and, many would argue, WI courses] in a structure that fundamentally resists it" (295).

The Case for WI Labels and Curricular Requirements

Even as the arguments against WI course requirements are made, an equally vocal contingent proclaims virtually the opposite. Proponents claim that WI requirements, when properly implemented, can cause faculty to realize the importance of writing, feedback, revision, well-designed assignments, and thoughtfully constructed assessment in the curriculum. The WI requirement, and the supporting apparatus that accompanies it (e.g., faculty workshops, consultation with WAC personnel, informal meetings of WI teachers to discuss problems and results), can serve as a catalyst for more writing across the curriculum in all courses, whether WI or not. Faculty on the whole can become better informed not only about writing but also about teaching and learning issues more broadly defined (e.g., peer review, collaborative learning, group projects). Institutions often use the WI designation as a rationale for reducing class size, making it possible for instructors to pay more attention to student writing.

Writing program personnel at various institutions report that the WI influence has "bubbled up" to the graduate level, that talk about the importance of writing to learning has turned up in unexpected campus committee meetings, and that once faculty have experienced success in their WI teaching, they can't "go back" to their previous methodologies. Others report that WI requirements begun at the general education level have positively influenced writing in the major. Still others go so far as to report a "culture change" on their campuses in which interest in and excitement about writing exist where they did not before. In contrast to the infusion model (no formal WI requirement, where all faculty agree to carry the load), a formal structural model of WI requirements can make this work visible to a wider audience. With WI courses flagged in the schedule and on student transcripts, students, faculty, administrators, and employers can be more attuned to specific measures in place at an institution, who is contributing to it, how many such courses students are taking, and so on. In sum, the WI course requirement (as with WAC in general) has served as a powerful vehicle for expanding attention to student writing as well as for conducting faculty development.

Selected Successful WI Programs

Writing intensive programs come in a multitude of configurations. The following range of examples is not intended to be inclusive, nor descriptive of any school's complete requirement, nor representative of what may work at another institution. It is intended to illustrate how a variety of institutions have creatively enacted different aspects of the WI requirement to fit their specific institutional needs. (These examples come from comments posted on WPA-L, [2] as well as from my own observation as a consultant. See also Toby Fulwiler and Art Young's *Programs That Work: Models and Methods for Writing Across the Curriculum* for further examples.)

- ◆ The University of Hawaii at Manoa requires five WI classes for graduation. Nonstipend faculty workshops are offered but not required; a newsletter and specifically chosen resource materials are sent to participating faculty.

- ◆ Eastern Connecticut State University has avoided faculty resistance to teaching WI courses by keeping class size small compared to non-WI courses.

- ◆ Southern Connecticut State University has taken a slow, thoughtfully deliberate approach to its newly revitalized "L" (for "literacy") course requirement. Among other SCSU programmatic aspects, faculty who successfully teach L courses three times will receive overload credits that factor into their workload assignments.

♦ Youngstown State University recently recommended that its upper-division, multisection general education courses be available in both WI and non-WI versions.

♦ The University of Rhode Island is attempting to create a culture for writing that transcends individual WI faculty by focusing on departments. Incentives being considered include direct departmental support for developing new WI courses, recognizing student writing achievement, and sending graduate teaching assistants to workshops. Perhaps most intriguing, URI is attempting to increase the profile, for program review purposes, of those departments that have developed a writing culture.

♦ Even though it doesn't have a structured WAC program, Tidewater Community College nonetheless has many WI classes, and half of the faculty have attended workshops conducted by writing center staff. Donna Reiss, coordinator of online learning, whose chapter with Art Young on electronic communication across the curriculum (ECAC) appears in this volume (Chapter 3), believes that new technologies have opened up new opportunities in the intersecting fields of WI, WAC, and ECAC: "Many of the instructional approaches that use WAC with communications technology began in writing classes, and many writing teachers have become leaders in instructional technologies for entire colleges" ("Comment" 722).

♦ Ohio State's second-year WI course requirement is taught in numerous departments across campus, but each carries the same course number. More information on these courses is available at www.ohio-state.edu through the Center for the Study and Teaching of Writing Web page.

♦ Western Washington University has eliminated its rising junior exam and is replacing its previously required WI course with a requirement for six writing "units" or "points." Courses that offer writing instruction will carry from one to three points; students need to accrue six points for graduation.

♦ At Muhlenberg College, in conjunction with their department heads, faculty determine whether a course will be WI in a given semester. A proposal is submitted the first time a course is offered to the Writing Committee to ensure that no one is unwillingly teaching a WI course.

♦ At the University of Missouri–Rolla, each course is reviewed each semester it's taught by each faculty member who teaches it, thereby ensuring oversight for course quality.

◆ At Washington State University, the All-University Writing Committee decided to focus its writing intensive courses at the upper-division level, calling them "writing in the major" courses and designing them to accommodate a variety of disciplinary approaches. The focus is on preprofessional writing tasks for students in the disciplines.

What Makes WI Courses Work?

The factors listed below, commonly cited by WAC directors and practitioners from both successful and not-so-successful WI initiatives, can help account for why some programs thrive while others languish or perish. Although it is impossible to claim that WI programs featuring all or most of these characteristics will ensure a robust program, nonetheless some combination of most of these does tend to predict a positive outcome.

1. *Strong faculty ownership of the WI system:* Such characteristics as a faculty-initiated course requirement, faculty peer review of WI course proposals, and faculty-established policies regarding WI criteria, workshop attendance, and faculty development activities seem essential.

2. *Strong philosophical and fiscal support from institutional administrators, coupled with their willingness to avoid micromanagement:* WI programs require influential officers who understand the principles behind WI courses and who can advocate consistently for them at high levels of institutional decision making. Administrators must also take an active role in securing resources to provide adequate staff support (trained WAC personnel to work with WI faculty), faculty development (funding for workshops, materials, and stipends for attendees), and graduate teaching assistants, if necessary (to assist faculty in dealing with the increased paper load). At the same time, if administrators get involved with the day-to-day management of the program, faculty will perceive a top-down approach that unnecessarily interferes with their work. Maintaining a healthy balance is critical.

3. *One and two above, in combination:* Neither of these two factors alone will allow for a truly successful WI program. If either group is unwilling or uninterested, the project is probably doomed to fail, sooner rather than later. Hearkening back to Fullan and Miles's Lesson Six in "Eight Basic Lessons for the New Paradigm of Change" summarized by McLeod and Miraglia in Chapter 1, both top-down and bottom-up strategies are necessary.

4. *Symbiosis with other institutional programs/missions:* It's likely that the more cooperation and links a WI program has with other initiatives the better, assuming that WI program leaders keep the WI focus in balance. Conscientious integration with the campus mission statement, writing center, service learning, other campus teaching and learning programs, campus assessment activities, technology, general education, graduate programs (by employing graduate students in the disciplines to assist with WI courses), and so on go a long way toward creating a curricular requirement that is tightly woven into the institutional fabric.

5. *A reward structure that values teaching:* This is one of the thorniest issues for many campuses to deal with, especially large research universities. Faculty need to perceive that their work is valued by their peers, departments, institutions, and disciplines. For the vast majority who undertake teaching in a WI format, the workload does increase. All too often, rewards for research are easier to attain than rewards for teaching. Some WI program directors may have few incentives to offer except the indirect programmatic support they can provide to WI teachers, coupled with the intrinsic satisfaction faculty typically derive from WI teaching (through students' engagement with topics, livelier class discussions, knowledge that students are thinking more critically about content, observing improved papers). Change may be on the horizon thanks to the aid of sources such as Boyer's *Scholarship Reconsidered: Priorities of the Professoriate* and Glassick, Huber, and Maeroff's *Scholarship Assessed: Evaluation of the Pro-*

fessoriate, as well as the Boyer Report, *Reinventing Undergraduate Education: A Blueprint for America's Research Universities.* But WI leaders should be aware that faculty members' perception of little or no reward for their increased effort may be a major roadblock to WI success.

6. *Knowledgeable, diplomatic WAC program personnel:* Faculty in the disciplines need access to well-informed specialists when they are designing writing assignments and grading criteria. More often than not, they also need help coordinating the writing with course goals and objectives and with their individual teaching styles. A dedicated and well-meaning—but not professionally schooled—faculty committee is not prepared to perform this function. As one savvy dean put it in a recent conversation, "WAC programs and WI courses don't run by committee; they need somebody who knows what's going on and who worries about them all day every day." At the same time, because WI course development intersects so thoroughly with faculty development, WAC personnel must have the interpersonal skills to work with sensitive faculty egos and personalities.

7. *Regular internal assessment procedures combined with periodic external program review:* These may be two of the most overlooked and under-attended-to features of a strong WI system. Yet having them in place will allow inevitable questions to be addressed. Most administrators and, increasingly, governmental agencies want evidence that academic programs are "working" so they can demonstrate "accountability" to their constituents. The old assessment adage "multiple measures, over time" is an excellent starting place for WI programs (see Condon, Chapter 2, this volume).

8. *A low student-to-WI-instructor ratio, along with TA help if necessary:* If writing is to be meaningful and teachers are to give feedback that leads to revision, large-enrollment WI classes cannot be effective. Successful programs manage to

hold enrollment to somewhere between fifteen and twenty-five students. When enrollment compromises must be made, graduate teaching assistants are necessary to alleviate a portion of the faculty marking and feedback burden, although care must be taken to ensure that overall responsibility remains in faculty's hands.

9. *Integration of WI assignments with course goals and instructor's pedagogical methods:* Ideally, this characteristic should be at the top of the list. The purpose of integrating writing into disciplinary-based courses, after all, is to enhance students' understanding of critical content in the subject-matter area. If the writing does not serve course goals or is at odds with the teacher's "style," it risks being a mere add-on for the sake of labeling the requisite number of WI courses. Realistically, though, without the characteristics above (1–8) firmly in place, even a WI program that features finely tuned, well-integrated assignments will probably be short-lived.

10. *Flexible but sound WI criteria:* A corollary to well-integrated assignments is rigorous yet flexible criteria for creating and evaluating WI courses. It is a challenge to establish overall programmatic and course integrity while allowing sufficient leeway for disparate disciplines to arrive at appropriate writing practices. Examples of how the University of Missouri addresses this issue are given in the following section.

11. *Patience and vigilance:* When all is said and done, WAC, especially in the form of WI courses, "attempts to reform pedagogy more than curriculum. . . . It asks for a fundamental commitment to a radically different way of teaching, a way that requires personal sacrifices, given the structure of American education, and offers personal rather than institutional rewards" (Russell 295). These commitments grow slowly and reforms take time. WI leaders must be simultaneously patient and perseverant while programs evolve.

MARTHA A. TOWNSEND

The University of Missouri–Columbia's WI Requirement: One Institution's Story

As on numerous other campuses, MU's WI requirement was born of a faculty perception that student writing needed more attention than it was getting. At the faculty's request, the dean and provost jointly convened an interdisciplinary Task Force on English Composition, chaired by English professor Winifred Horner, charged with reviewing the status of composition on campus and making recommendations. A year's worth of study later, the task force's 1984 report became the founding document for MU's WAC program, a program that included, among other components, the establishment of a WI requirement for all undergraduates as a condition of graduation. An eighteen-faculty-member interdisciplinary Campus Writing Board was constituted, a full-time director was hired to oversee the new Campus Writing Program, and a three-year pilot phase began.

The task force report also recommended that the program and its director be accountable to three sectors of the university: (1) the provost, because this office funds the program and because the program must be recognized as a campuswide endeavor; (2) the dean of the College of Arts and Science, because this college generates about half of all WI courses and because writing instruction is naturally situated in the liberal arts; and (3) the Campus Writing Board, because academic policy should rest in the hands of faculty. Although the three-way reporting appears cumbersome in description or on an organizational flowchart, in reality it works remarkably well. Both the dean's and the provost's offices are in positions to advocate for the program when necessary, but all decision making is done by faculty. In its fifteen-year existence, the program has reported to five provosts and three deans, all of whom have championed the WI cause. Board members, who serve three-year rolling terms, are jointly appointed by the provost and dean based on suggestions from Campus Writing Program staff. The board has come to be known as one of the most proactive faculty committees on campus. The program, as distinct from the board, consists of five full-time staff members (two of whom hold faculty appointments in English), ten part-time graduate student tutors (all from different disciplines), and a group of one hundred or so ever-changing graduate teaching assistants who work with the faculty teaching WI courses (so that a 20:1 student-to-teacher ratio is maintained).

The three-year pilot phase was critical for WI faculty, board members, and program staff in determining new policies and procedures and in allowing everyone time to experiment with WAC principles. The formal one-course WI graduation requirement did not become effective until 1988. The program then spent five-and-a-half years honing this requirement before moving to a two-course WI graduation requirement in 1993. MU's writing requirement for all students, then, is one semester of first-year composition, followed by two WI courses, one anywhere in the curriculum and one in the major at the upper-division level. This slow, thoughtful, deliberate progression is one key to the program's longevity. Participants had ample time to solve the inevitable problems; they conscientiously did not assume they could do a lot quickly—a common error of many WI initiatives.

The first board, with the guidance of founding director Doug Hunt, drafted MU's *Guidelines for WI Courses*, a document that has stood the test of time but that has also undergone some careful revision over the years. MU's guidelines incorporate all of the features identified by Farris and Smith summarized earlier in this chapter, albeit in somewhat different order and with somewhat different emphasis:

1. WI courses should be designed and taught by faculty members at a 20:1 student-to-faculty ratio. This recommendation precludes consideration of graduate students as primary instructors.

2. Each course should include multiple assignments that are complex enough to require substantive revision for most students. Students should submit a draft of other preliminary writing, consider responses from a teacher (and, whenever possible, from other students), revise, and finally edit. The final versions of these assignments should total at least 2,000 words (eight pages).

3. Writing for the entire course should total at least 5,000 words (twenty pages). This writing may take many forms and includes the drafts of preliminary writing and final versions of the assignments in guideline 2.

4. Each course should include at least one revised writing assignment addressing a question for which there is more than one acceptable interpretation, explanation, analysis, or evaluation.

5. Writing for the course should be distributed throughout the semester rather than concentrated at the end.

6. Written assignments should be a major component of the course grade.

7. Faculty members may use graduate teaching assistants to bring the student-to-faculty ratio down to a manageable level.

8. In classes employing graduate teaching assistants, professors should remain firmly in control not only of the writing assignments, but also of the grading and marking of papers.

A preamble to the guidelines sets forth the program's philosophy, and each of the guidelines is accompanied by a paragraph of explanatory text that anticipates questions faculty may have in preparing a WI course proposal. These sentences in italic immediately precede the eight points: *"The guidelines below are not inflexible, but they give applicants a picture of the sort of course the Board envisages. Alternative means to the same end will certainly be considered."* Although these words are intended as a specific invitation for faculty to creatively alter the guidelines to meet the needs of their discipline or their teaching style as long as they stay within the spirit of the document, few actually take advantage of it. In fact, Campus Writing Program (CWP) staff call this invitation to faculty awareness more often than faculty use it on their own.

Guidelines 1 and 4 have been revised from the original version. In guideline 1, the clarification that "this recommendation precludes consideration of graduate students as primary instructors" was added shortly after the second WI course requirement became effective. Although faculty had always been the only instructors allowed to teach WI courses, pressure to offer nearly double the number of WI courses created a wave of WI course proposals, presented for the first time with graduate students listed as the instructors of record. The Campus Writing Board allowed only a few exceptions to the longtime policy in order to enable departments to meet their short-term obligations for WI courses for their majors, but sent out notice with this new language advising that the long-standing policy would be enforced. At the same time, the provost and dean were able to remind colleges and departments that the faculty "rule" was important by asking that Request to Hire New Faculty forms show how departments would use their new hires to help meet departmental WI teaching obligations.

Guideline 4 originally read, "Each course should include at least one revised writing assignment addressing a question *about which reasonable people can disagree.*" When the second WI requirement—calling for an upper-division course in each major—became effective, the board began to get complaints from faculty that students in the sciences are not prepared to challenge the axioms of the discipline or take a stand on unsettled issues. Still, board members believed that even science students should tackle "live" questions in their academic disciplines, and the present language was drafted by Marty Patton, CWP consultant to WI courses in the natural and applied sciences. The new language still requires occasional explanation, but it is language that the science faculty can understand and live with.

In 1992, in preparation for instituting the second WI course, CWP undertook its first comprehensive program evaluation, which consisted of a year-long self-study and culminated in an external review by the WPA's Consultant/Evaluator Service. (For an explanation of the project's social constructivist theory, data collection methodology, and outcomes, see Townsend.) During the process of articulating program goals for ourselves and our reviewers, it became clear that a number of CWP's activities coincided with a newly developed university mission statement. We began framing our work by calling overt attention to these correspondences, and over time we have come to realize that the framework has helped others better understand what we do. A new provost, a new dean, a new member of the Board of Curators, newcomers to the Campus Writing Board, and others outside the university have commented that the fact that we have articulated our work by referencing MU's mission statement has allowed them to get a fuller picture of this WAC program that is organized around WI courses.

Of the multiple missions in MU's formal statement, the four we link to are undergraduate education, graduate education, faculty development, and research.

1. Undergraduate education is the starting point. Our primary responsibility is ensuring that academically rigorous WI courses are available for all students in both general education and the majors. Quoted here at some length is an e-mail recently sent to MU Mechanical and Aerospace Engineer Professor Aaron Krawitz by a student who had taken his WI course. Krawitz is known for his attention to both the conceptual and the technical aspects of student writing assignments. The student's remarks are not unusual feedback for WI faculty to receive:

> I wanted to write and let you know about my experience this summer and the effect of your composite materials class. I am working for a very large law firm's patent department. I have been reading and editing as well as assisting in the drafting of patent applications and amendments. Your composite materials class has been a huge factor in my ability to do this effectively. The patent attorneys have been amazed at how many mistakes I have been finding in their applications. These applications are highly technical and require thorough and careful editing before they are sent to the U.S. Patent Office. Having the experience of carefully writing and revising technical papers in your composites class was, I think, a huge help. I just wanted to let you know. Thanks. (Wiegmann)

Direct support for students enrolled in WI classes is provided by CWP's WI tutorial service. Students may schedule a fifty-minute one-on-one appointment with a graduate student in our writing center. Typically, these graduate students have served as WI TAs in their disciplines; taught classes of their own in that discipline; met with the instructors of the WI courses for whom they are tutoring; read the course texts; and seen the syllabus, assignment, and grading criteria before the student comes in. CWP offers two- or three-day faculty workshops each semester for new WI faculty, offers unlimited follow-up consultation to WI faculty, and coordinates all logistics with Registration personnel to ensure timely listing of WI courses in the schedule. A workshop feature popular with faculty is our giving each participant a copy of John Bean's excellent *Engaging Ideas: The Professor's Guide to Integrating Writing, Critical Thinking, and Active Learning in the Classroom.*

2. Graduate education is a vital part of MU's life as a Research I institution. We now make greater efforts to ensure that when graduate teaching assistants work with WI faculty or in CWP's tutoring center, they know they are receiving valuable professional preparation for their future careers. Quoted here, again at some length, is an illustration we use often, one that speaks volumes in helping many of MU's constituents understand why the WI requirement benefits graduate students as well as undergraduates. After earning his master's degree and securing a highly desirable position in his field, one student wrote:

> As a former Journalism WI TA of—was it six semesters?—and WI tutor of three semesters [I am] overcome by a need to [acknowledge] how I got to where I am not just with the *help* of my work with CWP, but *because* of it. . . . My approach to [my new position as assistant editor of *Aramco World* magazine] can be traced directly to training received not so much in a newsroom but as a WI TA. It was as a TA that I learned, most of the time without knowing it, how to be an editor.
>   Part of my interview process was to test-edit an article. Later, after I was hired, I was told that I was the only candidate who, upon receiving the article, asked the Editor what *kind* of editing he wanted. To me it was a logical question, straight out of starting a new WI class: What kind of marking do we do? . . . The result was impressive enough to get me the job; the techniques are now the ones I apply every day with professional writers. As a WI TA, I learned not just how something "should" read or look, but how to bring out the best in a writer, and how to articulate my criticisms and questions. (Doughty)

3. WAC has long been recognized as an effective faculty development tool by those working within the movement. But some institutions are reluctant to highlight this aspect, preferring to focus mainly on WAC's relationship to student writing. But when MU's mission statement specifically mentioned offering faculty continuing opportunities to develop their expertise, we thought it appro-

priate to acknowledge this link as well. CWP workshops and discussions explore the connections between writing, critical thinking, and problem solving. They don't focus so much on improving teaching as they do on understanding learning. Workshop attendees are offered a small stipend, and we have documented that even those participants who do not subsequently offer a formal WI course nonetheless use writing in their courses in more thoughtful ways. CWP's newsletter *The Writery* features articles on exemplary WI teachers and the innovative ways they teach WI classes. (All *Writery* issues are available online at http://cwp. missouri.edu; a slightly expanded explanation of CWP's links to MU's missions appears in Vol. 1, No. 1.) Thinking about the discipline-specific nature of knowledge has led many faculty to note that WI teaching has opened up new ways of approaching their own scholarship. Many Campus Writing Board members, too, comment that their three-year term on the board teaches them more than they could have imagined. In reviewing hundreds of WI course proposals, they read and evaluate a range of teaching ideas and WI assignments that inevitably cause them to reflect on their own practices. Even serving on the campus committee that prepared us for our WPA external review proved to be a learning experience for one non-WI faculty member. Journalism professor Steve Weinberg documented his and others' changes in attitude toward WI courses in "Overcoming Skepticism about 'Writing Across the Curriculum.'"

4. Befitting MU's Research I designation, CWP conducts and encourages a variety of projects related to WI teaching. Teams of WI faculty have presented their work at the two most recent national Writing Across the Curriculum conferences. The first team—a nurse, a mechanical and aerospace engineer, and a wildlife expert—saw their piece published in *Language and Learning Across the Disciplines* (October 1998) and the second—an architect, a Romance languages teacher, and an English teacher—have an article in progress. WI faculty are regular presenters at the Conference on College Composition and Communication, and numerous others have published essays in their respective disciplinary-based journals. CWP staff projects include examining what works—and what doesn't—in specific courses, as well

as consulting for other institutions on WI course development, integrating writing into general education, and using WI assignments in community learning courses. And an earlier research project, conducted at MU, led to a more enlightened form of research at Indiana University. In "Adventures in the WAC Assessment Trade: Reconsidering the Link between Research and Consultation," Raymond Smith and Christine Farris describe their attempts to determine the effect of WI courses on students' writing and critical thinking. They maintain that the results of their work "will have immediate and long-lasting consequences for pedagogy on our campus and are born of our questions about the researcher-subject relationship; specifically, whose needs drive the inquiry: those of WAC programs, composition specialists, or faculty members teaching WI courses?" (174).

Lest the CWP/mission statement framework and the relative vigor of MU's WI requirement convey too rosy a picture, we reinvoke Ed White's caution that "no one should minimize either the difficulties or the expense involved over the long term" (*Teaching* 164). Like virtually every other institution, MU faces budgetary quandaries that have no simple solutions. Our resources for providing WI TAs to the burgeoning number of WI classes are strained. Pressure to win grants and publish research increases yearly, taxing faculty's ability to develop new WI courses. The percentage of "nonregular" faculty rises each year, making it difficult for the board to enforce its policy of WI classes being taught by tenured or tenure-track faculty only. More and more students transfer into MU and submit requests to waive one of the two required WI courses, causing the board to revisit its long-standing policy of requiring both WI courses to be taken on campus. Similarly, more students are completing an international study component and requesting that one of the two WI courses be satisfied through study abroad. We should be doing much more with assessment. We would like to strengthen WI TA training more than we have. We need a solution to the reward problem, and we need to be constantly vigilant for faculty burnout. Obviously, we hope that the fifteen-year history of WI teaching on our campus will continue. We enjoy strong support from faculty, administrators, members of the Board of Curators, and even students. But future success depends on visionary thinking, creative problem solving, as well as all the goodwill we can muster from our constituents.

New Directions for WI Courses

In "The Future of WAC," Barbara Walvoord indicates challenges she believes WAC—and by extension, I would argue, WI courses— faces: "to change, to set goals, to address macro issues, to re- think old answers to micro issues, to deal with assessment" (74). As McLeod and Miraglia point out in Chapter 1, given its aim of pedagogical change, WAC is notoriously good at aligning itself with ongoing developments in academe. I elaborate here on two areas in which I believe WI courses could have significant impact.

One concerns the issue of students from varied language and cultural backgrounds and their mastery of academic discourse. WAC personnel are far more likely than WI faculty in the disci- plines to be aware of policy statements on language put forward by groups such as CCCC and NCTE. WAC personnel can, through their consultation with WI faculty, create greater aware- ness and sensitivity that can then translate into action in the class- room in the form of, say, innovative assignments and less judgmental thinking about "error." As Geneva Smitherman notes in her historical review of CCCC's advocacy for students on the linguistic margins, "What we are witnessing [now] . . . is a devel- oping sociolinguistic sophistication and political maturity about language rights issues" (369). Faculty in the disciplines will not be knowledgeable about the CCCC National Language Policy, but WAC personnel can be. Moreover, as professionals in the field, we have an obligation to understand and promote the in- tent behind such statements. Smitherman continues,

> The National Language Policy stresses the need not just for marginalized Americans but all Americans to be bi- or multilin- gual in order to be prepared for citizenship in a global, multicultural society. More than a policy for students of one par- ticular color or class, this policy recognizes that the ability to speak many tongues is a necessity for everybody. (369)

WI teaching provides one avenue for faculty in the disciplines not only to become more attuned to language issues generally, but also to practice them as part of their new WI teaching repertoires (see Villanueva, Chapter 7, this volume).

The second area is assessment. After more than a decade of national attention to assessment, particularly on the part of legislative bodies calling for "accountability" of one kind or another, groups around the country are beginning to protest (Bayles). Parents, students, faculty, and even school administrators are beginning to vocalize their opposition to what Robert Tierney, director of Ohio State's School of Teaching and Learning, calls "proficiency test madness" (Bayles 10a). No matter how effective these individual and organized protests may be in the long run, however, educators will still have to propose acceptable alternatives to the standardized tests now so prevalent on our educational scene. One answer, of course, is writing in WI courses. Many institutions, MU among them, require WI classes in both general education and major field courses. Writing from either curriculum could be used as a means of determining student achievement and programmatic effectiveness. Alternatively, writing from both curricula could be combined to serve as exit documentation of student proficiency. Admittedly, developing such portfolio systems would require expert guidance, resources, and time not associated with standardized testing. But the findings, not to mention what faculty would learn in the process, could provide a healthy counterbalance to the prevailing test madness. Using writing from WI courses could offer a genuine method that allows the research to feed back into the teaching and learning loop (see Condon, Chapter 2, this volume).

James Kinneavy concluded in an essay on WAC,

> The fact remains that the jury is out on writing across the curriculum. . . . Further cases must be brought to the courts to test the movement. At the present, the promise seems most favorable—writing across the curriculum may be the best academic response to the literacy crisis in English-speaking countries, though it cannot be a total social response. (377)

This summation, though now some thirteen years old, may be a fitting one for WI courses within the WAC movement as well.

WI courses are not without controversy. But in numerous places they have also proved an effective means indeed for enhancing undergraduate and graduate education, faculty development, and research. WI courses cannot be a complete response to any educational mission, but they can provide a significant contribution to an overall educational plan.

Notes

1. These guidelines may be found online in the WPA-L Archives, http://lists.asu.edu/archives/wpa-l.html, in posts by Linda Shamoon (University of Rhode Island, 8/5/97) and by Elizabeth Sawin (Missouri Western, 7/15/98).

2. These posts may be found in the WPA-L Archives, http://lists.asu.edu/archives/wpa-l.html. The dates for the posts are, respectively, 1/31/97, 3/27/97, 10/30/97, 12/2/98, 1/28/99, and 1/31/99.

Works Cited

Bayles, Fred. "Standardized Exams Coming under Fire." *USA Today* 11 June 1999: 10a.

Bean, John C. *Engaging Ideas: The Professor's Guide to Integrating Writing, Critical Thinking, and Active Learning in the Classroom.* San Francisco: Jossey-Bass, 1996.

Boyer, Ernest. *Scholarship Reconsidered: Priorities of the Professoriate.* Lawrenceville, NJ: Princeton UP, 1990.

Boyer Commission on Educating Undergraduates in the Research University. *Reinventing Undergraduate Education: A Blueprint for America's Research Universities.* SUNY Stony Brook for the Carnegie Foundation for the Advancement of Teaching, 1998.

Doughty, Dick. Letter to the author. 11 Nov. 1994.

Farris, Christine, and Raymond Smith. "Writing Intensive Courses: Tools for Curricular Change." *Writing Across the Curriculum: A Guide to Developing Programs.* Ed. Susan H. McLeod and Margot Soven. Academic.Writing Landmark Publications in Writing Studies:

http://aw.colostate.edu/books/mcleod_soven/ 2000. Originally published in print by Sage (Newbury Park, CA), 1992.

Fullan, Michael. *Change Forces: Probing the Depths of Educational Reform.* Bristol, PA: Falmer, 1993.

Fulwiler, Toby, and Art Young, eds. *Programs That Work: Models and Methods for Writing Across the Curriculum.* Portsmouth, NH: Boynton/Cook, 1990.

Glassick, Charles E., Mary Taylor Huber, and Gene I. Maeroff. *Scholarship Assessed: Evaluation of the Professoriate.* San Francisco: Jossey-Bass, 1997.

Horner, Winifred, et al. "Recommendations of the Task Force on English Composition." Unpublished document, 1984.

Kinneavy, James L. "Writing Across the Curriculum." *Teaching Composition: Twelve Bibliographical Essays.* Rev. and enl. ed. Ed. Gary Tate. Fort Worth: Texas Christian UP, 1987.

Latona, John. "What Do We Mean by 'Writing Intensive'?" *Composition Chronicle* (Oct. 1991): 8–9.

McLeod, Susan. "Re: Faculty Development in WAC." Online posting, Writing Program Administration. 1 Dec. 1998 <WPA-L@ASUVM.INRE.ASU.EDU>.

Reiss, Donna. "A Comment on 'The Future of WAC.'" *College English* 58 (1996): 722–23.

Russell, David. *Writing in the Academic Disciplines, 1870–1990: A Curricular History.* Carbondale: Southern Illinois UP, 1991.

Smith, Raymond, and Christine Farris. "Adventures in the WAC Assessment Trade: Reconsidering the Link between Research and Consultation." *Assessing Writing Across the Curriculum: Diverse Approaches and Practices.* Ed. Kathleen Blake Yancey and Brian A. Huot. Greenwich, CT: Ablex, 1997.

Smitherman, Geneva. "CCCC's Role in the Struggle for Language Rights." *College Composition and Communication* 50 (1999): 349–76.

Townsend, Martha A. "Integrating WAC into General Education: An Assessment Case Study." *Assessing Writing Across the Curriculum: Diverse Approaches and Practices.* Ed. Kathleen Blake Yancey and Brian A. Huot. Greenwich, CT: Ablex, 1997.

Walvoord, Barbara E. "The Future of WAC." *College English* 58.1 (1996): 58–79.

Weinberg, Steve. "Overcoming Skepticism about 'Writing Across the Curriculum.'" *Chronicle of Higher Education* 16 June 1993: B2–B3.

White, Edward M. "The Damage of Innovations Set Adrift." *AAHE Bulletin: A Publication of the American Association for Higher Education* 43.3 (1990): 3–5.

———. "Re: Descriptions of Writing Intensive Courses." Online posting, Writing Program Administration. 27 Mar. 1997 <WPA-L@ASUVM. INRE.ASU.EDU>.

———. *Teaching and Assessing Writing.* Rev. and exp. ed. San Francisco: Jossey-Bass, 1994.

Wiegmann, Chad. E-mail to Aaron Krawitz. 28 July 1999.

CHAPTER ELEVEN

Where Do the Naturalistic Studies of WAC/WID Point? A Research Review

DAVID R. RUSSELL
Iowa State University

One of the most significant developments in writing research over the last fifteen years has been the large number of naturalistic studies of college-level writing in the disciplines inspired by the WAC movement. In this chapter, I selectively review some of the over one hundred studies to suggest what conclusions we might tentatively draw at this stage and what avenues for further research they open.

Qualitative studies have predominated in recent years because the early attempts to perform quantitative experimental studies yielded confusing results (for reviews and analyses, see Schumacher and Nash; Ackerman; Geisler). When these studies attempted to test a central claim of WAC, that writing improves learning or thinking (Emig), they found that writing does not automatically improve either. Indeed, when writing was used to improve students' performance on the usual kinds of school tests, it often had no effect or a negative effect. Ackerman concludes his meta-analysis of twenty-six studies thus: "Writing simply may not perform well in the relatively brief and unrelated learning episodes that appear both in research and in practice" (359).

When students were given tasks differing significantly from "the standard knowledge-transmission purposes of the schools," however, writing helped students learn (Geisler 48). Simple fact-based learning may be better achieved through other study strategies (Durst; Penrose). But when students need to learn to solve what psychologists call "ill-structured problems," where there are no single right answers—as in most professional workplaces—

writing seems to help (Ackerman 359). Moreover, when we "distinguish between the literacy practices required in schools and those used in the . . . professions," Geisler argues, the experimental studies suggest that writing helps students become more involved in the activities, values, and expert practices of professions, as students appropriate—and sometimes critique—the written genres with which those professions do much of their work (44).

Experimental studies also suggest that it makes all the difference what kind of writing (genre, in Carolyn Miller's formulation of it) is used to support learning and how that writing is used (process in the broad sense). Students who are not motivated or challenged by a genre of writing do not profit from it, and some genres of writing support some kinds of learning better than others. For example, Cooper and MacDonald found that students in a Chinese-literature course who wrote journals directed by a series of cumulative, discipline-based prompts leading them through the readings did much better on analytical course papers than students who wrote undirected or "dialogic" journals. The journal prompts helped the students read the material in terms of the discipline of literary analysis.

"Writing does complicate and thus enrich the thinking process," as Ackerman concludes his 1993 research review, "but will result in learning only when writing is situationally supported and valued" (359). In other words, there is nothing magic about writing. As anthropological and sociological studies of literacy worldwide have shown, writing is not autonomous (Street). It does not work in one way, with one set of effects, but in many ways, with many and varied effects, given the specific system(s) of human activity in which a particular text or specific genre functions. Writing facilitates all kinds of social actions using all sorts of textual forms, in combination with nontextual forms (machinery, apparatus, architecture, gesture, drawing, etc.).

Writing is not a single generalizable skill, then, learned once and for all at an early age, but a complex range of accomplishments, variously tied to myriad human practices, which may develop over a lifetime as the desire or need to do new things with new genres of writing arises. Just as a scientist who can write one genre (say, an experimental article) might find it daunting or even impossible to write an acceptable article for a mass circulation magazine—even on the same subject—so students moving from course to course must learn new genres (McCarthy, "Stranger"). Writing is a potentially powerful tool of teaching, as it is a tool of many other modern systems of activity, but an immensely plastic tool that can be used well or poorly, for good or for ill.

That is why researchers have turned to qualitative studies to tease out of the immensely varied and complex human relationships that writing facilitates those factors that students and teachers and program builders might attend to when deciding where and how to use writing. As I summarize representative studies, I will try to answer the question posed in the title. The qualitative studies point faculty and program directors beyond the search for universal or autonomous approaches toward much more messy—and human—factors. To help students learn to write for some new social practice(s), we must look at how writing variously mediates the activities of specific classrooms as they intersect with other activities that use writing—those of curricula, institutions, disciplines, professions, and the wider personal and public spaces where writing is used to get things done. The studies consistently point to four factors that condition and shape writing and learning in secondary and higher education: (1) the students' motives as they move through and beyond formal schooling, negotiating their future directions and commitments with those of the disciplines and professions that faculty and classrooms represent; (2) the identities that students (re)construct as they try on new ways with the written word; (3) the pedagogical tools that faculty provide (or don't provide) students; and (4) the processes through which students learn to write and write to learn in formal schooling.

I have organized this review in reverse chronological order, looking at writing first in professional workplaces that most students will enter and eventually transform, then in graduate and internship education, then in introductory and intermediate courses for majors, and finally in general or liberal education courses. Though this organization is counterintuitive, I admit, we must see where students are headed with their writing before we can understand the ways schooling helps (or hinders) them getting there. If, as it has traditionally been assumed, writing were autonomous—a neat, once-and-for-all skill applicable to any social practice—then looking at writing in the social practices students will enter and eventually transform with their writing would be unnecessary. But because school writing is immensely conditioned and shaped by myriad social practices, we must understand how social practices such as professions and disciplines intersect with schooling at various points in students' development as writers.

I must note here that I do not take up the important research on faculty learning to use writing to improve their teaching. Walvoord et al.'s recent study of faculty, *In the Long Run*, provides an excellent overview and critique of that literature, as well as an exemplary addition to it. Nor do I take up studies of general composition courses, except were they specifically look at students writing across the curriculum (e.g., McCarthy, "Stranger"; Ronald).

Workplace Writing—As Immensely Varied as Professional Work

Qualitative research on how students write and learn to write has been profoundly influenced by cultural-historical ethnographic and discourse-analysis studies of how professionals write and learn to write, and I begin with these studies because a central goal of higher education (and WAC/WID programs) is to prepare students to enter and transform systems of professional activity, mediated in large part by a vast range of written genres.

Bazerman began the tradition of cultural-historical ethnographic research into workplace writing by looking at the humble undergraduate research paper, taught in first-year college writing courses for a little over a century ("Relationship"). He asked what kinds of writing go on among researchers in various disciplines and how writing helps disciplines work. The sociology, history, and philosophy of science provided resources for looking closely at the ways scientists write, and Bazerman began asking how communications were organized in disciplines, how texts of various genres "fit in with the larger systems of disciplinary activity" (*Shaping* 4). Through comparative studies of single articles, discourse-based interviews with physicists, and analyses of the citation practices of social scientists, he explored how writing practices (and genres) are regularized in various fields for various purposes (*Constructing*). His historical work on the origins of the scientific experimental article and on Thomas Edison's uses of writing to build the immense technological systems of our modern world has shown how writing has come to play the various roles it has in our lives—and our students' lives (*Languages*). Bazerman's research theorizes writing in workplaces as systems of genres, connected intertextually, circulating among various people and institutions to get work done. The humble research paper and most other classroom genres have their origins and their ends in these dynamic systems of professional genres without which modern society would be impossible. Bazerman's work has been extended by a number of researchers who have examined texts in various social practices.

Myers traces the textual genres and negotiations in biology research (*Writing*). He begins with grant proposals, the most overtly persuasive genre of scientific writing and the most essential. He follows two biologists revising proposals to align themselves with the mainstream of the discipline while carving out a space for their own attempts to modify the course of that stream; he investigates the negotiation of the status of the two biologists' knowledge claims in the reviewing process of a journal; and he chronicles the controversies among specialist "core researchers" as they reinterpret each others' work. Myers also moves beyond the activity systems of core researchers to consider the textual practices of popular science journal editors and scientists as they reposition or translate their highly specialized genres into genres that give them power in the wider society, and adapt research to it. Similarly, he looks at science textbooks to see the commodification of scientific knowledge as it is "translated" to serve educational ends ("Textbooks"). And at the furthest reach of commodified expert knowledge, Myers examines a scientific controversy and public policy debate in popular magazines and newspapers (*Writing*) to see how the rhetoric of science, translated into popular genres, extends to the genres of "public" discourse ("Out"), where core researchers participate only indirectly. (The commodification of expert knowledge in expanding systems of activity also occupies Fahnestock, who analyzes the changes in information as it passes from one activity system to another in increasingly commodified form.) The ways that knowledge circulates textually in professions and disciplines helps us see the complex pathways students must trace to arrive at competence in writing in some field.

MacDonald analyzes representative research articles from three disciplines in the humanities and social sciences to connect highly specific grammatical features (e.g., substantives, nominalization) to the epistemology of a disciplinary subfield (Renaissance New Historicism, Colonial New England social history, and child-caregiver attachment research in psychology). The textual differences, she shows, are more than differences in "jargon," in formal features. Textual differences are constructed by and construct the epistemology of the subfield, its ways of cooperating to identify and solve problems, to make and remake knowledge—or, in the case of literary criticism, to realize an epideictic rather than an epistemic motive. Students must pick up not only textual features as they learn to write, but also the ways specialists think, their identity and motive as members of a disciplinary community.

Other studies examine workplaces less directly related to academia. In the tradition of Odell and Goswami's groundbreaking studies of workplace writing, Yates chronicles the rise of modern organizational communication from the early nineteenth century through the 1920s. She examines its functions (control of far-flung organizations such as railroads), technologies (typewriter, rotary press, carbon paper, and the most powerful of all, the vertical file), and genres (memos, letters, reports, company newsletters, printed forms, timetables, etc.). Yates and Orlikowski have combined Giddens's structuration theory with genre theory to critique contemporary management communication theory from a genre perspective, including the genre of e-mail (Orlikowski and Yates). The ways people communicate textually in and among organizations change over time, and students entering a field enter an unfolding historical process in which their futures are bound up with changing communicative practices.

Studies of the genres and genre systems of a range of workplaces have followed. For example, McCarthy ("Psychiatrist") examines the epistemological and textual consequences of the *Diagnostic and Statistical Manual of Mental Disorders (DSM)*, psychiatry's charter document, on a psychiatrist's evaluation of a client. McCarthy and Gerring trace the negotiations that led to *DSM*'s revision. They followed the working group on eating disorders for three years, documenting the struggle to create a new diagnostic category, Binge Eating Disorder, and the stakes involved in the decision: status, research funding, and so on. The recognition of a new disorder by the profession was an intensely rhetorical/political process. Berkenkotter and Ravotas continue that line of investigation as they follow the construction of categories in the written genres of clinicians.

Van Nostrand traces the genres of research and development in the U.S. Department of Defense, charting the recursive flow of knowledge between customers and vendors through the flow of six genres, such as the Request for Proposal. A similar historical interest is evident in Huckin's studies of changes in a professional organization's convention program, the evolution of a scholarly journal, and the complex cycles of peer review in a scientific journal (Berkenkotter and Huckin). These and similar studies of the microlevel textual negotiations that workplace writing mediates show the deeply political nature of written communication in which students will become enmeshed when they enter disciplinary and professional networks.

Brandt is carrying on a large-scale study of the literacy of people from many walks of life over many decades to see how the writing in homes, churches, civic organizations, and so on intersects with the writing in school and workplace. She finds that people's life experience of literacy is immensely various and complex, ranging over a lifetime ("Remembering," "Accumulating").

In sum, writing is clearly not a single, autonomous skill, learned once and for all, but a varied and developing accomplishment. It is bound up with complex questions of motive, identity, tools, and processes. And writing in formal schooling can prepare—or fail to prepare—people for a lifetime of involvements in modern culture—personal, civic, religious, and artistic as well as intellectual and professional.

Writing in Graduate School and in Internships

Ordinarily, students must see themselves as students, mastering a discrete body of information and skills—until they find themselves in contact with professional networks. But in making the transition from school to work, school writing takes on added importance and complexity. Perhaps the best place to see the difficulties students have learning to write in the disciplines is in studies of graduate students and interns. Both emphasize how idiosyncratic, gradual, and "messy" (in Prior's phrase [*Writing/ Disciplinarity*]) it is to learn to write, even when students have chosen a profession and are motivated to identify themselves as professionals and to learn its discursive tools and communicative processes.

There have been many remarkable recent studies of internships (e.g., Winsor; Anson and Forsberg; Dias et al.; Freedman, Adam, and Smart; Smart, "Genre," "Knowledge-Making"; Paré, "Discourse," "Writing") that describe students/professionals in transition, struggling to make sense of a professional networks' writing using the tools they picked up in their schooling. Similarly, studies of the transition from undergraduate to graduate education have broadened our understanding of the complex play of power and identity within writing processes in complex, hierarchical, professional activity systems.

In the seminal study of graduate student writing, Berkenkotter, Huckin, and Ackerman follow the rhetorical development of one student during his first year in a prestigious Ph.D. program in rhetoric. Their quantitative discourse analysis of his five course papers written that year showed that "Nate" (co-author Ackerman) gradually came to produce texts that used more and more of the tools of the discipline: its expository patterns, syntactic complexity, avoidance of hyperbole, and sentence subjects referring to the disciplinary object and not himself.

Yet Nate had difficulty producing consistent cohesive ties, logical connections, and thematic unity. The authors trace this difficulty to his unfamiliarity with the discipline's activity system. And they examine, through qualitative methods, his processes in learning to write the genres of social science research through reading in the field and interacting with faculty. Nate drew on his history as a teacher of composition, a role in which expressive, personal genres are valued, to learn the much more impersonal, formal genres of expository social science writing. He reached back through informal writing in notes to himself and memos to professors to generate ideas and—crucially—to wrestle with issues of identity and motive. He finally came to (uneasy) terms with the necessity to adopt the observer stance of the discipline and its social-scientific detachment from the student writers it studies.

This article announced a central theme in future work: that newcomers to a genre/activity bring their cultural history to their writing and take an active role in learning as they wrestle with new genres. The studies of graduate students' writing that followed also suggest that disciplinary enculturation may be less a gradual absorption or assimilation and more a messy struggle.

Drawing heavily on Bakhtin's theory of speech genres, Paul Prior's studies of graduate students' development in applied linguistics, sociology, geography, and American studies extended the analysis to "the ways historical activity is constituted by and lays down sediments in functional systems that coordinate with various media with different properties" ("Contextualizing," "Redefining," "Response," "Tracing," *Writing/Disciplinarity* 36). He looks at the interactions of persons, artifacts (semiotic systems and material artifacts), institutions, practices, and communities to analyze the messy flow of graduate students' literate activity over time in multiple "streams of activity."

In Prior's accounts, the multiple and often conflicting motives and goals of participants in graduate programs, their personal and disciplinary histories, shape their mutual appropriation of tools and their dynamic representations of writing tasks—and of their own identities. Students and their teachers engage in a process of "genrification"—reclassifying texts, attributing resemblance—in the process "aligning" themselves with others. Agency is distributed in streams of activity as participants appropriate voices in the networks of disciplinary practice. Their images of authorship change as they negotiate authorship among themselves in their oral and written interactions, redrawing disciplinary boundaries as they redraw their personal boundaries and align themselves with—and sometimes reject—powerful disciplinary social practices.

Ann Blakeslee builds on the work in situated cognition to analyze how graduate students learn to write experimental articles in physics—focusing on their failures. She points to the limitations of situated cognition theory's emphasis on the weakness of intentional or prescriptive pedagogy. Indirect support "often seems insufficient to newcomers who have no previous experience engaging in the tasks they are asked to perform," she argues ("Activity" 145). Newcomers have residual writing practices and approaches to learning drawn from formal schooling that they appropriate—often unsuccessfully and unreflectively—to genres of research writing that have subtly different motives and conventions. And students' lack of authority makes it hard for them to fully engage in the domain's activity or challenge its direction, even "though they may be completely competent intellectually" ("Activity" 156). Blakeslee argues that explicit, direct support, reflective mentioning, making goals and motives explicit, and an earlier sharing of authority may be necessary support for engagement in the discipline's activity or allow some newcomers to understand, embrace, and transform the discipline and its genres.

Casanave also tells the story of a graduate student wrestling unsuccessfully with writing demands, this time a Hispanic sociology student who could not reconcile the conflict between disciplinary and personal values played out in her attempts to write assignments in theory courses. "Everyday" English and Spanish "came to be less valuable to her over time as tools for communicating her ideas about her work with friends and family in that they were not valued as resources for communication within the [sociology] department" ("Cultural" 161). Moreover, contradictions within sociology between positivist and hermeneutic approaches (made salient in the writing assignments) left her unable to reconcile the motive that drew her into the discipline—helping women, minorities, and educators in culturally mixed neighborhoods—with the motive of the most powerful wing of sociology. Alienated, she dropped out to become a researcher in a nonprofit Puerto Rican educational organization in New York. But she regretted leaving because she felt she would have less power to make a difference if she didn't stay with the more powerful core of the disciplinary practice. "Having a Masters in sociology is not enough to get people to listen to the ideas of a young Puerto Rican woman" ("Cultural" 173).

Chin traces the material conditions of communication—phone access, office placement, and so on—for graduate students in journalism. Their "failures" to write the genres research-oriented professors demanded of them arose from the sociologic of their ambiguous dangling between the activity systems of working journalists and professors of journalism, unsure of their identity as writers—and future professionals.

The most in-depth treatment of interns' writing is Winsor's four-year longitudinal study of four engineering students. Taught by their discipline to ignore the rhetorical character of their education and work, they nevertheless gradually appropriate the genres of professional writing and come to realize the importance of rhetorical expertise in the complex textual negotiations through which their profession—and the large corporate organizations it serves—is dynamically reconstructed. Each student follows a different path in his or her appropriation of written genres, paths laid out by their different personal histories and reflected in the very different professional roles and identities within engineering that each finds. What is competent writing at one point in their education, at one position in the vast activity systems of engineering, may be radically different from competent writing at some other point, some other node in the professional network. Given this local and variable character of writing, would-be insiders have great difficulty stepping back in order to understand and critique the rhetoric of their discipline, though Winsor finds such critique emerging in these young engineers.

The most comprehensive research on interns is being carried on by a group of Canadians who are exploring the transition from formal schooling to work in banking (Smart, "Genre," "Knowledge-Making"; Dias et al.; Freedman and Smart), finance (Freedman, Adam, and Smart), law (Freedman, "Reconceiving"), social work (Dias et al.; Paré, "Discourse"), engineering (Beer), architecture (Medway, "Language"; Dias et al.), and other related professions. They combine North American genre theory, situated learning, distributed cognition, and Engeström's systems version of activity theory to trace the profound ways school writing differs from workplace writing—and the ways student writers become professionals writing.

Beginning with the notion that people learn to write through activity-with-others, social engagement, Freedman and Adam describe school activity—the collaboration of teachers and learners—as "facilitated performance," in which the goal of the activity itself is learning. In nonschool workplaces, writing "occurs as an integral but tacit part of participation in communities of practice, whose activities are oriented towards practical or material outcomes," which the authors call "attenuated authentic performance," modifying Lave and Wenger's (1991) categories (Dias et al. 199). This difference profoundly affects people and their uses of texts in a host of ways: the psychology of instructor-learner interactions, the sociologics of power relations, the genres people write and read, the nature of assessment and sorting, and the writing processes they use, with improvisatory learning and "document cycling"—feedback and revision loops—being much more important in nonschool workplaces.

Smart and Freedman's work on banking explores the ways in which cognition in organizations is "enacted, preserved, communicated, and renegotiated through written texts" in systems of genres that mediate the routine actions of bankers and economists. They look at interns, senior managers learning a new genre, staff analysts, and others (Smart, "Genre," "Knowledge-Making"; Dias et al.; Freedman and Smart).

Paré's studies of social workers in hospitals and legal settings also suggest the extraordinarily broad range of genres/uses for writing, and the ways genres mediate power and authority (Dias et al.; Paré, "Discourse," "Writing"). Within a hospital or a court system, a large number of professions organize their work around shared written records, and in the writing and use of those records Paré traces competing and often contradictory motives. Social workers must negotiate various administrative, financial, legal, and medical interests and accountabilities—along with the interests of individual clients—in the routine but always changing genres of written records. Fledgling social workers, in internships and practicums, struggle mightily to find and create their place among these professional communities through writing, in which even the most seemingly trivial phrases in reports can have life-changing consequences for clients. Fortunately, newcomers are guided by traditions of induction that support them, in tacit ways, as they learn what to write/do—and who they are in the process.

Medway's studies of architecture students (Medway, "Language"; Dias et al.) emphasize another theme in North American genre research: the relation of alphabetized text to other media of inscriptions. He traces the ways students use a wide range of genres in alphabetized text that are "casual or undeclared" (informal and private jottings on drawings, notes, etc.) in conjunction with genres of graphical signs and diagrams that have a spatial as well as syntactic arrangement. In the "unofficial texts the students are rehearsing both the ideational content and the rhetoric—the terms and argumentative structures—of the discipline" (Dias et al. 29).

These qualitative studies of the transition from schooling to work get at the microlevel relations between school and society, in Dewey's phrase (Russell, "Vygotsky," "Rethinking"), and put into a wider—and starker—perspective the debates over transfer of learning and explicit versus implicit instruction (Freedman, "Show"; Williams and Colomb). The motives, identities, tools, and processes that students appropriate as they move from formal schooling to work are by no means linear or neat. They do not simply transfer knowledge of writing to new environments, nor do they learn to write through either explicit precepts and formulae or implicit trial and error. Rather, they learn to write through a complex negotiation between people and tools as they expand their involvement with some powerful system(s) of human activity mediated by dynamic systems of texts.

Writing in Intermediate and Beginning Courses in the Disciplines

Questions of the motivation for writing are central to students who have just begun their involvement with a discipline that they imagine might become their life's path. In studies of students in intermediate and beginning courses in a major, it is clear that writing is not a single skill, learned once and for all at an early age, as the autonomous view of literacy would have it. Instead, students appropriate (or ignore or resist) the genres of a class or discipline (pick up or reject its discursive tools) to the extent that they find them useful for further involvement with the discipline and its motives—or with other disciplines or peer groups, families, churches, hobbies, etc. This is often at odds with the motives of their teachers.

Professors, as representatives of a discipline, generally see students as professionals-in-training (Walvoord and McCarthy). They often assume—like the blind men and the elephant—that their particular genres represent the whole of academic writing. Since modern secondary and higher education developed in the late 1800s, school writing has settled into a relatively few "classroom genres" (Christie): the research paper, the essay (exam), and the laboratory report, each of which reflects, however dimly, the writing of professionals (scholarly articles and essays, experimental reports) (Russell, *Writing,* "Rethinking"). Yet these classroom genres vary immensely by discipline, such that a student must "psych" the teacher to divine the expectations for a particular discipline and course. What pushes students to do that?

The most immediate motive for students and teachers is the getting and assigning of grades, the institutional motive of selection. Students are writing first "for the grade," not for further involvement. Sometimes, however, students come to identify with (want further involvement with) one or more of those disciplines, and are motivated to appropriate its ways with words (learn to write new genres, to put it simply). They begin writing out of some motive beyond the grade.

As undergraduates in North American universities move from course to course, discipline to discipline, they are like "strangers in strange lands," as McCarthy ("Stranger") put it in one of the best cross-disciplinary comparative case studies of writing in undergraduate education. Her participant, Dave, experienced great difficulty when asked to write in radically different genres in biology, poetry, and composition classes, with little sense of the scholarly and research activities of the disciplines that motivated those genres. Despite some similarities among the genres of the different disciplines, he experienced them as totally different from one another. Because he was more interested in biology, and because the teacher furnished him more tools for involvement with the discipline than did the poetry professor, he more readily appropriated the genres of biology and came to see himself as a potential scientist (rather than a potential literary critic).

Faigley and Hansen's study of students writing social science papers in psychology, sociology, and English reveals the complexity of recognizing and appropriating disciplinary motives and discursive tools. Students in the social science courses found it difficult to understand the motive of the writing from the professor's (disciplinary) point of view. "To tell you the truth, I really don't understand what he's trying to do," one complained (143). An English professor helping a student write a sociology paper did not understand the sociological motive for analyzing the penal system, and the English professor's only comments on the student's paper dealt with surface features rather than "the depth of [the student's] encounter with the probation system," which the sociology professor was interested in (as well as the student, whose motive was becoming a lawyer) (147). Though the English teacher could understand the motives of writing to a general reader (journalistic genres), he could not evaluate the student's grasp of the penal system from a sociological perspective (and therefore the student's success in writing sociological analysis). Similar misunderstandings about "task representations" occur within courses in the same discipline.

Herrington's ("Writing") comparison of upper-level students writing in a lab course and a design course in chemical engineering found that the "courses did represent different classroom contexts or forums" (340). Lines of reasoning differed between the two courses' reports (340–41), as did the students' perception of the role of writing: epideictic and evaluative in the lab course, where the assignment did not have a plausible professional context and the students were writing for the instructor (or a less-informed version of the instructor), and deliberative in the design course, where the students were writing to influence an imaginary client's decision and the professor took the role of project design chief. In the lab course, students were not often conscious of having an identity beyond that of a student pleasing a professor. In the design course, they took on the role of practicing engineers—"suddenly we're experts" (349). They cited their own knowledge much more frequently, but displayed less knowledge of basic engineering (since a professional audience would assume it). Herrington concludes:

> Members of each community did not always agree on the conventions appropriate to that forum. Professors' perceptions of the conventions sometimes differed from those of the students. In the design course, the professor presented [the] audience as [a] project design chief, in a corporate setting, and students responded accordingly. Faculty shaped these roles, viewing the lab exercises as a learner-centered exercise to get concepts straight. Students saw it as tedious exercise in giving teachers what they want. (342)

Herrington's ("Teaching") study of two students in an introductory literary criticism course suggests how crucial it is for students to appropriate the motive of the discipline, as well as its discursive tools, in order to write successfully. The teacher wanted the students to "learn how to read [and write] like English majors," but the "individual students' own backgrounds and interests" profoundly influenced their "perceptions of functions and how they respond to the teacher" (152). Students who had already appropriated the motive of literary study, who already understood the object of the game, made argumentative claims and marshaled evidence for a discipline-sanctioned argumentative purpose—"not just a spit-back, [but] some reason you should be writing this paper," as one student put it (156). They were working out problems not only for themselves (their personal motives) but also for the disciplinary community. Herrington suggests that a more explicit writing pedagogy might give students a way to link their interests to those of the discipline and appropriate discursive tools for greater involvement, fostering independent inquiry rather than merely doing it for the grade.

Greene's ("Role") study of two groups of upper-level European-history students using six sources and their prior knowledge to write two different classroom genres (report and problem-based essay) also points to students' difficulty in going beyond the activity system of formal schooling. Neither the group writing reports nor the group writing problem-based essays used more prior knowledge than the other (or much at all). Both merely attempted to "demonstrate that they had done the reading, that they knew what the key issues and problems were" (67). Even on the problem-based essay, most students did not feel free to go beyond sources and venture an opinion, only demonstrating that they had read the sources. "You leave yourself open far more," said one student, who had been criticized by teachers when she ventured an opinion. But another student with prior experience in a debate club "constructed an image of the teacher as someone who valued the ideas of students and appreciated students' willingness to go beyond the task" (61). Though the students writing problem-based essays used more items from sources (perhaps because the prompt was more involving), both groups tended to use citations as "sources of information rather than as resources for supporting an argument or locating a faulty path" (68). Neither group did better on a pre-/post-test of learning, perhaps because even the problem-based task was perceived as a school exercise, not as a professional genre that involved students with the processes and motives of the discipline, as the researchers had hypothesized.

Jolliffe and Brier's study of upper-level (and some graduate) nursing and political science students writing abstracts of research literature supports their proposition that "a person's participation in the intellectual activities of an academic discipline directly affects his or her acquisition, use, and awareness of these kinds of knowledge"—including writing (35). "For the political science writers, the degree to which they read texts on subjects similar [to the article they wrote abstracts on] significantly predicted a higher summed holistic score on abstracts" (67). But nursing students did better on the summaries (e.g., discussed methodology more often), perhaps because they had almost all worked in nursing, all wanted to be nurses, and their curriculum required more writing in professional genres (68–79). Political science students, by contrast, "take political science courses for a number of personal and professional reasons" and have more electives. "Thus, political science professors may not feel the need to socialize students into the language . . . of the field." "Even the more advanced writers [graduate students] in this study suggested little unanimity on what it means to write successfully as a political scientist." Nursing students, with their intensive socialization in a more specialized and "crowded" curriculum, appropriated genres more quickly (71). The student nurses and their teachers saw themselves as soon-to-be professionals in action; the political science students were still doing school, not yet actively involved in professional work and lacking identity as professionals-in-training.

Hare and Fitzsimmons found that undergraduates from nursing who had read research literature from their field, analyzed its IMRD (instruction, methods, results, discussion) structure, and written papers using that structure were much more adept at writing a missing discussion from a research article in *education* than were undergraduates in education who had not read, analyzed, or written research articles in their own field using the IMRD structure. The nursing students appropriately recognized the genre as an experimental article and appropriated useful discursive tools. They related claims to data and in some cases provided warrants and backing. Moreover, they reported the results and discussed how the results filled the gap in research. Their discussion sections, however, clearly showed their lack of involvement with the activity of educational research. They made far more unsubstantiated claims than graduate students in education, and were "unable to make incisive and original claims," even compared to the undergraduate students. Hare and Fitzsimmons conclude:

> On the strength of their literacy experiences in nursing, they were able to invent discussion sections for an educational research article that were structurally comparable to the ones written by masters' students in education. On the other hand, education students with virtually no experience in the research discourse community were unable to invent the community's discourse successfully. (375)

The choice of a life path clearly affects students' motivation, sense of identity/agency, and choice of tools in writing. Chiseri-Strater offers a moving book-length portrait of two students, Anna and Nick, who use writing as a tool to make decisions on major and career, and two professors trying out changes in the way they use writing to teach general education. Anna has trouble meeting the writing demand of an art history professor that she move beyond incoherent description and biography ("Cuisinart" writing) to disciplinary-sanctioned analysis (97). On a final paper, however, Anna begins to connect art to the ecofeminism movement, uniting the personal, political, and academic dimensions of life. She becomes an art history major as a result. Nick, by contrast, uses writing to try on identities, to pose, as he moves from major to major, but he never overcomes his view of academic writing as competitive display, and never becomes involved in a discipline.

> In the end, Anna becomes a successful learner, not because she adapts to the mastery model but because she makes a conscious effort to "connect" her course work, an approach documented by feminist scholars looking at the different learning styles of women students. Nick, however, remains the separate knower within the academic setting, compartmentalizing and isolating his course work. (146)

The teachers helped little in these processes, she concludes: "From the students' perspective the literacy norms within most fields—the reading, writing, talking, and thinking patterns of the discipline—most often remain powerfully invisible, not offering ready access for them to earn membership in any discourse community" (144).

Similarly, in a four-year study of one biology student, Haas traces Eliza's growing sophistication as a reader of biology texts. Eliza gradually increased her involvement with a wider network of human agents and texts, "a growing cast of characters in the 'drama' of her interaction with texts" (71). In her summer job as a professor's lab assistant, for example, she got a sense of the sociocultural settings of biology.

Walvoord and McCarthy's book-length study of four courses in different disciplines suggests the complexity involved in understanding students' writing challenges and helping them to meet them. For example, when a production management professor had students evaluate various sites for a stadium, he expected them to write using the quantitative tools of his field in a genre similar to those of his discipline/profession, in the role of a business decision maker. He was dismayed to find they wrote in genres of the popular press and peer groups, without reference to the genres of the discipline he was teaching them. They had trouble seeing themselves as professionals-in-training, appropriating instead model genres and strategies from their other courses, such as the term paper or reflection paper, rather than learning to write a new genre, the business plan. Walvoord and the professor found that the students had difficulty gathering sufficient information for the case study; instead of using information from the textbook to develop problem-solving procedures (the how), they merely harvested declarative knowledge (the what). Their conversations with peers pushed their writing in the direction of dorm room or street corner debate rather than disciplinary analysis. And they often lacked topic-specific knowledge that would allow them to gather information in useful ways for later analysis—and see themselves as professionals-in-training as well as students completing another course assignment.

Walvoord and the professor traced the difficulties to mismatches between students' and teacher's expectations. They set about expanding and restructuring the assignment sheet, explicitly teaching—early in the process—strategies for writing, and modeling more useful strategies for gathering information, analyzing it in discipline-specific ways, and writing the genres expected in the language they wanted students to use.

Similarly, a biology professor's students had difficulty defining roles for themselves and their audience as they wrote lab reports on an experiment they had designed and conducted to evaluate a product. Some took the role of moralizing parent or storyteller, for example, or cast readers in the role of sports fans. Students had trouble stating a position, using discipline-based methods to arrive at and support it, managing complexity, gathering sufficient specific information, constructing operational definitions, and organizing the paper in the IMRD structure. When the professor taught the course three years later, she had developed a series of teaching strategies such as regularly spending class time doing group exercises and presentations on relevant writing tools (e.g., graphics and organization). The students' performance, as measured by external raters, increased.

As more teachers and researchers come to recognize the importance of disciplinary—and social—activity, qualitative research in undergraduate general education courses is expanding to trace the ways motives, identities, tools, and processes are appropriated (and ignored and rejected) by students exploring different disciplinary involvements leading to life paths—and the ways with words these entail.

Writing in General Education

Students just entering college and encountering its discourses in general education or liberal arts courses have an even more difficult task than students who have the direction—the identity and motive—that a major affords, because they are even further from involvement in the activity systems of disciplines, from the day-to-day actions that motivate its writing. Poised between the discourses of their networks of home, peer group, and mass media and the specialized discourses and activity systems of disciplines and professions, they must, as Bartholomae puts it in his ideological analysis of college students' entrance essays, begin "inventing the university" in their writing. They must "appropriate (or be appropriated by) specialized discourse" (135) to become part of some disciplinary project (system). Students "have to speak in the voice and through the codes of those of us with power and wisdom; and they not only have to do this, they have to do it before they know what they are doing, before they have a project to participate in, and before, at least in the terms of our disciplines, they have anything to say" (156). Required performance before active involvement, the need to imagine different identities and motives and the power that comes with involvement, causes errors to increase as students "find some compromise between idiosyncrasy, a personal history, on the one hand, and the requirements of convention, the history of a discipline, on the other" (135). To succeed, "a writer would have to get inside of a discourse that he could in fact only partially imagine" (160), and students in this in-between state, shuffling from one discipline and its genres to another, experience particular difficulty negotiating their futures and their identities through writing.

An important article by a group of first-year students and their teacher, Susan Miller (Anderson et al.), suggests that the "loudest voice" in students' descriptions of their motives was "that of the institution. The students were not, with the exception of Brandt [who had clear career expectations], planning schedules around related intellectual interests, but cooperating with the institution's provision of paths toward degrees," choosing from a menu of required courses and writing for the grade in them (16). This "generated feelings of frustration and singularity." They originally chose courses out of a diffident sense of duty combined with interest in a course's "uses." But these innocent motives reinforced "'me against this system' views of the pedagogical cultures they entered" (16). Psyching the teacher, divining expectations, and doing a "cost-benefit" analysis of study time and techniques, such as note taking, was central to writing. Writing was more difficult because "teachers across the curriculum did not define knowledge-making as an interactive process, with [a few] notable exceptions" (17). "Learning in these courses was assumed to be a private, competitive action" (17), and knowledge was commodified into hard facts and concepts without competing voices from the discipline that might motivate students' further involvement in its activities. In this environment, they "must compete for admission to major programs while they sustain their interest in introductory courses" (29).

Against this backdrop of an institutional system, North describes three students in an introduction to philosophy course negotiating disciplinary authority and their own personal motives in their required (and graded) journals. They appropriate the tools of philosophy, Alison to affirm her authority as a fundamentalist Christian; Mark to wrestle with his rebellion against his combative father and his inability to make a life commitment; and Yvette, a Jamaican immigrant, to find authority as an independent learner in a new institutional culture. The professor wanted the course to "achieve a general education function, personal values clarification, self discovery," but at the same time he wanted the students "to be philosophers themselves: to articulate their personal philosophies in the context of Western and Eastern thought as represented for them by their textbook" (229). In their struggle to reconcile personal and disciplinary authority and thus identity, students wrestled mightily with the writing, "to get a grip on what we're supposed to do in the journal" (245), as Yvette put it, to sound or not sound like a philosopher: to write garbled textbook paraphrase in an attempt to please the professor, or common phrases from their "personal" activity systems that risked the professor's criticism.

Such double binds are even more dramatically illustrated in a series of studies by Fishman and McCarthy chronicling Fishman's development as a philosophy professor using writing ("Community," "Teaching," *John Dewey;* McCarthy and Fishman.) He is torn between a desire to give students authority and their "own" language, and his love of philosophy's tools of analysis and his sense of duty to the discipline. As he grants and withholds authority (and grades) to students, he explores the limits of radical pedagogy, of traditional pedagogy, of expressivism, of diversity, and, finally, of a Deweyan pedagogy he tries to formulate:

> That's the problem with starting with personal experience. . . . Students are going to leave this course thinking they've done philosophy. And that's not fair to them. They've not done the reading, so they've not really tasted the challenge and rigor of philosophy. If they're to become sophisticated in their own discussions, they've got to understand something of what's already been said. (Fishman and McCarthy, "Community" 76)

The students attempt to figure him out as they write. Fishman's classroom was "a gathering of novices without an elder," McCarthy writes. "However, it was their very success in establishing their own voices and roles within the group which led students to resist the reading [and philosophical writing]. . . . They saw the texts [of philosophy] as unwelcome intruders" in their personal and collective searches ("Community" 76).

Disciplinary texts are more than repositories of knowledge; they are part of a dynamic system of disciplinary activity, and general education students are outsiders. Geisler offers an activity theory critique of cognitive psychology's autonomous spatial modeling of writing processes—which dominated empirical research in composition for almost a decade—by modeling writing processes in terms of temporal action. Expertise, she argues, is rhetorical. Experts don't merely know and apply rules or structures or norms; they constantly recreate and reinterpret them over time in dynamic social/historical conditions using writing and other semiotic means. She analyzes the development of expertise in the discipline of philosophy by comparing students in a general education philosophy course and graduate students in philosophy on the "same" task, an analytical philosophy paper.

The graduate students did much better on the task because they had already appropriated the motives, identity, and genres of the discipline, which extend back to William James's curious shuttling between academic and nonacademic activities and genres in his philosophical writing. They wrote as insiders, even when they used personal material and narrative. The general education undergraduate students, in stark contrast, constructed the writing task in terms of more overtly personal motives and goals, and wrote narratives closer to the genres of English classes, with which they were more familiar. The liberal arts students were not doing philosophy, but working out, for example, personal religious or family issues using some of the discursive tools of philosophy—but in a way not sanctioned by the discipline.

Walvoord and McCarthy's book looked at two general education courses, in history and psychology, as well as two upper-level courses. Like other professors in upper-level courses, the history and psychology professors viewed students as professionals-in-training—as debaters in history and as social scientists or counselors in psychology (though the psychology course also allowed for nonprofessional roles). The process of historical argument (stating a position, supporting it with evidence, and handling counterarguments) was taught in large part through oral classroom debates, which modeled the process and served as prewriting—though the process had to be taught and refined to make the students' writing more than mere text processing and to facilitate involvement in the activity of history through its genres.

Finding classroom genres that allow both disciplinary and personal or civic involvement is difficult. In a general education psychology course on human sexuality, the students were assigned to write a letter to a friend about to marry, giving advice on "how to have a good marital sex life" (Walvoord and McCarthy 150). The assignment presumed four complex and interrelated roles: "social scientist, counselor, mentor/friend and self who uses professional knowledge for personal decision-making" (150). Students found it difficult to construct an audience and identity as writers. Yet these roles encompassed the various motives that the students in an introductory psychology course might have, and supported the instructor's general education goals of incorporating and testing personal experience in light of disciplinary knowledge. Students tended to adopt the role of "text processor addressing a teacher checking textbook knowledge," or the role of a layperson, rather than the role of professional-in-training. And they appropriated models from other settings (e.g., essay test answer, dorm conversation) that were not sufficient from the teacher's disciplinary point of view (153). The professor and Walvoord looked for strategies to strengthen the expert stance of the student writers and find an appropriate tone that would allow them to integrate discipline-based methods and support a position while still negotiating the complex rhetorical stance the letter required.

Students and teachers in general or liberal education learn and teach and write in an institution where specialization and rigor constitute the highest value, but general or liberal education courses can offer only an introduction. The ambiguous role of writing in general or liberal education, and the genres students and teachers choose and reject, put students' and professors' motives and identities into a complex negotiation as they choose, reject, and transform discursive tools appropriated from the disciplines and personal lives they bring to the classroom.

Where the Literature on WAC/WID Points

The most striking aspect of the qualitative WAC/WID research literature is that it suggests again and again that when writing mediates further involvement with the activity—the social life—of the discipline, it is more successful, both for inviting students to go further intellectually and personally and for selection (helping them and other stakeholders make informed decisions about their future involvements). The literature suggests that for students to achieve the kind of involvement necessary in order to write a new genre successfully, they need four things:

1. Motivation: A motive for involving themselves with the people who write in new ways (genres), people pursuing different disciplinary objects of study, is central in drawing students beyond the ways they have written before into new written genres of involvement.

Because institutions of formal education are set up to help professions select students and help students select professions, the grade (officially enabling further involvement) will be a motive and object at all levels. And instructors must acknowledge this and take it into account in assigning, teaching, and evaluating writing. As studies repeatedly show, when instructors do not demonstrate that the writing is important by making it central to teaching and evaluation, most students do not involve themselves with it (writing intensive WAC programs acknowledge the need for such motivation by requiring that writing count significantly in the grade). The tendency to assume that students will write well or learn content through writing simply because they are writing—with or without the motivation to invest the time and effort in writing well—is a legacy of the autonomous view of writing so widespread in our culture.

Though grades may be an initial motive and objective, they are only crude spurs toward further involvement. The writing must help students realize more substantive motives in working with new disciplinary objects of study if it is to be valuable beyond the grade. The motives for and objectives of writing may be those of the discipline, its problems and social values, as students come to select and be selected for further involvement in a profession. And the clearer the relation between the ongoing activity of the profession and the writing in the classroom, the greater the potential for involvement in the profession, for appropriating its objectives and motives, for learning to enter and transform that profession.

Alternatively, students' motives for and objectives of writing may be what has been called "personal" or "public"—further involvement with already-existing activity systems of family, friends, religion, art, politics, gender, race, culture, or another discipline, as students use writing in some discipline to realize motives that may have little or nothing to do with the profession the course represents. Studies point again and again to students who use writing for objectives and with motives that are not those of the professor or the discipline. Students work out personal and public issues through writing in unpredictable ways; the task the professor has in mind may be very different from the task students are doing from their perspective on the assignment. In a sense, the mismatches and double binds this creates for teachers and students—whether from confusion or downright resistance—can be important to students' development, as they search out paths of future involvement, appropriating, rejecting, and transforming what they are offered in courses (Ronald; Greene, "Making"). Writing is intensely multivalent (in a way multiple-choice tests are not), and the research suggests that these differing motives for and objectives of writing—even on the same assignment—be taken into account.

2. Identity: To understand the ways in which students write and learn to write differently than they have before, researchers have found it crucial to understand the ways in which students construct their identities as writers in particular disciplines and genres. Writing (unlike multiple-choice exams) demands that students have a voice, a sense of themselves as empowered to say some things (and not others). In choosing an identity in their writing, a sense of agency, they enter a complex negotiation with the instructor (and perhaps other students), with the social practices they are already involved in and empowered to write in, and with the more powerful social practices of the discipline that they may choose or choose not (and be chosen or not chosen) to enter. Students must see themselves (past, present, or future) in the writing. Instructors tend to see students as potential professionals-in-training or as vessels to be filled with information (whose potential uses are too veiled in myriad futures to take into account). Students tend to see themselves as students, after a grade and perhaps a life direction, or at least a job. Some will come to identify with the discipline and want to become a part of it, perhaps even involved enough to help transform it.

Studies repeatedly point to students' and instructors' confusion about what identity to assign to themselves and each other in the writing and reading. Where the writing, teaching, and learning seem most successful, instructors and students have a clear sense of their identity and agency, what they can do and say now and what they cannot. And the clearer this is—whether because of a specialized curriculum or extraordinary efforts by the instructor to empower students—the greater the success of writing for learning.

Identity is deeply involved with issues of gender, age, social class, and ethnicity, which have just begun to be studied. As we have seen, writing is a messy activity. It is conditioned—but never determined—by a huge range of historical involvements and by the expectation of future involvements, stretching into an indeterminate future. The few studies that have considered gender, age, social class, and ethnicity suggest that the most powerful influences are families, neighborhoods, and friends. Again and again in the literature we see that the changes resulting from contact with formal education are polyvalent. Change may be "learning" for the teacher but "selling out" for parents and friends. The literature on writing and learning is replete with accounts of deep identity struggles in individuals and groups (e.g., women, African Americans) as they sort out their life directions in relation to "personal" activity systems of family, peer groups, and so on, and as they (re)construct their identities from among contradictory motives of various systems of human activity (Velez; Haas; North; Casanave; Chiseri-Strater). Writing is difficult in part because the process of appropriating certain tools-in-use and not others implies—implicates students and teachers in—certain life directions, certain affiliations, with long-term consequences for their identity (Walvoord and McCarthy).

3. Tools: Qualitative research strongly suggests that students need a range of tools for writing that lead to further involvement. Motive is insufficient by itself (Hare and Fitzsimmons). The most crucial choice of tools is that of genre. In what ways will the kinds of writing students are asked (and allowed) to do involve them in the activity system of the discipline, or help them more usefully engage in activity systems beyond it? If the goal is memorization of facts and concepts, extended writing may not be the best choice. If faculty want something more, then they must choose genres that will bring students into contact with the uses of facts and concepts in their (students' and professors' and professionals') worlds. Fortunately, every discipline and every profession has a wide range of genres, from the most specialized experimental reports and esoteric academic journal articles to the least specialized mass-media magazine and newspaper articles, brochures, position statements, and so on, through which a discipline or profession makes its work useful to various publics. Faculty tend to stick to the traditional classroom genres of essay (exam), research paper, and canned lab report, which have often fossilized into sterile exercises, divorced from the myriad dynamic activities of the discipline. Choosing a genre for student writing is a way of opening students to the worlds of writing through which people work and live.

Other tools for learning to write and writing to learn take many forms in many media, such as explicit instructions and criteria, models, precepts, talk, and physical action. With enough time for trial and error, students can appropriate a genre successfully without explicit help. But most courses don't have that time (or provide sufficient feedback to show students what works and what doesn't). So students need other tools to demystify the discourse of a course or discipline and its uses in and beyond the course or discipline. These tools for helping students learn are all too rarely used in college courses.

Because faculty have been socialized in a discipline, they often assume that students share their perceptions and expectations about writing—what makes it effective and good. The writing, genres, and expectations of their disciplines have become second nature to faculty. But the studies of writing in the disciplines show that unsuccessful writing (from the point of view of faculty, students, or both) proceeds from misunderstandings about what constitutes good writing in a particular genre. Students need the central tool of clear instructions about the expectations of writing in the discipline, such as assignment sheets and grading criteria.

Another crucial tool is models or examples of the kinds of writing expected. Students have difficulty producing writing in a genre if they have not read examples of it—and understood them as examples of the kind of writing that works in the discipline (Fishman and McCarthy, "Community"; Herrington, "Writing"; Brooke; Greene, "Making"; Charney and Carlson; McCarthy, "Strangers"; Blakeslee, "Activity," "Readers," "Rhetorical"; Henry; Prior, "Contextualizing," "Redefining," "Response," "Tracing," *Writing/Disciplinarity;* but see Freedman, "Show"). Depending on the history and motives of the students, modeling may be implicit or explicit, but modeling is an essential—though often ignored—tool. And models may be used well (as invitations to involvement) or poorly (as forms to be mindlessly copied).

Another tool for demystifying writing is precepts or guide lines about how writing in a genre is done—through assignment sheets, grading criteria, explicit teaching of conventions, specific analysis of models, and so on. Without precepts, students may not understand the salient features of a genre from models presented (if any are), or they may appropriate unimportant features and ignore central ones. Precepts, like models, can be used effectively or ineffectively, as general cookbook recipes and formulas (based on the assumption that writing is autonomous), or as information on how a discipline works through its writing and how students can work with the discipline using what is valuable to them.

Talking together, either in large-group discussion or small-group work, is another important tool. Nystrand's research on secondary literature instruction confirms and expands research on classroom talk that strongly suggests students learn from open-ended dialogue about the content, as they can formulate and reformulate their understanding in preparation for, or as part of, a process of writing. Most classroom talk, however, is not open-ended dialogue on the content, but recitation, in which the teacher elicits previously known information (as on a test), or discussion not related to the content. Neither seems to involve students in the activity of the discipline in a way that permits them to do extended writing on ill-structured problems as well as they would do using open-ended dialogue (though they may do as well or better on recall tests, which recitation resembles).

Acting together is another tool that facilitates writing, particularly in fields that rely heavily on nonverbal tools, such as laboratory apparatus, and visual tools. Students in engineering, laboratory sciences, nursing, mathematics, and architecture, whose reading and writing are integrated with the goal-directed use of nonverbal tools, seem to appropriate writing along with their use of those tools (Medway, "Language," "Writing"; Haas; Winsor; Smagorinsky and Coppock). As powerful as writing is, it remains one tool among many for learning and cannot be separated from the other tools.

4. Processes: Earlier research on the processes of writing assumed that there is such a thing as *the* writing process. As with the autonomous view of literacy, writing processes were assumed to be universal—prewrite, write, revise, edit. But research on writing in the disciplines suggests that the process of writing (and learning to write) is multiple, as varied as the uses of writing. What works in composition or literature may not work in some other discipline that has different uses for writing and different traditions of teaching and learning. What does seem to work is a process of writing that involves students in the activity of a discipline, whether as consumer or client of its commodified products (as in writing a quick and unrevised response to an ad) or as potential participant (gathering data from a lab as "prewriting" for writing an experimental report).

Designing assignments and courses so that students engage in a process of learning to write and writing to learn over time, allowing them to build, refine, and reflect on their composing, seems to be more effective than assigning a paper and taking it up on the due date, with nothing in between—though what comes in between will vary enormously.

These four directions in which WAC/WID research seems to point all suggest that the question in designing writing experiences that go beyond rote recall has to be: What do we want students to be able to *do* with the material of the course? Not merely, What do we want them to *know*? The motive, identity, tools, and process—the why, who, and how—are as important as the content—the what—in learning to write and writing to learn.

The Future of Research in WAC/WID

A final word on the future directions of this research: The increasingly rich literature of individual case studies is being extended to groups, sometimes using quantitative as well as naturalistic methods. It will be useful for us to know through survey research, for example, whether and how prior exposure to the activity of a discipline is associated with success in writing in its genres. It will also be useful to know whether identification with the discipline's motives (an expressed intention to take subsequent courses in the field, for example) is associated with success in writing in its genres.

Richer discipline-specific studies of writing will tease out the differences in learning to write in various disciplines, building on the work of Velez, Haas, Geisler, and others. Large-corpus quantitative discourse analysis, of the type Susan Conrad is undertaking in biology and history, will also be helpful in understanding the ways in which students' reading and writing change over time to more resemble that of professionals in a discipline.

The work already going on in qualitative studies of the relation between academic and workplace writing (such as that of the Canadian researchers) is being extended over time both forward, to young professionals expanding into wider and wider involvements (and genres), as well as backward, through longitudinal and retrospective analysis of previous writing experiences that shape students' entrance into and rejection of (and by) various professions. (Some five longitudinal studies of cohorts of undergraduate students are now in progress.)

Finally, researchers have repeatedly found that the very process of studying writing in conjunction with faculty helps faculty to critically reflect on their practice and change that practice. It is important to continue to document the development of faculty—individually and as part of a department, an institution, and a profession—as they change over time, so that we can bring the fruits of our research to inform educational practices across disciplines and institutions. Walvoord et al.'s longitudinal study of faculty at three institutions (*In the Long Run*) is a major step in this direction.

Learning to write, then, is an extraordinarily "messy" activity, to return to Prior's term. Yet that very messiness comes out of the persuasiveness of writing in (post)modern societies. Writing mediates so many human actions, is central to so many collective human activities, that it is as diverse and messy as the (post)modern world itself. Yet in spite of the daunting task ahead for research in WAC/WID, we should not lose sight of the fact that naturalistic studies of WAC have created an entirely new object of disciplinary study: the workings of writing in society and culture. And by carefully tracing the comings and goings of students' writing in many walks of life, these studies, messy and difficult to generalize though they are, can have important implications for a wide range of human activities—not only in education but also in government, industry, business, the nonprofit sector, and advocacy groups, as well as in families, neighborhoods, and the deepest personal relationships. Through naturalistic studies of writing, we are developing expertise of real value to others: our students certainly, but also our students when they are no longer students but professionals entering and eventually transforming our culture through this immensely plastic tool called writing.

Works Cited

Ackerman, John M. "The Promise of Writing to Learn." *Written Communication* 10 (1993): 334–70.

Anderson, Worth, et al. "Cross-Curricular Underlife: A Collaborative Report on Ways with Academic Words." *College Composition and Communication* 41 (1990): 11–36.

Anson, Chris M., and Lee Forsberg. "Moving beyond the Academic Community: Transitional Stages in Professional Writing." *Written Communication* 7 (1990): 200–31.

Bartholomae, David. "Inventing the University." *When a Writer Can't Write: Studies in Writer's Block and Other Composing-Process Problems.* Ed. Mike Rose. New York: Guilford, 1985. 134–65.

Bazerman, Charles. *Constructing Experience.* Carbondale, IL: Southern Illinois UP, 1994.

———. *The Languages of Edison's Light.* Cambridge: MIT P, 1999.

———. "A Relationship between Reading and Writing: The Conversation Model." *College English* 41 (1980): 656–61.

———. *Shaping Written Knowledge: The Genre and Activity of the Experimental Article in Science.* Madison: U of Wisconsin P, 1988.

Beer, Anne. "Diplomats in the Basement: Graduate Engineering Students as Negotiators of Genre." *Transitions: Writing in Academic and Workplace Settings.* Ed. Patrick X. Dias and Anthony Paré. Cresskill, NJ: Hampton, 2000.

Berkenkotter, Carol, and Tom N. Huckin. *Genre Knowledge in Disciplinary Communication: Cognition/Culture/Power.* Hillsdale, NJ: Erlbaum, 1995.

Berkenkotter, Carol, and Doris Ravotas. "Genre as a Tool in the Transmission of Practice over Time and across Professional Boundaries." *Mind, Culture, and Activity* 4 (1997): 256–74.

Berkenkotter, Carol, Tom N. Huckin, and John Ackerman. "Social Context and Socially Constructed Texts: The Initiation of a Graduate Student into a Writing Community." *Textual Dynamics of the Professions: Historical and Contemporary Studies of Writing in Professional Communities.* Ed. Charles Bazerman and James Paradis. Madison: U of Wisconsin P, 1991. 191–215

Blakeslee, Ann M. "Activity, Context, Interaction, and Authority: Learning to Write Scientific Papers In Situ." *Journal of Business and Technical Communication* 11 (1997): 125–69.

———. "Readers and Authors: Fictionalized Constructs or Dynamic Collaborations?" *Technical Communications Quarterly* 2 (1992): 23–35.

———. "The Rhetorical Construction of Novelty: Presenting Claims in a Letters Forum." *Science, Technology, and Human Values* 1 (1994): 88–100.

Brandt, Deborah. "Remembering Writing: Remembering Reading." *College Composition and Communication* 45 (1994): 459–79.

———. "Accumulating Literacy: Writing and Learning to Write in the Twentieth Century." *College English* 57 (1995): 649–68.

Brooke, Robert. "Modeling a Writer's Identity: Reading and Imitation in the Writing Classroom." *College Composition and Communication* 39 (1988): 23–41.

Casanave, Christine P. "Cultural Diversity and Socialization: A Case Study of a Hispanic Woman in a Doctoral Program in Sociology." *Diversity as a Resource: Redefining Cultural Literacy.* Ed. D. E. Murray. Alexandria, VA: TESOL, 1992. 148–82.

Charney, Davida H., and Richard A. Carlson. "Learning to Write in a Genre: What Student Writers Take from Model Texts." *Research in the Teaching of English* 29 (1995): 88–125.

Chin, Elaine. "Redefining 'Context' in Research on Writing." *Written Communication* 11 (1994): 445–82.

Chiseri-Strater, Elizabeth. *Academic Literacies: The Public and Private Discourse of University Students.* Portsmouth, NH: Boynton/Cook, 1991.

Christie, Francis. *Language Education.* Waurn Ponds, Victoria, Australia: Deakin UP, 1985.

Conrad, Susan. "Corpus-Based Linguistic Studies and the Teaching of Reading and Writing." Diss. U of Northern Arizona, 1996.

Cooper, Charles, and Susan Peck MacDonald. "Contributions of Academic and Dialogic Journals to Writing about Literature." *Writing, Teaching, and Learning in the Disciplines.* Ed. Anne Herrington and Charles Moran. New York: MLA, 1992. 137–55.

Dias, Patrick X., et al. *Worlds Apart: Acting and Writing in Academic and Workplace Contexts.* Mahwah, NJ: Erlbaum, 1999.

Durst, Russell K. "Cognitive and Linguistic Demands of Analytic Writing." *Research in the Teaching of English* 21 (1987): 347–76.

Emig, Janet. "Writing as a Mode of Learning." *College Composition and Communication* 28 (1977): 122–28.

Engeström, Yrjö. *Learning by Expanding: An Activity Theoretical Approach to Developmental Research.* Helsinki, Finland: Orienta-Konsultit Oy, 1987.

Fahnestock, Jeanne. "Accommodating Science: The Rhetorical Life of Scientific Facts. *Written Communication* 3 (1986): 275–96.

Faigley, Lester, and Kristine Hansen. "Learning to Write in the Social Sciences." *College Composition and Communication* 36 (1985): 140–49.

Fishman, Stephen M., and Lucille McCarthy. "Community in the Expressivist Classroom: Juggling Liberal and Communitarian Visions." *College English* 57 (1995): 62–81.

———. "Teaching for Student Change: A Deweyan Alternative to Radical Pedagogy." *College Composition and Communication* 47 (1996): 342–66.

———. *John Dewey and the Challenge of Classroom Practice.* New York: Teachers College P, 1998.

Freedman, Aviva. "Reconceiving Genre." *Texte* 8/9 (1990): 279–92.

———. "Show and Tell? The Role of Explicit Teaching in the Learning of New Genres." *Research in the Teaching of English* 27 (1993): 222–51.

Freedman, Aviva, and Christine Adam. "Proving the Rule: Situated Workplace Writing in a University Context." *Transitions: Writing in Academic and Workplace Settings.* Ed. Patrick X. Dias and Anthony Paré. Cresskill, NJ: Hampton, 2000.

Freedman, Aviva, Christine Adam, and Graham Smart. "Wearing Suits to Class: Simulating Genres and Genres as Simulations." *Written Communication* 11 (1994): 193–226.

Freedman, Aviva, and Graham Smart. "Navigating the Current of Economic Policy." *Mind, Culture, and Activity* 4 (1997): 238–55.

Geisler, Cheryl. *Academic Literacy and the Nature of Expertise: Reading, Writing, and Knowing in Academic Philosophy.* Hillsdale, NJ: Erlbaum, 1994.

Greene, Stuart. "Making Sense of My Own Ideas: The Problems of Authorship in a Beginning Writing Classroom." *Written Communication* 12 (1995): 186–218.

———. "The Role of Task in the Development of Academic Thinking through Reading and Writing in a College History Course." *Research in the Teaching of English* 27 (1993): 46–75.

Haas, Christina. "Learning to Read Biology." *Written Communication* 11 (1994): 43–84.

Hare, Victoria Chou, and Denise A. Fitzsimmons. "The Influence of Interpretive Communities on Use of Content and Procedural Knowledge." *Written Communication* 8 (1991): 348–78.

Henry, Jim. "A Narratological Analysis of WAC Authorship." *College English* 56 (1994): 810–24.

Herrington, Anne J. "Teaching, Writing, and Learning: A Naturalistic Study of Writing in an Undergraduate Literature Course." *Writing in Academic Disciplines* Ed. David A. Jolliffe. Norwood, NJ: Ablex, 1988. 133-65.

———. "Writing in Academic Settings: A Study of the Context for Writing in Two College Chemical Engineering Courses." *Research in the Teaching of English* 19 (1985): 331–61.

Jolliffe, David A., and Ellen M. Brier. "Studying Writers' Knowledge in Academic Disciplines." *Writing in Academic Disciplines.* Ed. David A. Jolliffe. Norwood, NJ: Ablex, 1988. 35–77.

Lave, Jean, and Etienne Wenger. *Situated Learning: Legitimate Peripheral Participation.* Cambridge: Cambridge UP, 1991.

MacDonald, Susan. *Professional Academic Writing in the Humanities and Social Sciences.* Carbondale: Southern Illinois UP, 1994.

McCarthy, Lucille P. "A Psychiatrist Using DSM-III: The Influence of a Charter Document in Psychiatry." *Textual Dynamics of the Professions: Historical and Contemporary Studies of Writing in Professional Communities.* Ed. Charles Bazerman and James Paradis. Madison: U of Wisconsin P, 1991. 358–78.

———. "A Stranger in Strange Lands: A College Student Writing Across the Curriculum." *Research in the Teaching of English* 21 (1987): 233–65.

McCarthy, Lucille P., and Stephen Fishman. "Boundary Conversations: Conflicting Ways of Knowing in Philosophy and Interdisciplinary Research." *Research in the Teaching of English* 25 (1991): 419–68.

McCarthy, Lucille P., and Joan P. Gerring. "Revising Psychiatry's Charter Document, *DSM-IV.*" *Written Communication* 11 (1994): 147–92.

Medway, Peter. "Language, Learning and Communication in an Architect's Office." *English in Education* 28 (1994): 3–13.

———. "Writing and Design in Architectural Education." *Transitions: Writing in Academic and Workplace Settings.* Ed. Patrick X. Dias and Anthony Paré. Cresskill, NJ: Hampton, 2000.

Miller, Carolyn R. "Genre as Social Action." *Quarterly Journal of Speech* 70 (1984): 151–67.

Myers, Greg. "Textbooks and the Sociology of Scientific Knowledge." *English for Specific Purposes* 11 (1992): 3–17.

———. *Writing Biology: Texts in the Social Construction of Scientific Knowledge.* Madison: U of Wisconsin P, 1990.

North, Stephen M. "Writing in a Philosophy Class: Three Case Studies." *Research in the Teaching of English* 20 (1986): 225–62.

Nystrand, Martin. *Opening Dialogue: Understanding the Dynamics of Language and Language Learning in the English Classroom.* New York: Teachers College P, 1997.

Odell, Lee, and Dixie Goswami, eds. *Writing in Nonacademic Settings.* New York: Guilford, 1985.

Orlikowski, Wanda J., and JoAnne Yates. "Genre Repertoire: The Structuring of Communicative Practices in Organizations." *Administrative Science Quarterly* 39 (1994): 541–74.

Paré, Anthony. "Discourse Regulations and the Production of Knowledge." *Writing in the Workplace: New Research Perspectives.* Ed. Rachel Spilka. Carbondale: Southern Illinois UP, 1993. 111–23.

———. "Writing as a Way into Social Work: Genre Sets, Genre Systems, and Distributed Cognition." *Transitions: Writing in Academic and Workplace Settings.* Ed. Patrick X. Dias and Anthony Paré. Cresskill, NJ: Hampton, 2000.

Penrose, Ann M. "To Write or Not to Write: Effects of Task and Task Interpretation on Learning through Writing." *Written Communication* 9 (1992): 465–500.

Prior, Paul. "Contextualizing Writing and Response in a Graduate Seminar." *Written Communication* 8 (1991): 267–310.

———. "Redefining the Task: An Ethnographic Examination of Writing and Response in Graduate Seminars." *Academic Writing in a Second Language: Essays on Research and Pedagogy.* Ed. Diane Belcher and George Braine. Norwood, NJ: Ablex, 1995. 83–110.

———. "Response, Revision, Disciplinarity: A Microhistory of a Dissertation Prospectus in Sociology." *Written Communication* 11 (1994): 483–533.

———. "Tracing Authoritative and Internally Persuasive Discourses: A

Case Study of Response, Revision, and Disciplinary Enculturation." *Research in the Teaching of English* 29 (1995): 288–325.

———. *Writing/Disciplinarity: A Sociohistoric Account of Literate Activity in the Academy.* Hillsdale, NJ: Erlbaum, 1998.

Ronald, Kate. "On the Outside Looking In: Students' Analyses of Professional Discourse Communities." *Rhetoric Review* 7 (1988): 130–49.

Russell, David R. "Rethinking Genre in School and Society: An Activity Theory Analysis." *Written Communication* 14 (1997): 504–54.

———. "Vygotsky, Dewey, and Externalism: Beyond the Student/Discipline Dichotomy." *Journal of Advanced Composition* 13 (1993): 173–97.

———. *Writing in the Academic Disciplines, 1870–1990: A Curricular History.* Carbondale: Southern Illinois UP, 1991.

Schumacher, Gary M., and J. Gradwold Nash. "Conceptualizing and Measuring Knowledge Change Due to Writing." *Research in the Teaching of English* 25 (1991): 67–96.

Smagorinsky, Peter, and John Coppock. "Cultural Tools and the Classroom Context: An Exploration of an Artistic Response to Literature." *Written Communication* 11 (1994): 283–310.

Smart, Graham. "Genre as Community Invention: A Central Bank's Response to Its Executives' Expectations as Readers." *Writing in the Workplace: New Research Perspectives.* Ed. Rachel Spilka. Carbondale: Southern Illinois UP, 1993. 124–40.

———. "Knowledge-Making in a Central Bank: The Interplay of Writing and Economic Modeling." Diss. McGill U, 1997.

Street, Brian B. *Literacy in Theory and Practice.* Cambridge: Cambridge UP, 1985.

Van Nostrand, A. D. *Fundable Knowledge: The Marketing of Defense Technology.* Mahwah, NJ: Erlbaum, 1997.

Velez, Lili F. "Interpreting and Writing in the Laboratory: A Study of Novice Biologists as Novice Rhetors." Diss. Carnegie Mellon U, 1995.

Walvoord, Barbara F., et al. *In the Long Run: A Study of Faculty in Three Writing-Across-the-Curriculum Programs.* Urbana, IL: NCTE, 1997.

Walvoord, Barbara F., and Lucille P. McCarthy. *Thinking and Writing in College.* Urbana, IL: NCTE, 1990.

Williams, Joseph M., and Gregory G. Colomb. "The Case for Explicit Teaching: Why What You Don't Know Won't Help You." *Research in the Teaching of English* 27 (1993): 252–64.

Winsor, Dorothy A. *Writing Like an Engineer: A Rhetorical Education.* Mahwah, NJ: Erlbaum, 1996.

Yates, JoAnne. *Control through Communication: The Rise of System in American Management.* Baltimore: Johns Hopkins UP, 1989.

Yates, JoAnne, and Wanda J. Orlikowski. "Genres of Organizational Communication: A Structurational Approach to Studying Communication and Media." *Academy of Management Review* 17 (1994): 299–326.

CHAPTER TWELVE

Theory in WAC: Where Have We Been, Where Are We Going?

CHRISTOPHER THAISS
George Mason University

First, a rationale for this chapter: Why talk about "WAC theory"? After all, every chapter in this book deals with "theory" in some fashion since theory provides reasons, based in scholarship and teaching practice, for the methods it describes. The focus of this chapter, however, will be on first principles: the assumptions behind the reasons—the theories beneath the theories, if you will. Moreover, in the almost three decades since explicit workshops on writing across the curriculum began, the shape of WAC has undergone significant change. It is therefore reasonable to attempt to define both (1) a core of consistent WAC principles over that span, and (2) the theoretical influences that have worked changes on the concept.

I proceed as follows: in keeping with the notion of first principles, I work toward extensive definitions of the three terms— "writing," "across," and "the curriculum,"—that make up the operant phrase. Each term is defined historically within the context of WAC programmatic and teaching practice; changes are explored and trends emerge. Where appropriate, I cite other essays in this volume that further illuminate my observations. I close by speculating, in the spirit of this millennial volume, about a few further developments in WAC theory. (For suggestions of further reading, see the brief annotated bibliography of major texts in WAC theory that follows this chapter.)

And so . . .

"Writing"

The public, including many academics, talks about writing as if it were a simple concept and as if everyone meant the same thing by it. Sweeping pronouncements, usually negative, are made: "Students can't write," "The writing is poor," and so forth, and generalizers rarely specify, nor are asked to specify, exactly what the trouble is. Nevertheless, anyone who studies writing is familiar with the surprise of reading allegedly "poor" and "good" samples and wondering on what bases the evaluator reached the judgment. When I conduct discussions of standards with my colleagues, we routinely fill the chalkboard with criteria for successful writing of experienced-based essays; we disagree about priorities, even though we are discussing, mind you, only a single—though varied and complex—genre.

Writing does appear simple to define: the use of graphic characters, "letters," to render language. This illusion of simplicity and consensus may explain the consternation of the faculty at Harvard who after 1870 felt it necessary to make composition a required, remedial course in its own right (Berlin, *Writing*; Halloran) and thus set in motion the U.S. composition industry. The illusion is also responsible for the easy acceptance of "good writing," an equally elusive term, as a virtue and as a goal of education. Most pertinent to this chapter, this illusion helps to explain why writing across the curriculum has gained such widespread acceptance—at least in concept—in colleges and schools. Faculty and administrators readily pay lip service to the "need" for students to "write well," and they tend readily to pass motions and even earmark funding for various forms of faculty inservice training and curricular mandating. Yet, as always, the devil is in the details, and programs bog down when the significant differences in real definitions become apparent. (I would speculate that schools that have faced the most difficulty in even starting WAC programs have been those that have addressed the definitional question at the outset, and the resulting conflict of definitions has stalled any initiative.)

What most safely can be said is that "writing" in writing-across-the-curriculum programs has been many things, not all of them compatible, exemplifying Naisbitt's theory of the "trends and countertrends" that he saw as characteristic of the movement of ideas in a society (Naisbitt and Aburdene). Even within one institution—even, I would argue, in the deliberations of a single teacher—we can almost perceive definitions and goals of writing moving in opposite directions.

Conformity versus Originality

I will label these opposite directions the "drive to conformity" and the "drive to originality." These are certainly nothing new— the basic yin/yang, tree/serpent of the cultural anthropologists— but how they are played out in the teaching of writing, and especially in WAC programs, helps us understand the variety of meanings given to such spin-offs of "writing" as "good writing," "learning to write," and "writing to learn."

First, the drive to conformity. Some faculty and governing boards are attracted to WAC because it promises greater conformity: to these advocates, "learning to write" means learning correct usage of Standard English, the learning of modes and formats characteristic of a discipline, consistency of documentation, and consistency of application of disciplinary research methodology.

Conversely, others see in WAC the potential for the student's growth as thinker and stylist; this direction is toward the more individual, less easily defined or prescribed, more evanescent development of style and confidence characteristic of insiders in a discourse. David Bartholomae's notion of "inventing the university" involves this more profound theory of "learning to write" ("Inventing"), similar to Kenneth Bruffee's adaptation of the age-old notion of university education as allowing one to "join the ongoing conversation" of ideas. Several common aspects of "good writing" exemplify this trend: among them, (1) the ability to integrate the writings of others into one's own vision, (2) the ability to envision how one might adapt one's writing to the needs of diverse readers, (3) the ability to take a writing project through an unpredictable "process" that encourages revisioning and reshaping, and (4) the ability to cross conventions—reinvent them, as it were—in order to make connections with styles and genres of other fields. Genre theorists (e.g., Bishop and Ostrom) explore this process, and this growing research field clearly will have more and more impact on WAC development in coming years.

It is in this less-conformist sense of "learning to write" that the definition of "writing" includes that other epigrammatic notion popular in WAC: "writing to learn." Although "writing to learn" has been frequently isolated from "learning to write" in workshops, often by means of a split between so-called "formal"("learning to write") and "informal" ("writing to learn") assignments, conscientious workshop leaders try to keep the connections before the minds of participants. Certainly the work of the theorists who were most influential in the rise of WAC integrated these ideas. For example, Mina Shaughnessy's (1977) developmental progression from "fluency" to "correctness" saw the conformist goal of "learning to write" as dependent on the use of writing as a tool of thought, as did James Britton's earlier formulation (1975) of the "expressive" mode of writing (for the self, as an exploratory tool) as the "matrix" out of which grew the ability to write "transactionally" to others (Britton et al.). I count it one of the failings of theory in recent years that our sense of the connectedness of "writing to learn"/"the expressive"/"the informal" and of "learning to write"/"the transactional"/"the formal" has been lost to some extent in the drive of some scholars to stress the distinctions between theories more than their connections. This loss may have been best illustrated by the 1995 "debate" between Peter Elbow and David Bartholomae in the pages of *College Composition and Communication*, but this focus on the disconnect, rather than on the profound links, between concepts is played out continuously in uninformed, off-the-cuff critiques of the expressive as "soft," "touchy-feely," and "self-indulgent" and of the transactional/formal as "rigid," "formulaic," and "superficial." While it has been useful analytically for composition theorists to specify differences between, as Patricia Bizzell described them, so-called "inner"- and "outer"-directed theories, the loss of a unified theory has not been helpful to teachers trying to plan a coherent course.

While I have characterized "writing to learn" as related to the growth of the student as thinker and stylist, I should also point out opposing trends in this aspect of WAC. On the one hand, "writing to learn" includes the conforming goals of recall and memorization, manifest in note-taking and journaling exercises directed to better performance on standardized tests. This "lower-order" thinking (Perry) contrasts with, and to some extent runs counter to, "higher-order" uses of writing, also often pursued in some form of regular writing such as a journal, including doing synthetic or divergent writing, thought experiments, metaphorizing and other creative invention, and what cultural studies theorists (see Berlin and Vivion, for example) call "critical work"—examining and questioning ("deconstructing," if you will) those very terms and concepts that one strives so conscientiously to memorize and assimilate. The annual symposia on "Writing and Higher Order Thinking" at the University of Chicago in the 1980s have been thus far the most explicit attempt to relate WAC theory and practice to these theories of psychological development, but they are played out tacitly in the variety of assignments arrayed under the "writing to learn" umbrella.

Overall, what we mean by "writing" and by "learning to write" and "writing to learn" varies from school to school, teacher to teacher, class to class, assignment to assignment, even from thought to thought within a teacher's response to a group of papers or to a single paper.

Dominance of the Transactional

Nevertheless, the concept can be narrowed to some degree. The "writing" that is most often meant in the phrase "good writing" can be safely, if nebulously, defined as what James Britton and his colleagues called "transactional" writing, or what Janet Emig in 1971 termed "extensive" writing: "the mode that focuses upon the writer's conveying a message or a communication to another; the domain explored is usually the cognitive; the style is assured, impersonal, and often reportorial" (*Composing* 4). Further refining the term to the school context, we can accept Bartholomae's definition of successful academic writing in "Inventing the University":

> What our beginning students need to learn is to extend themselves, by successive approximations, into the commonplaces,

set phrases, rituals and gestures, *habits of mind*, tricks of persua-
sion, obligatory conclusions and necessary connections that determine the "what might be said" and constitute knowledge within
the various branches of our academic community. (145; emphasis added)

The conformist vision clearly dominates in this definition; however,
in the phrase "habits of mind," which I have italicized, lurks the
drive toward originality. Bartholomae later in the essay explains
one of the key "habits" of the successful academic writer: "The key
distinguishing gesture . . . is the way the writer works against a
conventional point of view, one that is represented within the essay
by conventional phrases that the writer must then work against"
(152). Nevertheless, since this type of originality marks the successful academic, it too is an expected part of the transaction.

This greater emphasis on the transactional has been consistent in WAC. Even though the informal and the expressive have
received considerable attention in WAC programs, as best illustrated by Toby Fulwiler's early work on journals (e.g., in *The
Journal Book*), the earliest impetus to WAC was signaled by the
1970s furor created by concern about correctness. The 1975
Newsweek cover story, "Why Johnny Can't Write," is typically
cited as epitomizing the mood at that time; "Johnny's" explicit
shortcomings were in syntax, spelling, vocabulary, and organization. Moreover, the assessment/accountability fashion of the
1990s, part of the many-faceted reaction to the free-spending
1980s, has made "transaction" far more emphatic in WAC programs than "expression." Certainly, the increase in the number
of writing intensive requirements illustrates this trend. Where
"writing to learn" exists as a key element of the definition of
"writing" in WAC, more and more it exists as a stage of student
progress toward that transactional "good writing," rather than
as an end in itself.

Technology: Changing All the Rules

But if traditional concerns have kept the definitions of "writing"
and "good writing" somewhat narrow, the force of technological advancement is expanding those definitions and will no doubt

continue to do so. When Janet Emig wrote "Writing as a Mode of Learning" (1977), which helped conceptualize "writing to learn" as theory, she carefully distinguished between writing and three other language modes—speech, reading, and listening—in order to support the "uniqueness" of writing. But the "writing" she assumed was of words as conventionally defined; to wit:

> Making such a case for the uniqueness of writing should logically and theoretically involve establishing many contrasts, distinctions between (1) writing and all other verbal languaging processes—listening, reading, and especially talking; (2) writing and all other forms of composing, such as composing a painting, a symphony, a dance, a film, a building. (7)

Emig's formulation antedates the emergence of other tools, such as the computer monitor, invisible storage on disks, and the mouse, that have changed in still undetermined ways the relationship between writer and text. (One question, for example: does the operation of the hand on the mouse, as one imports text from one source into another or moves text around in a document, still reinforce learning to the extent claimed by Emig for the physical act of writing using old tools?) Even more profoundly, Emig's definition antedates the virtual fusion—at least hybridization—of talk and writing by means of e-mail (Spooner and Yancey). Anyone attempting to define first principles of WAC must confront the e-mail explosion. Some practical questions, for example: In determining the prevalence of WAC at a school, does one "count" the e-mail exchanges between student and professor regarding answers to test questions or ideas for a presentation? Does one count—and how might one count, even if one wished to—e-mail exchanges between students preparing for that same test or presentation?

When WAC was new in the 1970s, surely no one foresaw the difficulty of distinguishing writing from other modes of communication that exist today. Talk was talk and writing was writing—indeed, it can be argued that the concept of writing across the curriculum grew up in this country precisely because writing seemed so clearly different from talk. Interestingly, the British, our predecessors in identifying both writing and talk as subjects for study across the curriculum (Martin et al.; Martin), persistently linked the two in the term "language across the curriculum." In the United States, however, where the preeminence of multiple-choice and short-answer testing had devalued both writing and speaking in curricula (Russell), most teachers had little practical experience of the mutually reinforcing effects of the two, and so their differences were much more obvious than their connections. In the late 1970s, a few U.S. writers (e.g., Goodkin and Parker) argued for synthesis, but "language across the curriculum" or "communication across the curriculum"—the sense of a reforged link between speech and written composition—has yet to take hold in institutions, except in rare instances (Thaiss and Suhor; Sipple and Carson), whereas WAC has flourished. Hence, e-mail poses a conceptual difficulty for WAC planners, a difficulty that will disappear in an integrated language-across-the-curriculum (LAC) environment, one which, I predict, technology is forcing us to conceptualize and eventually accept.

The Multimedia Swamp

If e-mail muddies the definition of writing, consider the swamp created by multimedia composing. When I try out different colors for the background of a Web page and ask one of my sons, a visual artist, to design a logo, am I "writing"? If another son, in tenth grade and a guitarist, attaches an alternative rock music file to an e-mail message to a friend in order to illustrate a point about that rock group, where does the "writing" end and something else take over? If the final product in an electrical engineering course that meets a school's writing intensive requirement (see Townsend, Chapter 10 in this volume, for definitions of "writing intensive") is a multimedia (video, sound, words) Web page designed by a six-person team of students from three universities, how and how much does that work count, how does the teacher evaluate it, and is it "writing"? Should the university WAC committee question its validity and demand something different, or does the entity demand new theory? (See Chapter 3 in this volume by Reiss and Young and the volume by Reiss, Selfe, and Young for more on this issue.)

If we define "writing" conventionally as words, sentences, paragraphs, pages, and so forth, then multimedia composing creates problems for the teacher/evaluator and the administrator. If program guidelines say, for example, that for a course to be writing intensive every student must write four thousand graded words, then the teacher and the committee must do some clever rationalizing to justify the product. But if the definition of writing is broadened to, let's say, "creative use, for communicative purposes, of the various tools available to the electronic composer," then the challenges change. The teacher of a dramatic literature course must, for example, weigh the comparative communicative power within a critical essay of a video clip from a production of *Hamlet* versus a written description of the same excerpt. Using the clip may make the essay a clearer, more emphatic piece of "writing"; but if we define writing in this more inclusive, technologically current way, then we are setting up new standards for "good writing" that have many consequences. Among these, "teaching writing" will now include teaching a broad range of computer skills—an issue even now facing all administrators of writing programs; hence, teaching these skills means that all students must have access to sophisticated hardware and software, and teachers must be well-"versed" (to use an old-tech metaphor) in them. The broader definition will now mean that the act of writing means choosing among a huge array of images and forms, only some of which are "words." Ideas such as "syntax," "organization," "accuracy," "clarity," "style"— the list includes all the conventional criteria and more—will all come to be defined in multimedia terms. "Style," for example, would come to mean the distinctive way a writer designs and organizes sound, video, static visuals, spoken words, and so forth. How quickly are we approaching the day when the class of "good writers" will not include anyone who composes only with words, even if that person is a virtuoso on the instruments of "mere" literacy?

A More and More Inclusive Definition

Of course, the broader definition of "writing" may make the notion of "good writing" much broader. Rather than simply raising the bar, so that only those with the most eclectic, omni-media skills are rewarded, technological choice might allow a much greater variety of "written products" to succeed in the context of the academy. This multiplicity of media already flourishes outside the academy and there is no reason to believe that schools won't adapt, though they will never catch up to the commercial marketplace in technical or conceptual innovation—unless universities, through corporate funding, become (or become once again) the research arms of industry (e.g., Bleich). Just as printed books, visuals-and-text magazines, radio, television, CDs, live theater, Web sites, MOOs, and so on coexist today as venues for "writing" in the marketplace, so school parameters of "good writing" should broaden as these varied technologies continue to become cheaper and easier to use.

This technological broadening of the definition of writing is helped along, I would argue (as I have elsewhere [Thaiss, "WAC Theory"]), by the hesitancy (or neglect, possibly benign) of program directors and committees to impose detailed definitions of writing on WAC, or to enunciate detailed, narrowing criteria. As I stated at the beginning of this chapter, this lack of close definition is largely responsible for the growth of WAC programs. Allowing, even encouraging, different parts of a faculty to maintain divergent, often conflicting, goals for writing does serve the growth of the program, and it also serves the tendency of a concept to grow and change with technology. An intriguing paradox in the history of WAC has been that most programs have been funded because of deep and wide concern about the quality of student writing; nevertheless, few programs have systematically studied just what is wrong and what is good with that writing, nor prescribed in detail what is needed (as Condon, Chapter 2 in this volume, shows). Consciously or not, WAC theorists and program leaders have encouraged almost unlimited variety in terms of what counts as writing and how it is evaluated, and therefore have kept the door open for a vigorous, intimate relationship between technological advance and writing. Walvoord et al. argue that assessment of WAC programs should honor this diversity of teachers' definitions of "what works for them"; they criticize a potential tendency of program leaders and their supervisors to assess programs in terms of a narrow range of criteria. I would argue that the relative lack of rigorous assessment of WAC programs (again, see Chapter 2 in this volume) demonstrates that the vast majority of WAC programs already honor this laissez-faire principle, at least tacitly. Almost everyone agrees that "good writing" is hard to find among students, but most program participants also agree that definitions of good writing are best left to them, to individual teachers and members of professional groups trying to achieve meaningful, workable standards within shared contexts.

The Assessment Caveat

Hence, while some powers-that-be (presidents, boards of regents, state legislatures) may be calling for more rigorous assessment, we need to keep in mind that such accountability always carries with it the risk of making programs and instruction obsolete by making them inflexible. As Sosnoski argues in a recent volume about grading writing, the electronic writing environment calls into question all conventional assumptions about academic assessment:

> Yet as hazardous as grading in print environments is to the psyche of teachers, how much more perplexing it becomes in electronic environments where teacher/student roles characteristically shift. In computer oriented classrooms, students often teach their teachers. When boundaries of authority blur, grading can become an arbitrary use of power. (157)

I used the term "laissez-faire" deliberately in the previous paragraph because critics of WAC's indeterminacy have focused on the relationship between writing and economics. Regardless of one's views of and desires for that relationship, it is hard to ignore the usefulness of what has been variously called the "social-epistemic" (Berlin, "Rhetoric"), "cultural studies" (e.g., Berlin and Vivion), or "new historicist" approach to defining "writing," "good writing," "teaching writing," and so forth. As explained in Russell's essay in this volume (Chapter 11), an ongoing element of some WAC research (e.g., by Bazerman; Myers) has been to highlight the ways by which "learning to write" in a discipline means reproducing the existing hierarchies of power.

As Mahala contended, the willingness of WAC directors to allow departments and faculty to define standards of good writing in their own areas actually determined that the status quo would be maintained. To Mahala, the status quo meant that "instead of addressing the most contentious issues, WAC programs have often maintained a political invisibility, tailoring theory to institutional divisions . . . rather than really interrogating prevailing attitudes about knowledge, language, and learning" (773). In a rebuttal, Patricia Dunn argued that, given the diversity of disciplines and teachers, it was inaccurate and reductive to characterize faculty monolithically and as committed to the status quo: "they would not be involved in WAC if they believed they had nothing to learn" (732; see also the rebuttal of Mahala's arguments by McLeod and Maimon). I would argue that regardless of one's view of the motives of faculty, and regardless of one's view of how economic power is held and distributed, "writing" in WAC always is defined in terms of the relationship between what happens in academia and what happens in the "economy" of which it is a part and into which colleges graduate students. Moreover, WAC is a powerful concept precisely because it addresses that relationship.

The Marketplace as Driving Force

To show how WAC-defined "writing" directly addresses the question of economy, we might contrast it to writing as defined in the first-year (FY) composition class. When we seek to define writing in WAC, we should keep in mind that as a political movement, writing across the curriculum in the United States has meant "writing not only in required English composition courses." Implicitly manifesting awareness of the social construction of knowledge, WAC researchers and planners saw the teaching of writing in the typical FY comp class as disconnected from (1) the disciplines in which students would be writing later on (if not at the same time as they were taking the comp class), and (2) the careers for which, one presumed, the disciplines were preparing them (see, for example, Maimon; Thaiss, "WAC and General Education"). The basic rationale for WAC has always been that writing cannot be the same in an FY comp class as it is in a course in the major because all the key environmental factors differ:

- ◆ Ways of knowing (hence logic, evidence, organization) differ among disciplines—indeed, we define disciplines by these differences. (I use the term "disciplines" for convenience here; later I take up the difficulties with this term.)

- ◆ Terms are specialized, and even the connotations of familiar words change from discipline to discipline.

- ◆ The purposes of writing are different because of when the student takes the course and who teaches it. Basically, the FY comp class is part of the student's acclimation to the discourse of the academy only in its most general features; the writing is an end in itself, the teacher usually a specialist in language or literature. Conversely, writing in a course in the major is usually a means to the end of developing and demonstrating knowledge of methods and materials in the discipline; it is not an end in itself. The teacher is a specialist in those materials and methods.

- ◆ Further, even if the course in the major is also part of the student's acclimation to the academy, it primarily prepares the student for life after school, presumably within the marketplace, in a way that the FY comp course cannot approach.

In summary, then, writing within WAC can be defined historically in contrast to the British language across the curriculum. It can also be defined dynamically and unpredictably in terms of advances in technology, as well as somewhat more narrowly in terms of its distinction from writing in FY comp class. But even this "narrower" definition ineluctably admits of great variety since it is founded on the (antifoundational!) assumption that "writing" and its ethical corollary "good writing" differ from discipline to discipline, context to context.

"Across"

I don't want to make too much of this little word, but focusing on it briefly can help to clarify some points and make others helpfully cloudier. After all, "across" is not the same as "in" or "throughout" (not to mention "against," "over," "behind," or other delicious prepositions that conjure up intriguing ironies). The term "writing across the curriculum" has had remarkable staying power,[1] for which I think there are good reasons. "Across" connotes movement from place to place, time to time. It implies coverage, but not necessarily depth. "They moved across the country" means something very different from "They moved through the country." "Across" need not be profound; it can imply visited but did not stay.

Of course, its connotation depends on subjects and verbs. "The plague spread across Europe" feels very different from "The train sped across Europe." But even if it's a deadly disease that is "crossing," "across" feels less permanent and thorough than "The plague spread throughout Europe."

Why then does "writing across the curriculum" have staying power even though "across" is not a "stay-put" kind of word? I think it's because it sounds nonthreatening. Unlike "writing throughout the curriculum," which implies 100 percent compliance, "writing across the curriculum" implies an even presence, but not control. Variants such as "writing across the disciplines" and "writing across the university" have a similar feel. Note that when governing bodies want to get tough about the idea, the language becomes more aggressive: "writing intensive requirement" is the best example. "Writing across the curriculum" says to faculty, "See how this works in your own teaching and how it might work; no pressure."

A second connotation of "across" is best illustrated by contrast with "in," specifically in the phrase "writing in the disciplines." "Across" suggests a link—"hands across the sea," "telephone lines across the continent"—whereas "in" suggests presence but not connection, certainly not movement. Writers over the years have commented on the messianic, or at least peripatetic, nature of WAC (see Walvoord), and "across" expresses this dynamic character well. That the signal event of WAC programs has been the multi- or cross-disciplinary workshop, marked by discussions and exchanges of information, also fits with "across." ("Sharing," a 1960s word, was the vogue term for this mode until the 1980s backlash. We now "interact," but we don't "share.")

"In," as in the phrase "writing in the disciplines," suits well that aspect of WAC which is more concerned with the specific, differentiating features of disciplinary discourse than in their intersections or in the effort to establish a community of interest among faculty. As I explored in my attempt to define "writing," the notion that each discipline has its own distinctive epistemology and discourse has been a central argument in support of a cross-curricular writing movement. Without the "in" there is little argument for the "across." Or, to give a different answer to the old question, "Why did the chicken cross the road?"—because there really was another side.

"The Curriculum"

"The curriculum" is not the same as "curriculum"; in fact, these two might be more different than "the curriculum" and "the disciplines," at least as WAC has evolved in practice. In my first draft of this chapter, I planned to define "curriculum" as the third term of the phrase, but having discovered the resonance of "across," I became fascinated by the even smaller word "the." So please bear with me.

I have never heard the phrase "writing across curriculum"; what might it mean? I have heard National Writing Project colleagues who teach K–12 say, "I'm writing curriculum," as in "I'm writing a plan of study or designing a sequence of courses." But "curriculum" without the definite article implies tentativeness, a draft perhaps of what might, if all the officials sign off on it, become "the curriculum," at least until the next batch of standardized test scores comes in. "The curriculum," particularly in the context of colleges and universities, evokes hallowed halls, festoons of ivy, Greek lettering, and all the other trappings of surety, permanence, even immortality. "Writing across the curriculum," especially when paired with "writing in the disciplines," reinforces this emotion. ("Writing across the disciplines" is a nice conflation that captures this feeling and some of the flavor of both "in" and "across".)

Actually, "the curriculum," like an unambiguous "writing," is an illusion, an idyll of some rapidly receding golden age. I'm not sure for whom we continue to peddle phrases such as "the curriculum" or "the disciplines," since higher education, like every other aspect of culture, is in flux, and has been as far back as we can study it (Halloran; Ohmann). Even if the definite articles sustain some selling power with parents—usually concerned that the college experience provide at least some stability—and with some prospective students, I assume that faculty, at least those who have been around a while, automatically see through "the curriculum" and "the disciplines" to such fluctuating administrative expediencies as "the departments" or "the majors."

"The curriculum" is subject to the same destabilizing forces that make the definition of "writing" so volatile. Indeed, if we see "the curriculum" as embodied in its documents and its processes of communication (the postmodern versus Platonic perspective, as Villanueva points out in Chapter 7 in this volume), then changes in "writing" and "curriculum" must go together. Speaking practically, a theory of mutual change in "writing" and "the curriculum" implies, for example, that we should not look for fixity in a roster of courses labeled "writing intensive," just as we should not try to define our criteria for "writing intensity" too specifically. The theory also implies that changes in curriculum should signal to writing researchers and administrators changes in the writing environment and in forms of writing. Even the smallest change, say approval of a new course, may represent a deep change in faculty feeling about the discipline, about students, about technology, and about the outside community that can affect every facet of "writing" for those faculty, from purpose, to format, to potential audience, and so forth.

The Elusive WID

If "the curriculum" is a misleading term, "the disciplines" is no less so. Although our sense of the social construction of "writing" has advanced from our reliance on the one-size-fits-all composition course to the recognition of basic differences across disciplines, our sense of categorical differences does not yet extend within the so-called disciplines themselves. In the relatively short history of writing-in-the-disciplines (WID) research (Bazerman; Myers; Herrington; Henry; McCarthy), areas of study tend to be given traditional disciplinary names: chemistry, philosophy, biology, engineering, architecture, and so forth, and researchers continue to seek generalizable characteristics within those broad categories. Certainly WID textbook publishers have reinforced this level of generality (e.g., the several textbooks on "writing in psychology" or "writing in political science"), when they aren't dealing at an even more abstract level: e.g., "writing in the sciences." Although researchers have conscientiously explored the great differences from context to context within alleged disciplines, overall theory has basically ignored both (1) the proliferation of subspecialties within so-called disciplines (e.g., composition within English)[2] that render communication among "colleagues" almost nil, and (2) the rise of so-called interdisciplinary specialties that correspond to emergent professional descriptions in the workplace: e.g., law enforcement, recreation and leisure studies, career counseling. The usual notion of WID, when applied to program design and assessment, fails to question the level of generality that is either possible or meaningful. To cite an absurdly obvious example, if I record that the Department of Modern and Classical Languages has designated ten courses as "writing intensive," participation by those faculty looks different than if I record that for each of the ten languages taught in that department there is one WI course, different still if the ten break down into five in the Spanish literature of South America, none in the rest of Spanish, and five scattered among the nine other languages. Categorizing the distribution of writing in other disciplines, such as computer science, might not be so easy, and the difficulty points up the shortcomings of our current theory of WID, as well as WAC.

Helpful to our understanding of "the disciplines" would be the comparatively sophisticated theory of research in workplace writing (see Alred). This research has moved beyond such general categories as professions (e.g., writing by lawyers or engineers) and industries (e.g., textiles, aerospace) toward the definition of context based on multiple factors, such as "Electronic Mail in Two Corporate Workplaces" (the title of an essay by Brenda Sims, in Sullivan and Dauterman), in which technology ("electronic"), genre ("mail"), and setting ("two corporate workplaces") confine the study and its pretensions. The definition of writing assumes ethnographic limitations: the research does not presume to generalize about whole genres, technologies, or fields (in this case telecommunications and computers) based on the findings, but merely to compare features of the technology and the genre in two specific locales. If readers wish to extrapolate analogies to other contexts, such as to the entirety of "the computer industry," they may, but it is not the intent of the essay to do so.

From WID to WIC

This is not to say that many WID-type studies have not already adhered to this ethnographic lack of pretension; nevertheless, the fact that the WID category still exists shows that we have not yet moved beyond the so-called discipline as a meaningful marker of difference. More useful in looking at writing cultures in academia might be the notion of "WIC"—or "writing in the course" (analogous to "writing in the workplace"). This concept would allow researchers to observe the richness of each course context without having to fit that context within the arbitrary category of a so-called discipline. Certainly part of the research data might be the teacher's and the students' senses of how the course fits within their concepts of the field—which one would expect to differ from one another—but the theory would never assume that the course in any way represents a consensus definition of "the discipline." By removing the assumption of disciplinary "fit," the theory also allows other influences to be observed. If, for example, we look at a course called History 130—The New South and do not assume that the prefix "History" is essentially meaningful, then we can more openly question the origins, purposes, and methods of the course. We may find that the teacher draws theory from texts usually categorized according to other nebulous disciplines—public policy, economics, literature, sociology, not to mention popular media—and uses methods drawn from participants and guest lecturers at cross-university workshops. We would definitely not assume that, whatever we find, History 130 represents in any way the methods, purposes, and materials of any other course also prefixed "History." We might discover, with further research, that such a link does exist within the particular institution, but we would not be able to generalize about "the discipline"—nor, I should add, about the characteristic behaviors or attitudes of any disciplinary group of faculty toward writing. I have often heard WAC program leaders say things like "English faculty are hard or [easy] to work with," as if it were possible to make such "disciplinary" generalizations, and I invariably find these generalizations contradicted by the next conversation.

As theory, "writing in the course" operates on an ethnographic basis close to that of another subfield of composition studies, "teacher research" (see, e.g., Goswami and Stillman; Mohr and McLean). Teacher research also sees the relationship between the individual teacher and a group of students as the most meaningful locus of study about writing in the academic context. Teacher research goes further, of course, to see the teacher as the key researcher in the context, because the primary goal of the research is the teacher's knowledge, with the long-range objective being improved teaching and learning. While I believe that WAC research has benefited—and will benefit further—from applications of teacher research principles (e.g., the studies of Fishman ["Writing to Learn," "Writing and Philosophy"]), the most useful principle is the primacy of the individual course as the focus of the study of writing in an academic setting, regardless of the researcher.

Although I suggest here that the notion of "writing in the disciplines" has diverted attention from the most meaningful context of "writing across the curriculum," I would stress that most WAC programs, in their most common activities, support the theory of "writing in the course." The most common event of the WAC program has been some form of faculty development workshop, usually open to teachers from many departmental units. Even when workshops are conducted within single departments or among smaller units, the preponderance of workshop materials and topics has centered on the individual course, irrespective of discipline. Such common teacher concerns as workload, student motivation, productive feedback to students, and grading dominate both workshop discussion and the most popular workshop materials. Moreover, the typical "genre" of the inhouse

WAC newsletter (Thaiss, "Newsletters"), the "teacher practice" essay (although most of these hardly qualify as conscientious ethnography), is based on the theory of the individual course as a more meaningful locale of study about the role of writing in academia. Though writers of such essays routinely invoke their concept of "the discipline" as part of the rationale for their methods, the burden of such essays is usually to explain methods in relation to the teacher's goals. The audience for these essays is usually faculty across the institution, and the essays are published in order to inform and encourage this heterogeneous group to make individual adaptations, much as the workshop does.

Conclusion: Theory for a New Millennium

In defining "writing," I made some predictions about the future of WAC theory, primarily in response to advances in technology. By changing every facet of what we currently mean by "writing," technology will ineluctably change every aspect of "the curriculum" and what we mean by the dynamic term "across." In addition, I don't see any reason why the trend in higher education to adapt to the career interests of prospective students should be interrupted. As pointed out earlier, new degree programs correspond to emerging careers; why should this trend change? Further, just as electronic technology is bridging the physical separation of "the university" and "the community," so technology will facilitate further interplay between "student," "professor," "worker," and "manager," with blurring and perhaps eventual merger of aspects of these roles. For example, it is easy to see service learning, as explored by David Jolliffe in Chapter 4 in this volume, evolving from a college outreach program to an intrinsic part of education. There is no reason for this not to be so: technology facilitates communication by students working at an off-campus site with other students, the professor, and onsite supervisors. Inevitably, roles and lines of authority will blur and in some cases vanish, just as the concept of "distance education" is drastically changing the notions of "campus" and "classroom."

Theory will both respond to these changes and help to encourage them. I predict that the ethnographic similarity between "writing in the course" and "writing in the workplace" will enable further blurring of the differences between school and community. As the concept of "writing in the disciplines" gives way to theory that encourages a more open exploration of the influences on what and how we teach, curriculum will be freer to grow symbiotically with changes in work.

Notes

1. In the preface to Martin et al. (1976), the term is dated to as early as 1971.

2. Composition studies, of course, has developed its own rich literature on methods and style in the field itself—Asher and Lauer; Kirsch and Sullivan; Kirklighter, Vincent, and Moxley, etc. I use comp within English as an example, familiar to many readers of this essay, of "disciplinary" subdivisions that appear in all so-called disciplines and that likewise have developed their own literatures of method.

Works Cited

Alred, Gerald. *The St. Martin's Bibliography of Business and Technical Communication*. New York: St. Martin's, 1997.

Asher, William, and Janice Lauer. *Composition Research: Empirical Designs*. New York: Oxford UP, 1988.

Bartholomae, David. "Inventing the University." *When a Writer Can't Write: Studies in Writer's Block and Other Composing-Process Problems*. Ed. Mike Rose. New York: Guilford, 1985. 135–65.

———. "Writing with Teachers: A Conversation with Peter Elbow." *College Composition and Communication* 46 (1995). 62–71.

Bazerman, Charles. *Shaping Written Knowledge: The Genre and Activity of the Experimental Article in Science*. Madison: U of Wisconsin P, 1988.

Berlin, James. "Rhetoric and Ideology in the Writing Class." *College English* 50 (1988). 477–94.

———. *Writing Instruction in Nineteenth-Century American Colleges*. Carbondale: Southern Illinois UP, 1984.

Berlin, James, and Michael Vivion, eds. *Cultural Studies in the English Classroom*. Portsmouth, NH: Boynton/Cook, 1992.

Bishop, Wendy, and Hans Ostrom, eds. *Genre and Writing: Issues, Arguments, Alternatives*. Portsmouth, NH: Heinemann, 1997.

Bizzell, Patricia. "Cognition, Convention, and Certainty: What We Need to Know about Writing." *PRE/TEXT* 3.3 (1982): 213–43.

Bleich, David. "What Can Be Done about Grading?" *Grading in the Post-Process Classroom: From Theory to Practice*. Ed. Libby Allison, Lizbeth Bryant, and Maureen Hourigan. Portsmouth, NH: Boynton/Cook, 1997. 15–35.

Britton, James N., et al. *The Development of Writing Abilities, 11–18*. London: Macmillan , 1975.

Bruffee, Kenneth. "Collaborative Learning and the 'Conversation of Mankind.'" *College English* 46 (1984): 635–52.

Dunn, Patricia. "Response to 'Writing Utopias.'" *College English* 54 (1992): 731–33.

Elbow, Peter. "Being a Writer vs. Being an Academic." *College Composition and Communication* 46 (1995): 72–83.

Emig, Janet. "Writing as a Mode of Learning." *College Composition and Communication* 28 (1977): 122–28. Rpt. in *Cross-Talk in Comp Theory: A Reader*. Ed. Victor Villanueva, Jr. Urbana, IL: NCTE, 1997. 7–15.

———. *The Composing Processes of Twelfth Graders*. Research Report No. 13. Urbana, IL: NCTE, 1971.

Fishman, Stephen. "Writing to Learn in Philosophy." *Teaching Philosophy* 8 (1985): 331–34.

———. "Writing and Philosophy." *Teaching Philosophy* 12 (1989): 361–74.

Fulwiler, Toby, ed. *The Journal Book*. Portsmouth, NH: Heinemann, 1987.

Goodkin, Vera, and Robert Parker. *The Consequences of Writing: Enhancing Learning in the Disciplines*. Upper Montclair, NJ: Boynton/Cook, 1987.

Goswami, Dixie, and Peter Stillman, eds. *Reclaiming the Classroom: Teacher Research as an Agency for Change*. Portsmouth, NH: Heinemann, 1987.

Halloran, S. Michael. "From Rhetoric to Composition: The Teaching of Writing in America to 1900." *A Short History of Writing Instruction*. Ed. James J. Murphy. Davis, CA: Hermagoras, 1990. 151–82.

Henry, Jim. "A Narratological Analysis of WAC Authorship." *College English* 56 (1994): 810–24.

Herrington, Anne. "Writing in Academic Settings: A Study of the Contexts for Writing in Two College Chemical Engineering Courses." *Research in the Teaching of English* 19 (1985): 331–61.

Kirklighter, Christina, Cloe Vincent, and Joseph Moxley, eds. *Voices and Visions: Refiguring Ethnography in Composition*. Portsmouth, NH: Boynton/Cook, 1997.

Kirsch, Gesa, and Patricia Sullivan, eds. *Methods and Methodology in Composition Research*. Carbondale: Southern Illinois UP, 1992.

Mahala, Daniel. "Writing Utopias: Writing Across the Curriculum and the Promise of Reform." *College English* 53 (1991): 773–89.

Maimon, Elaine. "Writing Across the Curriculum: Past, Present, and Future." *Teaching Writing in All Disciplines*. Ed. C. W. Griffin. San Francisco: Jossey-Bass, 1982. 67–74.

Martin, Nancy. "Language Across the Curriculum: Where It Began and What It Promises." *Writing, Teaching, and Learning in the Disciplines*. Ed. Anne Herrington and Charles Moran. New York: MLA, 1992. 6–21.

Martin, Nancy, et al. *Writing and Learning Across the Curriculum, 11 16*. London: Ward Lock, 1976.

McCarthy, Lucille. "A Stranger in Strange Lands: A College Student Writing Across the Curriculum." *Research in the Teaching of English* 21 (1987): 233–65.

McLeod, Susan, and Elaine Maimon. "Clearing the Air: WAC Myths and Realities." *College English* 62 (2000): 573–83.

Mohr, Marian, and Marion McLean. *Working Together: A Guide for Teacher-Researchers*. Urbana, IL: NCTE, 1987.

Myers, Greg. *Writing Biology: Texts in the Social Construction of Scientific Knowledge*. Madison: U of Wisconsin P, 1990.

Naisbitt, John, and Patricia Aburdene. *Megatrends 2000: Ten New Directions for the 1990's*. New York: Morrow, 1990.

Ohmann, Richard. *English in America: A Radical View of the Profession.* New York: Oxford, 1976.

Perry, William G. *Forms of Intellectual and Ethical Development in the College Years: A Scheme.* New York: Holt, 1970.

Reiss, Donna, Dickie Selfe, and Art Young, eds. *Electronic Communication Across the Curriculum.* Urbana, IL: NCTE, 1998.

Russell, David. "American Origins of the Writing-Across-the-Curriculum Movement." *Writing, Teaching, and Learning in the Disciplines.* Ed. Anne Herrington and Charles Moran. New York: MLA, 1992. 22–42.

Shaughnessy, Mina. *Errors and Expectations.* New York: Oxford, 1977.

Sipple, Jo-Ann, and Jay Carson. "Reaching Out to the Business and Professional Community." *Composition Chronicle* 10.4 (1997): 9–10.

Sosnoski, James. "Grades for Work: Giving Value for Value." *Grading in the Post-Process Classroom: From Theory to Practice.* Ed. Libby Allison, Lizbeth Bryant, and Maureen Hourigan. Portsmouth, NH: Heinemann, 1997. 157–76.

Spooner, Michael, and Kathleen Yancey. "Postings on a Genre of Email." *Genre and Writing: Issues, Arguments, Alternatives.* Ed. Wendy Bishop and Hans Ostrom. Portsmouth, NH: Boynton/Cook, 1997.

Sullivan, Patricia, and Jennie Dauterman, eds. *Electronic Literacies in the Workplace: Technologies of Writing.* Urbana, IL: NCTE, 1996.

Thaiss, Christopher. "Newsletters." *The Harcourt Brace Guide to Writing Across the Curriculum.* Fort Worth: Harcourt Brace, 1998. Chap. 4.

———."WAC and General Education Courses." *Writing Across the Curriculum: A Guide to Developing Programs.* Ed. Susan McLeod and Margot Soven. Academic.Writing Landmark Publications in Writing Studies: http://aw.colostate.edu/books/mcleod_soven/ 2000. Originally published in print by Sage (Newbury Park, CA), 1992. 87–109.

———."Writing-Across-the Curriculum Theory." *Theorizing Composition: A Critical Sourcebook of Theory and Scholarship.* Ed. Mary Lynch Kennedy. Westport, CT: Greenwood, 1998. 356–64.

Thaiss, Christopher, and Charles Suhor, eds. *Speaking and Writing, K–12: Classroom Strategies and the New Research.* Urbana, IL: NCTE, 1984.

Walvoord, Barbara. "The Future of WAC." *College English* 58 (1996): 58–79.

Walvoord, Barbara, et al. *In the Long Run: A Study of Faculty in Three Writing-Across-the-Curriculum Programs*. Urbana, IL: National Council of Teachers of English, 1997.

"Why Johnny Can't Write." *Newsweek* 8 Dec. 1975: cover and 58ff.

Annotated Bibliography of Representative Works Relevant to WAC Theory

Bazerman, Charles. *Shaping Written Knowledge: The Genre and Activity of the Experimental Article in Science*. Madison: U of Wisconsin P, 1988. This groundbreaking study analyzes the conventions of scientific discourse and its teaching in terms of power relations within the disciplines of science. Bazerman's work has itself shaped much of the inquiry into writing in the disciplines.

Britton, James, et al. *The Development of Writing Abilities, 11–18*. London: Macmillan Educational, 1975. This influential work of the British Schools Council Project (1966–1975) introduced theories of cognitive and emotional development in writing on which much current writing process theory and practice are based. WAC workshops and writing intensive curricula in the United States and elsewhere continue to be founded on these theories.

Emig, Janet. "Writing as a Mode of Learning." *College Composition and Communication* 28 (1977): 122–28. Rpt. in *Cross-Talk in Comp Theory: A Reader*. Ed. Victor Villanueva, Jr. Urbana, IL: NCTE, 1997. 7–15. Based on Emig's earlier work in cognition and on her readings of Piaget, Vygotsky, Britton, and others, Emig's careful distinctions between writing and other language modes gave theoretical impetus to the nascent WAC movement in the United States.

Fulwiler, Toby, ed. *The Journal Book*. Portsmouth, NH: Heinemann, 1987. Although not primarily a work of theory, this comprehensive collection of practice essays by teachers across grade levels and disciplines fleshed out Fulwiler's earlier work on writing in this mode, thereby providing evidence that popularized the theory.

Martin, Nancy, et al. *Writing and Learning Across the Curriculum, 11–16*. London: Ward Lock, 1976. Another product of the British Schools Council Project (see Britton), this work, which describes and theorizes the effects of writing in different subject areas in British schools, conceptualized WAC for many U.S. educators, who made it a goal of U.S. schooling.

McCarthy, Lucille. "A Stranger in Strange Lands: A College Student Writing Across the Curriculum." *Research in the Teaching of English* 21 (1987): 233–65. This micro-ethnographic study created a methodological model and confirmed theory of the deep distinctions between disciplinary contexts in terms of modes of thought, uses of language, and teachers' expectations for student writing.

McLeod, Susan, and Margot Soven, eds. *Writing Across the Curriculum: A Guide to Developing Programs.* Academic.Writing Landmark Publications in Writing Studies: http://aw.colostate.edu/books/mcleod_soven/ 2000. Originally published in print by Sage (Newbury Park, CA), 1992. This collection of WAC program development essays, while not primarily theoretical, exemplifies McLeod's "stage" theory of WAC—the evolution of WAC programs in the 1980s from grassroots faculty development efforts to institutional requirements—and explores its many implications.

Reiss, Donna, Dickie Selfe, and Art Young, eds. *Electronic Communication Across the Curriculum.* Urbana, IL: NCTE, 1998. This recent collection of practical and speculative essays takes as its theme the merging of language modes in diverse disciplinary curricula through various uses of electronic technology (electronic mail, distance-learning courses, multimedia databases and Web sites, etc.) by teachers.

Russell, David. "American Origins of the Writing-Across-the-Curriculum Movement." *Writing, Teaching, and Learning in the Disciplines.* Ed. Anne Herrington and Charles Moran. New York: MLA, 1992. 22–42. Based on Russell's comprehensive history of WAC and WAC-like efforts in the United States over more than a century, this essay, paired with one by Nancy Martin on British "language across the curriculum," shows how U.S. educational politics and theory shaped U.S. WAC.

Thaiss, Christopher. "Writing-Across-the-Curriculum Theory." *Theorizing Composition: A Critical Sourcebook of Theory and Scholarship.* Ed. Mary Lynch Kennedy. Westport, CT: Greenwood, 1999. 356–64. This recent bibliographical essay explores WAC as a programmatic concept. It explains the rapid growth of WAC over three decades as attributable to the theorists' and organizers' preference for inclusiveness and avoidance of narrow prescription.

Walvoord, Barbara. "The Future of WAC." *College English* 58 (1996): 58–79. This speculative essay interprets WAC in terms of social movement theory. Walvoord envisions WAC eventually disappearing in many schools as a separate institutional entity and merging conceptually and practically with newer trends in education.

INDEX

Academia,
  changes in, 19–22
  economy of, 310
Academic discourse, 62
Academicspeak, 182
Academic.Writing, 80 n. 1
  Internet address of, 7
*Academic Writing in a Second
  Language* (Belcher and
  Braine), 161
"Accommodating Complexity"
  (Condon), 7
Ackerman, John M., research of,
  259–60, 266
Adam, Christine, research of, 270
Adler-Kassner, Linda, 90, 97–98, 98
Advancement Via Individual
  Determination, 22 n. 5
"Adventures in the WAC
  Assessment Trade" (Smith
  and Farris), 253
Agre, Phil, 77
ALN. *See* Asynchronous learning
  network
Alverno College, WAC assessment
  at, 43
"American Origins of the
  Writing-Across-the-Curriculum
  Movement" (Russell), 324
Appropriation, 105
*Assessing Writing Across the
  Curriculum* (Yancey and
  Huot), 32
Assessment, 6–7, 192–93, 244,
  309–10
  changing paradigm for, 33–39

of curriculum, 42
examples of, 35–36
in learning communities, 131–36
in linked course programs,
  129–30
performance, 43–44
tied to objectives, 133
"Assessment of Powerful
  Pedagogies" (MacGregor),
  130
Assimilation, 166
Asynchronous learning network, 70
Atkinson, Dwight, 148
  on critical thinking, 151
Audience, 63

Bailey, Carol A., 71
Bakhtin, M. M., 267
Banta, Trudy W., 35
Barker, Thomas, on collaborative
  classrooms, 66
Barnett, Robert, 188
Bartholomae, David, 301, 302
  definition of successful writing,
  303–4
  on student writers, 279
Basham, Charlotte, on ESL
  students, 150
Batson, Trent, 59
Bazerman, Charles, 104
  research of, 262
  on student writing, 125
Bean, John, 237, 251
Belcher, Diane, on second language
  errors, 153

Berkenkotter, Carol, research of, 265, 266
Beyond Outcomes (Haswell), 48 n. 1
Biochallenges, 64–65
Birkerts, Sven, 78
Bizzell, Patricia, on Freire, 172
Blair, Kristine L., 74
Blakeslee, Ann, on graduate students, 268
Blumner, Jacob, 188
Boyer, Ernest L., 243
on faculty scholarship, 94
Boyer Commission on Educating Undergraduates in the Research University, 3, 79, 80 n. 7, 244
Braine, George, 155
Brandt, Deborah, research of, 265
Braudel, Fernand, 168, 175 n. 3
Brier, Ellen M., research of, 275
Brigham Young University, writing program, 212, 220
Britton, James, ix, 5, 302, 303
"Broadening the Perspective of Mainstream Composition Studies" (Silva, Leki, and Carson), 145, 163
Brown University, Writing Fellows Program, 201–2
Bruffee, Kenneth, 5, 15, 301
on peer tutors, 210
on writing in collaborative learning, 122

CAC. *See* Communication Across the Curriculum
California Pathways (CATESOL), 161
California State Polytechnic University, 61
"Calling, The" (Rodríguez), 170–72
Camp, Roberta, 30
Campbell, Peter, 71

Campus Compact, 89
Campus Computing Project, The (Green), 57
Carino, Peter, 180–81
Carleton College,
peer tutoring program at, 15–16
writing program at, 201
Carlin, James, 93
Carson, Joan, 145
Casanave, Christine P., 268
on cultural diversity, 152
CBPT, 201
controversies concerning, 205–11
evaluation of, 220–21
implementation of, 215–18
problems with, 218–20
program stagnation, 219
Change Forces (Fullan), 20
Chaos theory, x, 20
Cheek, Madelon, on engineering student project, 59
Childers, Pamela, 68
Chin, Elaine, research of, 269
Chiseri-Strater, Elizabeth, research of, 276–77
Chomsky, Noam, 168
Citadel, Internet address of, 187
City College of New York, writing program, 204
Classical Rhetoric for the Modern Student (Corbett), 174
Clemson University, 60
Collaborative learning, 66–69
"Collaborative Learning and the 'Conversation of Mankind'"(Bruffee), 5
Colorado State, WI guidelines of, 236
Coming to Class (Shepard, McMillan, and Tate), 175 n. 4
Communication Across the Curriculum, 53, 54
future of, 72–80
Composition courses, 310–11
history of, 300
Computer conferences, 68

Condon, William, 7
Conferences, computer, 68
Connor, Ulla, 146
Conrad, Susan, 290
Contrastive rhetoric, 145
Contrastive Rhetoric (Connor), 161
Cooper, Charles, 260
Corbett, Edward P. J., ix
Cornell University, 60
Corporation for Public Service, 90
Corridor conversations, 188
Critical thinking, 151–52
Crooks, Robert, 90
Curriculum, definition of, 313–14
Curriculum-based peer tutoring
    programs. *See* CBPT
"Curriculum-Based Peer Tutors
    and WAC" (Soven), 16
Curriculum-based program,
    progress and change in,
    211–15

"Damage of Innovations Set
    Adrift, The" (White), 237
Deans, Thomas, 90–91, 96
Demographics, student, 11–12
*Development of Writing Abilities,
    The* (Britton), 323
*Diagnostic and Statistical Manual
    of Mental Disorders*
    (McCarthy), 265
Dinitz, Sue, on expert vs. generalist
    tutors, 207
Discourse, 66
    academic, 62
Discourse communities, 210
Diversity as a Resource (Murray),
    162
"Documenting Improvement in
    College Writing" (Haswell),
    34, 40
Drucker, Peter, 19
    on fate of universities, 2
Dunn, Patricia, on WAC faculty,
    310

Durst, Russell K., writing studies
    of, 259

ECAC. *See* Electronic
    Communication Across
    the Curriculum
Ede, Lisa, on collaboration, 67
Edison, Thomas, writing of, 263
*Education for Critical
    Consciousness* (Freire), 172
Ehrmann, Stephen C., 133–34
    on evaluation, 132
"Eight Basic Lessons for the New
    Paradigm of Change" (Fullan
    and Miles), 20, 243
Elbow, Peter, 302
Electronic communication, 78
Electronic Communication Across
    the Curriculum, 7–9, 53, 54
    history of, 57–60
*Electronic Communication Across
    the Curriculum* (Reiss, Selfe,
    and Young), 7, 324
Electronic Communication Across
    the Curriculum resources,
    Web site of, 80 n. 1
Electronic portfolios, 74
E-mail, 305
Emergent English-dominant
    students, 143–44
Emig, Janet, 5
    on writing, 305
    writing studies of, 259
Engaging Ideas (Bean), 251
English for academic purposes, 12
Epiphany Project, 59
ESL,
    theories of, 145
    Web sites for, 164
    writing programs, 148
ESL students,
    categories of, 142
    challenges of, 141
    helping faculty understand,
    148–53

"ESL Students and WAC
Programs" (Johns), 12
Evaluation, 132
"Expressive Media" (White,
Campbell, and Lyon), 71
Expressivism, ix

Faculty,
bashing of, 93–96
development, 10, 186–89
logs, 130
scholarship, 94
WAC, 125–26
workshops, 200
Fahnestock, Jeanne, research of,
263–64
Faigley, Lester,
on modern students, 179–80
research of, 273
Fanon, Frantz, 173
Farris, Christine F., 17, 234–37,
253
Federated learning communities,
137 n. 1
First-year composition. *See* FYC
Fischer, Ruth, 119–20
Fisherman, Stephen M., research
of, 281
Fitzsimmons, Denise A., research
of, 276
Flashlight Project, 111, 132
Forster, E. M., viii
Fossilization, 143
Foucault, Michel, 92
Fourth Generation Evaluation
(Guba and Lincoln), 46–47
Fox, Helen, on critical thinking,
151
Frank, Andre Gunder, 175 n. 3
Freedman, Aviva, research of, 270
Freire, Paulo, 16, 172, 175 n. 2
Freshman interest groups, 137 n. 1
Fullan, Michael, viii, 20, 243
Fulwiler, Toby, viii, 59, 187, 304
on enemies of WAC, 75

Fuss, Diana, 173
"Future of WAC, The" (Walvoord),
110, 254, 324
FYC,
linked to lecture courses, 115–17
linked to SL component, 119–20
linked to two or more courses,
117–19

Gabelnick, Faith, 109
Gaff, Jerry, 94
"Gain in First-Year College
Composition Courses"
(Haswell), 129
Geisler, Cheryl,
research of, 281–82
writing studies of, 259–60
"Genre as Social Action" (Miller),
103–4
Genres, 184, 260, 262, 267
classroom, 272
dual thrust of, 104
learning to write new, 283
as meaning-making templates,
103
Genre studies, 185
Genre theory, 102–6, 264
Genrification, 267
George Mason University,
WAC at, 111–12
WI guidelines of, 236
Gere, Anne Ruggles, 99
Gerring, Joan P., research of, 265
Gilbert, Steven W., 59
Giles, Dwight E. Jr., on history of
SL, 89
Gillespie, Paula, on e-mail
journals, 65
Gillmore, Gerald, 41
Giroux, Henry, 175 n. 1
Glassick, Charles E., 243
Gordon, Nicholas, on CAC,
59–60
Goswami, Dixie, research of, 264
Gould, Stephen Jay, 37

Graduate school, writing in, 266–71
Graduate students, study of writing of, 266
Green, Kenneth C., on technology, 57
Greene, Stuart, research of, 274–75
Guba, Egon G., 33, 46
Guidelines for WI Courses (Hunt), 247–48

Hansen, Kristine, research of, 273
Hare, Victoria Chou, research of, 276
Haring-Smith, Tori, 201
    on generalist tutor model, 209
    on problems in CBPT programs, 218
Harris, Jeanette, 187
Harris, Leslie, 59
Harris, Muriel, on engineering student project, 59
Haswell, Richard, 34, 40, 48, 129
Hawisher, Gail E.,
    on recommendations for teachers, 79
    on WAC and ALN, 70
Hawthorne, Joan, 184
Heilker, Paul, 96
    on genres in SL writing, 98
Herrington, Anne J., viii
    research of, 273–74
    on writing conventions, 274
Herzberg, Bruce, 98
    on journal writing in SL, 97
Hickey, Dona J., 65
Holder, Carol, 61
Honan, William H., 93
Hubbuch, Susan, 209
Huber, Mary Taylor, 243
Huckin, Tom N., research of, 265, 266
Hughes, Gail, 46
Hunt, Douglas, 247
Huot, Brian, 32, 46

"Idea of a Writing Center, The" (North), 14
Imitatio, 174
Immigration and Nationality Act of 1965, The, 22 n. 4
Information technology, 67
Inquiry Contract, 101
Integrated studies, team-taught, 137 n. 1
Interlanguage, 157 n. 6
International E-mail Debate, 66
International students, 144
Internships, writing in, 266–71
In the Long Run (Walvoord et al.), 262
"Is It Still WAC?" (Zawacki and Williams), 11
"Ivory Tower under Siege, The" (Honan), 93

Jaibería, 173–74
Johns, Ann M., 12
Jolliffe, David A., 10, 120, 318
    research of, 275
Jones, Robert, 59
Journal Book, The (Fulwiler), 323
Journals, 96
    e-mail, 65

Kail, Harvey, 213
Kairos, 93
Kaplan, Robert B., 146
    on voice of ESL writers, 151
Kellogg Commission on the Future of State and Land-Grant Universities, 185, 195–96
Kemp, Fred, on collaborative classrooms, 66
Keys for Writers (Raimes), 154, 163
Kiedaisch, Jean, on expert vs. generalist tutors, 207
Kiefer, Kate, 59
Kinds, John, 146

Kinkead, Joyce, 187
Kinneavy, James, ix
  on WAC, 255
Knowledge, social construction of,
  310
Knowledge-building communities,
  187
Krawitz, Aaron, 250
Kruck, Mary, 116

Langsam, Deborah, on
  biochallenges, 64–65
Language across the curriculum,
  306
LaSalle University, writing
  program, 212–15
Latona, John, 236
Law, Joe, 188
Learner English (Swan and Smith),
  163
Learning communities, 10–11, 69,
  121, 185, 187
  assessing WAC in, 128
  assessment in, 131–36
  definition of, 109
Learning environments, 185
*Learning Literature in an Era of
  Change* (Hickey and Reiss),
  65
Learning theories, 206–7
LeCourt, Donna, 168, 172–73,
  175 n. 1, 175 n. 2
Leki, Ilona,
  on second-language acquisition,
  145–46
  on sources of error, 145–46
Limited-English-proficient
  students, 142–43
Lincoln, Yvonna S., 33, 46
Linguistically diverse students,
  142–44, 156 n. 1
Linked courses, 137 n. 1
"'Linked-Courses' Initiative
  within a Multi-faceted WAC
  Program, A" (Thaiss), 113

Linked Courses Program, 110,
  113–15
Linton, Joan Pong, 99
Longview Community College, 60
"Look Back and Say 'So What'"
  (Kiedaisch and Dinitz), 207–8
Loren, F. O., on second-language
  errors, 153
Lowell L. Bennion Community
  Service Center, 97, 100
Lunsford, Andrea, on collaboration,
  67
Lyon, Marsha, 71

MacDonald, Susan Peck, 260
  research of, 264
MacGregor, Jean, 109, 130
Maeroff, Gene I., 243
Mahala, Daniel, on WAC programs,
  310
Maimon, Elaine, 54, 111
Making a Difference (Banta), 35
Management communication
  theory, 264
Mansfield, Susan, on CAC, 59–60
Matalene, Carolyn, 146
Matthews, Roberta, 109
May, Claire, 155
McCarthy, Lucille P., 125, 264–65
  research of, 277–78, 281, 282
McLaughlin, Tim, 113
McLeod, Susan, viii, 123, 136, 254
  on new WAC strategies, 55
  on response of WAC teacher, 36
McLuhan, Marshall, on secondary
  orality, 174
Medway, Peter, research of, 271
Mellon Multimedia Courses, 70
Metadiscourse, 146–47
Metalanguage, 144, 147
Michigan State University, SL at,
  194
Milam, John H., 133
Miles, Matt, 20, 243
Miller, Carolyn, on genre, 103

Miller, Susan, research of, 279–80
Minter, Deborah, 99
Miraglia, Eric, 254
  on new WAC strategies, 55
Mismeasure of Man, The (Gould), 37
Missouri Western State College, WI guidelines of, 236
Modeling, 288
Moran, Charles, viii
Moxley, Joseph, 69
Muchuri, Mary N., on voice in ESL writers, 151
Mulamba, Greg, on voice in ESL writers, 151
Mullin, Joan A., 15, 60, 114, 201
Multiculturalism, 169
Multimedia composing, 306–7
Myer, D. E., on second-language errors, 153
Myers, Greg, research of, 263

Naisbitt, John, 301
National and Community Service Act, 90
National and Community Service Trust Act, 90
National Center for Service Learning, 89
National Society for Experiential Education, 89
National Writing Project, ix
Ndoloi, Deoscorous B., on voice in ESL writers, 151
Needs-assessment surveys, 149
New Century College, 110
  integrated studies at, 120–27
Newman-James, Stephanie, 65
Noble, David, 78
North, Stephen M., 14, 280
Nshindi, G., on voice in ESL writers, 151

O'Connor, John, 122

Odell, Lee, research of, 264
Okawa, Gail, 173–74
Olson, Gary, 14
Ong, Walter, on secondary orality, 174
Online learning environments, 46
Online Writing Labs, 191
Orlikowski, Wanda J., research of, 264
"Overcoming Skepticism about 'Writing Across the Curriculum'" (Weinberg), 252

Palmquist, Mike, 59
Paré, Anthony, research of, 270
Patton, Marty, 249
Paulsen, Deidre, 202, 220
  on peer tutors, 212
Pedagogies,
  middle ground, 64
  one-on-one, 185
  writing center, 193
Peer tutoring, 15–16
  at Carleton College, 15–16
  curriculum-based programs, 201
Peer tutors, 201, 204
  burnout of, 218
  compensation of, 217
  controversies concerning, 205–11
  course-linked, 202
  expert, 211–13
  expert vs. generalist, 207–15
  generalist, 214
  reports of, 188–89
  role of, 205
  sample of report, 190
  selection of, 216
  training of, 216–17
  See also Writing fellows
Pemberton, Michael A., 70
Pennycook, Alastair, on plagiarism, 155
Penrose, Ann M., writing studies of, 259

Plagiarism, 155–56
Plan for Alternative General
    Education, 112
Plato, 167
Platonic mind-set, 166–68
Polanyi, Karl, 168, 175 n. 3
"Politics of Literacy Across the
    Curriculum, The"
    (Villanueva), 13
"Politics of Peer Tutoring, The"
    (Kail and Trimbur), 203
Portfolios, 130–31, 134, 192, 255
    developmental, 43
    electronic, 74
    writing, 39
Powell, Colin, 90
Powell, Malea, 173–74
Prior, Paul, 267
Proficiency tests, 255
ProfScam (Sykes), 93
Program for Excellence in
    Teaching, 71
Programs That Work (Fulwiler
    and Young), 187, 240
Project CONNECTS, 194
Protherow-Sith, Deborah, 194
Puerto Rican Jam (Grosfoguel,
    Negrón-Muntaner, and
    Georas), 173
Purdue, writing programs, 183
Purdue University, Internet
    address of writing lab, 191
Purley, James, 93
Purves, Alan, 146

Quintilian, 168, 174

Race, Rhetoric, and Composition
    (Gilyard), 173–74
Raimes, Ann, 12, 154
Raines, Helon Howell, 206
Ramanathan, Vai, 148
    on voice of ESL writers, 151
Rand Change Agent Study, 21

Ravotas, Doris, research of, 265
Ray, Ruth, on ESL students, 150
Reader-responsible texts, 146–47
"Reality Check for SLA Theories,
    A" (Sridhar), 145
Redd, Teresa M., 65
Reflective writing, 96
*Reinventing Undergraduate
    Education* (Boyer
    Commission), 79, 244
Reiss, Donna, 8, 65, 123
    on technological changes in
        WAC, 73
Remediation, 203
Resistance theory, 175 n. 1
Retention, 195
"Rethinking Genre in School and
    Society" (Russell), 104
Returning to Our Roots (Kellogg
    Commission), 185
Rhetoric, ix, 167–68
    contrastive, 145
Richter, Eva, 221
Rodríguez, Luis J., 172
Rudenstine, Neil L., on electronic
    communication, 78
Russell, David R., x, 1, 18
    on faculty studying writing, 58
    on faculty writing, 115–16
    on genres, 103, 104
    on goals of WAC, 74
    on importance of writing skills,
        58
    on resistance to WAC, 239
    on WAC, 89, 180–81
    on WAC movement, 3
    on writing tasks, 131

Santos, Terry, on second-language
    errors, 153–54
Sarah Lawrence College, 60
Scholarship Assessed (Glassick,
    Huber, and Maeroff), 243–44
Scholarship Reconsidered (Boyer),
    94, 243

School-to-Work Initiative, 185
Schwalm, Karen, 59
Scientific knowledge, modification
of, 263
Secondary orality, 174
Second language,
acquisition, 145
errors, 145, 153–54
*Second Language Reading and
Vocabulary Learning*
(Huckin, Haynes, and
Coady), 162
Selfe, Cynthia L., 59, 70
on recommendations for
teachers, 79
on writing-intensive learning
activities, 58
Selfe, Dickie, 59
Service learning. *See* SL
Shaping Written Knowledge
(Bazerman), 323
Shaughnessy, Mina, ix, 302
Sheridan, Harriet, viii, 15–16, 201
Sherman, Lawrence, on
technological strategies, 64
"Shifting Roles in Classroom
Tutoring" (Soliday), 205
Shires, Peter, 71
Silva, Tony, 12, 145
Situating Portfolios (Yancey and
Weiser), 74
SL, 9–10, 182, 185
connections to WAC, 91
definition of, 87–88
energy of, 92–95
genres of writing in, 95–102
origins of, 89–90
Smart, Graham, research of, 270
Smith, Barbara Leigh, 109
Smith, Charles, 59
Smith, Raymond S., 17, 234–37,
253
Smitherman, Geneva, on
multicultural society, 254
Social construction, ix
of knowledge, 310

Soliday, Mary, 206
on tutor roles, 205
Song, Bailin, 221
Sosnoski, James, on academic
assessment, 309
Soven, Margot, viii, 16, 189
Speech genres, theory of, 267
Sridhar, S. N., 145
"Stranger in Strange Lands, A"
(McCarthy), 324
Structuration theory, 264
Students,
assessment of, 6–7
demographics of, 11–12
emergent English-dominant,
143–44
ESL, 12
international, 144
limited English proficient,
142–43
nontraditional, 11–12
Style, 307
Swanson, Mary Catherine, 22 n. 5
Sykes, Charles, 93
Sylvester, Barbara, 202, 211

Takayoshi, Pamela, 74
Taking Flight with OWLS (Inman
and Sewell), 60
Teachers of English to Speakers of
Other Languages, 147
Teaching,
politics in, 166
and technology, 7–9
Teaching and Assessing Writing
(White), 237–38
*Teaching from a Multicultural
Perspective* (Roberts), 162
Teaching, Learning, and
Technology Group, 59
Technology, and teaching, 7–9
Tenure, 2
Texts,
reader-responsible, 146–47
writer-responsible, 146–47

Thaiss, Christopher, viii, 18, 111,
133
on the act of writing, 55
on technology techniques, 76
Theory,
gap between practice and, 192
WAC, 210
WID, 315
"Theory in WAC" (Thaiss), 18–19,
133
Tidewater Community College, 60
Tierney, Robert, on proficiency
tests, 255
TLT. *See* Teaching, Learning, and
Technology Group
Topics in Writing, 101
Townsend, Martha A., 17, 71
Transformation, 127
Trimbur, John, 213
Tutor-linked classrooms, 189
Tutor-linked courses, 201
"Tutor Needs to Know the
Subject Matter to Help a
Student with a Paper, A"
(Hubbuch), 209
Tutors. *See* Peer tutors

Undergraduate education, WI in,
250
*Understanding and Using English
Grammar* (Azar), 163
Understanding ESL Writers
(Leki), 145, 162
University of Hawaii at Manoa,
WI guidelines of, 236
University of Missouri, writing
center Internet address, 193
University of Missouri–Columbia,
Institute for Instructional
Technology, 71
WI guidelines, 246–54
University of North Dakota,
writing program, 184
University of Portland, writing
program, 220

University of Rhode Island, WI
guidelines of, 236
University of South Carolina,
writing program, 187–88
University of Toledo,
tutor reports at, 188–89
writing programs, 183
University Year for Action, 89

Vann, Roberta J., on second-
language errors, 153
Van Nostrand, A. D., research of,
265
Vaught-Alexander, Karen, 202, 205
Villanueva, Victor, 13, 152

WAC, 4–6
accommodating complexity in
evaluation of, 39–48
broader initiatives of, 54
budgetary concerns of, 195
changes in, vii–x, 1–3, 19–22
conflicts in, 186–87
connections to SL, 91
connections with writing
centers, 183
constructivist evaluations of,
34–35
discourse, 63
economy driven, 310–11
enemies of, 75
and ESL, 12
evaluation of, 32–33
faculty, 125–26
first faculty seminar for, 22 n. 1
future of, 3–4
future of research in, 290
history of, 179
integrating with assessment
programs, 44
movement of, 3
new strategies of, 55
program personnel, 244
qualitative studies in, 17–18

results of research, 283–90
self-assessment of, 36–37
theory of, 18–19, 210
and WC partnerships, 184–86
"WAC and the Restructuring of
First Year Composition"
(Mullin), 114
"WAC as Critical Pedagogy"
(LeCourt), 168
WAC/CAC,
drives change, 72
goals for, 56
legal issues concerning, 77
programs, 70–71
WAC Clearinghouse Web site, 236
"WAC on the WEB" (Kimball),
60
WAC-SL, 90–92
connections between, 91
"WAC Wired" (Reiss and Young),
8
Walker, Kristin, 188
Wallerstein, Immanuel, 169
Walley, Elizabeth, on ESL students,
150
Walters, Keith, on diverse students,
149
Walvoord, Barbara, viii, 22 n. 1,
254, 262, 308
on future of WAC, 3–4
on impact of information
technology, 54
on need for WAC programs, 58
research of, 277–78, 282
on survival of WAC, 110
Washington State University,
examples of writing
assessment at, 35–36
Watters, Ann, 90
Wax, Robin, on synchronous
computer conferences, 68
Weinberg, Steve, 252
Weisser, Christian R., 69
Western Washington University,
writing program, 211
Whassup with Suspension, 102

"Where Do the Naturalistic
Studies of WAC/WID Point?"
(Russell), 18
White, Andy, 71
White, April, on being a tutor, 213
White, Edward, 30, 233
on assessment, 33
on WI, 237, 253
"Why Johnny Can't Write"
(Newsweek), 304
WI, 16–17
assignments, 245
case against, 237–39, 253
case for, 239–40
defining requirements, 234–37
ensuring success of, 242–45
examples of successful, 240–42
faculty ownership of, 242
new direction for, 254–56
requirements of, 233
in undergraduate education, 250
WID,
elusiveness of term, 314–15
theory of, 315
WI guidelines,
Colorado State, 236
George Mason University, 236
Missouri Western State College,
236
University of Hawaii at Manoa,
236
University of Missouri–
Columbia, 246–54
University of Rhode Island, 236
Williams, Ashley Taliaferro, 11
Williams, Patricia, 70
Williamson, Judy, 59
Winsor, Dorothy A., research of,
269
Wiring the Writing Center
(Hobson), 60
Woest, June, 66
Wofford, Harris, 90
Working documents, 98, 100
Workplace writing, research in,
262–65, 315

Write for Your Life initiative, 194
Writer-responsible texts, 146–47
Writer's Workbench, 59
Writery, The, Internet address of, 252
Writing,
  act of, 55
  analysis of, 104
  assessment of, 124
  characteristics of good, 301–2
  definition of, 300–301, 307–9
  disciplinarity in, 189
  in the disciplines, 271–79
  effects of, 260
  factors that condition, 261
  faculty study of, 58
  general education, 279–83
  genres of, 260
  good, 309
  graduate school, 266–71
  graduate student, 268
  identity in, 285–86
  internship, 266–71
  learning new genres of, 283–90
  motivation for, 284–85
  originality vs. conformity, 301–3
  process of, 209, 289
  in professions, 266
  reflective, 96
  technological changes in, 304–6, 318
  as a tool, 261
  tools for, 286–89
  transactional, 303–4
  use of technology in, 307
  workplace, 262–65
Writing Across Curricular Cultures, 111, 137
Writing Across Languages (Connor and Kaplan), 146
Writing Across Languages and Cultures (Purves), 146
Writing across the curriculum. *See* WAC
Writing Across the Curriculum (McLeod and Soven), 324

"Writing Across the Curriculum and Service Learning" (Jolliffe), 10
"Writing-Across-the-Curriculum Theory" (Thaiss), 324
"Writing and Higher Order Thinking," 303
Writing and Learning Across the Curriculum (Martin et al.), 323
"Writing as a Mode of Learning" (Emig), 5, 305, 323
Writing center directors, as leaders of ECAC, 59
Writing Center Resource Manual, The (Law), 188
Writing centers, 13–15, 192
  budgetary concerns of, 195
  community connections of, 193–95
  conflicts of, 186–87
  connections with WAC, 183
  high school, 194
  history of, 179
  in military training, 181
  strategies for, 192
  student-centered pedagogy for, 182
Writing Centers (Olson), 14
"Writing Centers and WAC" (Mullin), 15, 201
Writing Centers and Writing Across the Curriculum Programs (Barnett and Blumner), 188
Writing Centers in Context (Kinkead and Harris), 187
Writing conventions, 274
Writing enhanced courses, 233
Writing fellows, 16, 204
  advertisement for, 225
  application for assistance from, 227
  evaluation form of, 232
  faculty nominations form for, 226

letter to potential, 228
selection of, 216
training of, 216–17
See also Peer tutors
Writing fellows programs,
evaluation form for, 229–30
form for faculty report on, 231
objectives of, 202
Writing for a Better Society, 99
Writing from Sources (Braine and
May), 155
Writing intensive courses. *See* WI
"Writing Intensive Courses and
WAC" (Townsend), 17
*Writing in the Academic
Disciplines, 1870–1990*
(Russell), x
Writing in the course, 316–17
Writing in the disciplines. *See* WID
Writing in the major, 233
Writing labs, 181
Writing online, 66–69
Writing Partnerships (Deans), 90
Writing portfolios, 39
Writing process, 120
Writing programs,
Brigham Young University, 212,
220
Carleton College, 201
City College of New York, 204
LaSalle University, 212–15
Purdue, 183

University of North Dakota, 184
University of Portland, 220
University of South Carolina,
187–88
University of Toledo, 183
Western Washington University,
211
Writing skills, importance of, 58
Writing tasks, 131
Writing teachers, as leaders of
ECAC, 59
Writing the Community
(Adler-Kassner, Crooks, and
Watters), 90
Writing to communicate, 5, 235
Writing to learn, 5, 235, 302
Writing to Learn (Thaiss), 111
Wutzdorff, Allen J., on history of
SL, 89

Yancey, Kathleen Blake, 32, 36, 46
Yates, JoAnne, research of, 264
Young, Art, viii, 8, 123, 187
on enemies of WAC, 75
Young, Dennis, on frame of
reference, 117
Young, Jim, 128

Zawacki, Terry Myers, 11
Zlotkowski, Edward, on SL, 87

EDITORS

Susan H. McLeod is professor of writing and director of the Writing Program, University of California, Santa Barbara. Her publications include *Strengthening Programs for Writing Across the Curriculum*; *Writing Across the Curriculum: A Guide to Developing Programs* (co-edited with Margot Soven); *Writing about the World*, a multicultural textbook for composition; and *Notes on the Heart: Affective Issues in the Writing Classroom*, as well as articles on writing across the curriculum and writing program administration.

Eric Miraglia is a Web design manager for a young Internet company in Silicon Valley. In his work as an instructional technologist at the university level, Miraglia has focused on the creation of innovative virtual learning spaces. He has published articles in *InLand, Journal of Basic Writing,* and *Journal of Advanced Composition,* and he and Susan McLeod have published a follow-up study of successful writing-across-the-curriculum programs, "Whither WAC? Interpreting the Stories/Histories of Enduring WAC Programs," in *WPA: Writing Program Administration.* Eric's current writing projects focus on the imbrication of technological literacies and academic textual literacies.

Margot Soven is professor of English at La Salle University and is currently director of the New Core Curriculum and the Writing Fellows Program. Her essays have appeared in journals such as *College Composition and Communication,* the *Journal of the Council of Writing Program Administrators,* the *Journal of Teaching Writing,* and *Freshman English News.* She is the author of *Write to Learn: A Guide to Writing Across the Curriculum* and *Teaching Writing in Middle and Secondary Schools.* She has co-edited two texts: *Writing Across the Curriculum: A Guide to Developing Programs* and *Writings from the Workplace.* Soven has conducted numerous workshops at the high school and college level on writing across the curriculum.

Christopher Thaiss is professor of English at George Mason University, where he chairs the department and where he formerly directed the composition and writing-across-the-curriculum programs. Active as a consultant in cross-curricular writing in schools and colleges since 1978, Thaiss also coordinates the National Network of WAC Programs and works with teachers in elementary, middle, and high schools through the Northern Virginia Writing Project. Books he has written or edited include *The Harcourt Brace Guide to Writing Across the Curriculum, Language Across the Curriculum in the Elementary Grades,* and *Speaking and Writing, K–12* (co-edited with Charles Suhor). He has also written or co-authored several textbooks, the most recent of which are *Writing about Theatre* (with Rick Davis), *Writing for Law Enforcement* (with John Hess), and *Writing for Psychology* (with James Sanford).

CONTRIBUTORS

William Condon is director of Campus Writing Programs—Writing Assessment, Writing Across the Curriculum, and the Writing Center—at Washington State University. He is co-author of *Writing the Information Superhighway* (with Wayne Butler) and *Assessing the Portfolio: Principles for Theory, Practice, and Research* (with Liz Hamp-Lyons). Condon has also published several articles on writing assessment, program evaluation, and computers and writing.

Ann M. Johns is professor of linguistics and writing studies at San Diego State University and director of the Center for Teaching and Learning. She has published widely on ESL and novice student reading and writing, including a volume entitled *Text, Role, and Context: Developing Academic Literacies.*

David A. Jolliffe is professor of English and director of the First-Year Program at DePaul University in Chicago. He regularly teaches courses in cooperation with DePaul's Center for Community-Based Service Learning.

Elaine P. Maimon is chief executive officer and professor of English at Arizona State University West. In the early 1970s, she initiated and then directed the Beaver College writing-across-the-curriculum program, one of the first WAC programs in the nation. She was a founding Executive Board member of the National Council of Writing Program Administrators (WPA). She has co-authored three books and directed national institutes (sponsored by the National Endowment for the Humanities) to improve the teaching of writing. Maimon's current project is a spiral-bound first-year composition handbook, co-authored with Janice Peritz, forthcoming in 2002.

Joan A. Mullin, associate professor of English and director of WAC and the Writing Center at the University of Toledo, started both programs in 1987. She publishes in various journals across the disciplines. Her co-edited collection, *Intersections: Theory-Practice in the Writing Center,* won the 1994 National Writing Center Association Award for Outstanding Scholarship, and the co-authored book, *ARTiculating: Teaching Writing in a Visual Culture,* indicates her current research interest in visual literacy across the curriculum. Past president of the National Writing Centers Association, she co-edits the *Writing Center Journal.*

Donna Reiss is coordinator of online learning at Tidewater Community College (Virginia), where she teaches computer-enhanced and Web-based writing, literature, and humanities. Recent presentations and workshops focus on electronic communication throughout the curriculum. With Dickie Selfe and Art Young, she edited *Electronic Communication Across the Curriculum,* and with Dona Hickey she co-edited *Learning Literature in an Era of Change: Innovations in Teaching.* Reiss has edited regional books and written features for regional publications, including restaurant criticism for Norfolk's *Virginian-Pilot.*

David R. Russell is professor of English at Iowa State University, where he teaches in the Ph.D. program in rhetoric and professional communication. His book *Writing in the Academic Disciplines, 1870–1990: A Curricular History* examines the history of U.S. writing instruction outside of composition courses. He has published many articles on writing across the curriculum, and co-edited *Landmark Essays on Writing Across the Curriculum* and a special issue of *Mind, Culture, and Activity* on writing research. He was the first Knight Visiting Scholar in Writing at Cornell University. Russell is currently conducting research on Kentucky's twelfth-grade portfolio writing assessment; editing AgComm, an Internet clearinghouse of teaching materials on communication in agriculture (www.ag.iastate.edu/grants); and co-editing a collection of essays describing the role of writing in the transition from secondary to higher education in seven national education systems.

Martha A. Townsend is director of the University of Missouri's sixteen-year-old Campus Writing Program and a member of the Department of English. A former literacy consultant to the Ford Foundation, she has offered faculty writing workshops at a wide variety of postsecondary institutions. She has also consulted on writing in the disciplines at universities in Romania, Korea, Thailand, South Africa, and China. Her CV includes publications on WAC/WID, writing and general education, and writing program assessment and administration.

Victor Villanueva is professor and chair of the Department of English at Washington State University, where he also teaches rhetoric and composition studies. He is the winner of two national awards on research and scholarship for *Bootstraps: From an American Academic of Color*, winner of the Young Rhetoricians Conference Rhetorician of the Year for 1999, editor of *Cross-Talk in Comp Theory: A Reader*, author of numerous articles, and past chair of the Conference on College Composition and Communication. Other than that, he likes to watch movies.

Ashley Taliaferro Williams is visiting assistant professor of integrative studies in New Century College at George Mason University. She is the writing-across-the-curriculum consultant for New Century and also has responsibility for portfolio assessment. Prior to the establishment of New Century College, Williams taught in the Department of English and helped establish linked courses at George Mason. In addition to work with writing across the curriculum in interdisciplinary and learning community settings, her research interests include shared authority in collaborative teaching, Appalachian literature, and literature and the environment.

Art Young is Campbell Chair in technical communication and professor of English and professor of engineering at Clemson University in South Carolina. He coordinates Clemson's Communication-Across-the-Curriculum program, and he is co-editor with Donna Reiss and Dickie Selfe of *Electronic Communication Across the Curriculum*. He has conducted workshops on writing across the curriculum at more than seventy colleges and universities.

Terry Myers Zawacki is on the Department of English faculty as well as director of the University Writing Center and Writing Across the Curriculum at George Mason University. Prior to assuming the latter responsibilities, she developed and directed the Linked Courses Program. With Chris Thaiss, she has co-authored "How Portfolios for Proficiency Help Shape a WAC Program" in Yancey and Huot's *Assessing Writing Across the Curriculum: Diverse Approaches and Practices*. In addition to WAC and learning communities, her scholarly interests focus on gender and writing. Her article "Telling Stories: The Subject Is Never Just Me" appears in Adler-Kassner and Harrington's *Questioning Authority: Stories Told in School*.

This book was set in Sabon by Electronic Imaging.
Typefaces used on the cover include Runic, Arquitectura, and Officina.
The book was printed on 50 lb. Williamsburg Offset paper by Versa Press.